The Counterintuitive Writer

A Writing Guide for Students ... and for Others

Joan Flaherty

Rock's Mills Press
Oakville, Ontario
2018

The Counterintuitive Writer
A Writing Guide for Students ... and for Others

Published by
Rock's Mills Press

Copyright © 2018 by Joan Flaherty
All rights reserved. Published by arrangement with the author.

The author gratefully acknowledges the assistance of the following in granting permission to reprint material included in this book:

Fast Company for "A Core Curriculum to Create Engaged Entrepreneurs," which appeared in *Fast Company*, July 11, 2012, and was subsequently reprinted under the title "A New Curriculum for Real-World Success" in *The Globe and Mail*, October 13, 2012.

Penguin Random House LLC for excerpt from *Catch and Release: Trout Fishing and the Meaning of Life* by Mark Kingwell, copyright © 2004 by Mark Kingwell. Used by permission of Viking Books, an imprint of Penguin Publishing Group, a division of Penguin Random House LLC. All rights reserved. Any third party use of this material, outside of this publication, is prohibited. Interested parties must apply directly to Penguin Random House LLC for permission.

Eric C. Girard for "What I Learned at Law School: The Poor Need Not Apply," which appeared in *The Globe and Mail*, November 17, 2013;

For information about this title, please contact:
Rock's Mills Press
2645 Castle Hill Crescent
Oakville, ON L6H 6J1
www.rocksmillspress.com
customer.service@rocksmillspress.com

This is for Anne and Brian

Contents

	Acknowledgments	vii
1.	Establishing a Strong Foundation	1
2.	Developing Your Topic	8
3.	Structuring Your Paper	31
4.	Developing Your Content	42
5.	Avoiding the Common Pitfalls that Weaken Your Paper's Content	68
6.	Writing the Introduction	93
7.	Writing All the Rest: Paragraphs, Conclusion, and Summary (or Abstract)	112
8.	Editing	138
9.	Grammar	147
10.	How to "Get" a Good Grade	189
	Glossary	197
	Index	209

Acknowledgments

Writing isn't lonely. In fact, it's crowded with people, places and circumstances that help you figure out what to say and how to say it – and, in some cases, maybe even prompt you to say it in the first place.

I've been lucky to have so much of that help, and I'm grateful for it:

David Stover of Rock's Mills Press is the best possible publisher for this book because he recognizes that taking the road less travelled is sometimes the best, perhaps even the only, option.

Chris Helsby encouraged me from the start to pursue this project – and, in doing so, he taught me that what we say to others can have a significant impact on their lives.

David Ward I thank for his kindness and guidance in helping shape the ideas – and the title – of this book.

Leah-Ann Lymer provided me with conscientious advice.

Hazel McGuiness told me to write this book – and kept telling me, until I finally started. I'm thankful for her persistence.

The University of Guelph and, specifically, the College of Business and Economics, allowed me a generous sabbatical leave to write, unburdened by competing work demands.

The University of Guelph's School of Hospitality, Food and Tourism Management, all its staff, faculty and students, has created such a supportive place to learn, to take risks – and to be inspired.

My family and friends have been my most important teachers. I hope this book reflects all the good, really valuable lessons they've taught me.

Chapter 1
Establishing a Strong Foundation

> It's not that I'm so smart.
> It's just that I stay with problems longer.
> Attributed to ALBERT EINSTEIN

This chapter will help you ...

- Consider an approach to writing that may contradict what you've heard, read or been taught before
- Identify – and leave behind – obstacles that prevent you from writing well
- Understand why you need – really need – to start writing right now

THE COUNTERINTUITIVE PRINCIPLE

Choose one name from the list below. Your choice can be based on any reason you like: perhaps it's the only name you recognize, a person whose work you admire, or someone who, for whatever reason, strikes a resonating chord.

- Alice Munro
- Steve Jobs
- Albert Einstein
- Jerry Seinfeld
- Robert Frost

Alice Munro, one of only two Canadians to have won a Nobel Prize for Literature, ignored her publisher's conventional view that serious – and successful – writing naturally evolves from short stories to novels. She persisted in her calling as a short story writer. And she won not just the Nobel Prize but also, one can safely predict, a lasting place in literary history.

Steve Jobs, whose name is often prefaced with the **adjective** "visionary," revolutionized how we communicate when he created the Macintosh computer. He attributed an important spark of inspiration for the Mac to a course he audited in calligraphy – a subject that most people would view as far removed from computing.

Albert Einstein's name has been synonymous for years with scientific genius. Today, as a quick Internet search of his name – or a visit to any poster shop – would suggest, many of his writings are linked to an area beyond the realm of the stereotypical scientist: New Age wisdom.

Jerry Seinfeld, the American comedian, co-created and wrote a television show so popular that it continues to be part of popular culture years after its final episode aired in 1998. The show that made such an indelible imprint in his audience's memory was famously described as being "about nothing."

And poet Robert Frost wrote the words that link all these disparate individuals:

> Two roads diverged in a wood, and I –
> I took the one less travelled by,
> And that has made all the difference.[1]

Each of them embraced a perspective that went against conventional wisdom or followed a path that ran counter to what someone in a similar position might do. And in doing so, each of them met with great success. One word sums up the principle that implicitly guided them toward this success: **counterintuitive**. The term means "contrary to expectations; not in accordance with what would naturally be assumed or expected."[2]

Much of this writing text is based on the counterintuitive principle. Following it means you may have to discard some notions about writing that you've learned before. You may even be asked in these pages to do the opposite of what you've been doing so far as a writer. In other words, your effort to become a better writer might require that you take the path "less travelled."

If that prospect makes you feel uncertain, skeptical or curious, just keep

---

1. Robert Frost, "The Road Not Taken," in *Mountain Interval* (New York: Holt & Co., 1920).
2. "Counterintuitive," in *MSN Encarta: Online Dictionary* (Redmond, WA: Microsoft Corporation).

reading. This book aims to clarify how you can use the counterintuitive principle to strengthen your writing.

If that prospect makes you feel disoriented or completely alone, because it asks you to give up the writing approach you're used to and replace it with the counterintuitive principle, then keep reading. This book aims to help you forge a connection with yourself as a writer and with your reader through the counterintuitive principle.

And if that prospect leaves you feeling bored or indifferent, consider this: the person whose name you chose from the list above walked this counterintuitive path ahead of you. It helped define his or her success. This book aims for you to achieve success as a writer through the counterintuitive path – so keep reading.

HOW TO START

You start applying the counterintuitive principle *before* you sit down to write your essay, report or any other document you need to produce – because good writing doesn't start with words on a page. It starts with the thoughts in your head.

> I feel I'm always struggling with the material, whether it's a concert or a poem or a prayer or a conversation. It's very rarely that I find I'm in a condition of grace where there's a kind of flow that is natural. I don't inhabit that landscape too often.
> —*Leonard Cohen*[3]

If Leonard Cohen could admit it, then so can the rest of us. Writing well can be a struggle. It requires the sort of sustained focus and deep thinking that many of us prefer to avoid. It requires the discipline to sit quietly and concentrate on filling a blank sheet or computer screen with our own carefully chosen, coherent – and original – arrangement of words, sentences, and paragraphs. And it requires the will power to resist distractions, such as e-mail, texting, Facebook, and the entire world, really, in the form of the Internet.

No wonder the distractions sometimes win out over the hard work. Consider these statements:

> *I typically start my essays the night before they're due.*

---

3. Retrieved from http://www.leonardcohenfiles.com/sward.html.

A significant part of my paper's content isn't my own writing at all. It's information that I've copied and pasted from the Internet.

When we have a group writing assignment, I prefer that someone else from the group do the actual writing.

I like writing, but I often have difficulty starting – and finishing.

If you can relate to any of them, you're not alone. On one level, wanting to delay or completely avoid writing makes sense. It is, after all, a time consuming and challenging task. On another level, however, procrastination and avoidance are completely counterproductive strategies. For example, when we don't give ourselves enough time to write the essay, we likely end up feeling stressed by the encroaching deadline – and annoyed at ourselves, knowing we could have done better if we had devoted more time to the paper. When we look for shortcuts by copying and pasting whole excerpts from the Internet, we probably feel anxious and vulnerable to accusations of plagiarism. When we routinely pass on the responsibility of writing the group assignment to another team member, we're likely to start believing that we're incapable of doing the job ourselves. And when we abandon the paper altogether, we deprive ourselves of a chance to shine at something we enjoy.

We end up, in other words, not feeling good about ourselves because stress, guilt, and a sense of incompetence and lack are all negative emotions that undermine our confidence.

The American writer Sinclair Lewis famously suggested we could overcome this problem by "apply[ing] the seat of the pants to the seat of the chair."[4] Just sit down and write. It's good advice, but it requires a fair bit of mental effort to overcome the temptation to procrastinate or to avoid writing altogether. That's why the counterintuitive writer adds a two-part preamble to Lewis' advice.

First, resist the predictable gambit of trying to shore up your confidence by convincing yourself that the paper you have to write is straightforward, and the writing process will go smoothly. That kind of false optimism is probably going to result in your giving up when the going inevitably gets rough. False optimism is a shaky foundation. Instead, learn from Leonard Cohen. Accept right from the start that writing well is challenging. Then

---

4. This quotation, although widely attributed to Lewis, has also been linked with other authors, including Kingsley Amis.

you're starting off on solid ground because you're starting with the truth.

Second, to give you the fuel to start that challenging task, try embracing a credo that may contradict a central tenet of other writing texts: focus on yourself, not on your reader. *Just for the time being,* forget your reader. Instead, place your own interests front and centre – and those interests revolve around feeling good about yourself.

You may think this advice is easy to follow, but ask yourself if you've ever begun a paper by thinking, "I want to get an 'A' "; "I want to impress the instructor with my insights and superior intellect"; "I want to get the highest grade in the class"; or, conversely, "I need to do well on this paper to pass the course." Perhaps you believed these goals were attainable or perhaps not, the statements simply being a reflection of wishful thinking. In either case, if you answered "yes" to any of those statements, you have some work to do, because those goals do not serve your interests at this beginning stage. None of them is likely to make you feel good about yourself. Writing is already an inherently challenging task. There's no need to make the challenge even heavier by adding to it the weight of all your hopes, fears, and anxieties about how others will judge your writing.

Concerns about the grade you'll receive or how the paper will be judged have their place. But that place comes later. Right now, start the writing process by embracing one central goal: "I want to feel good about myself." And then *focus on how good you'll feel by putting a genuine effort into writing the best paper you can*: not a paper that got written at the last minute, not a "copy and paste from the Internet" essay, not a document that never actually got completed, but a paper that represents your best effort. When you start with this mindset, you're affirming your own best self: not someone who's undisciplined or duplicitous or lacking in confidence, but someone who rises to the challenge.

And with that mindset firmly in place, you can then "apply the seat of the pants to the seat of the chair." Start writing. Now, however, you're not just writing an essay; you're also working on feeling good about who you are. That's the best feeling in the world, and the best possible motivation, therefore, to get you started writing.

Exercise 1.1

If you're reading this book, you've probably been assigned a paper to write. From the following list, circle all the challenges you face in starting – or completing – this paper.

I don't have enough time.

I don't know what to write.

I'm afraid what I write won't be any good – or good enough.

I tend to procrastinate.

I lack discipline.

I have no interest in this paper.

And now add any others:

....

....

Your list of challenges, I'm guessing, revolves around four main themes: fear, apathy, inaction, and lack – terms that spell the acronym "FAIL," by the way. Consider that these themes do not serve your best interests. They undermine your confidence and your sense of well-being. Consider, also, that overcoming them involves a straightforward, simple strategy: think differently. Instead of focusing on thoughts that point you in the direction of failing, focus on thoughts that point you in the direction of feeling good about yourself.

In other words, reframe each challenge into its opposite:

I manage my time wisely.

I have the intelligence to figure out what to write.

I always put forth my best effort.

I take action now.

I am disciplined.

I have a natural curiosity that means I'm never bored.

Complete the list.

Now repeat each statement aloud – or not (reading it quietly to yourself works just as well); and consider how it makes you feel.

Good.

That's the starting place. We've just laid the foundation for you to begin writing. Our next step is to figure out how to build on that foundation. That's the focus of Chapter 2.

SUMMARY

Everyone agrees that writing well is challenging. Counterintuitive writers address this challenge by taking "a path less travelled." They don't start in the conventional place, by focusing on their reader. Instead they start by focusing on themselves, on feeling good about who they are. And that's the best reason – and the best motivator – to get you started writing. It affirms that you have the discipline, the confidence and the creativity to tackle what everyone knows is a challenging task: writing.

Chapter 2
Developing Your Topic

This chapter will help you start writing by ...

- Re-considering the role of uncertainty, writer's block and boredom
- Following a two-part pre-writing plan that's been shaped by various successful writers, real and fictitious
- Figuring out a specific theme or purpose to focus your paper

SOME PRE-WRITING GUIDELINES
Embrace uncertainty

We've been conditioned to see uncertainty as an undesirable state. That's why so many students become upset when they can't *quickly* decide on a topic or, once they do have their topic, how to develop it. Uncertainty has become synonymous with weakness, and consequently the statement "I don't know" becomes associated with all manner of negative qualities, such as dimwittedness, apathy, inertia – and even despair.

That's the conventional view. The counterintuitive writer, however, does not take the conventional view – and neither did 17th-century writer Sir Francis Bacon (whose gender-biased language we forgive because he is, after all, writing in the 17th century):

> If a man begins with certainties, he will end with doubts, but if he begins with doubts, and is patient with them, he will end with certainties.[5]

There is, in other words, an unexpected potential to being uncertain.

What this potential means for you, facing a writing assignment, is simple: if you're not sure how to proceed with your paper, don't berate yourself, don't panic, and don't use it as an excuse not to keep going. Good writers are often uncertain. It saves them from becoming complacent. Their willingness to say "I don't know" – and to be patient with themselves in the midst of not knowing – means they're open to exploring ideas until they come up with the most insightful ones; they're willing to fuss with the arrangement of words until they come up with the most logical, coherent

---

5. Francis Bacon, *The Advancement of Learning* (1605).

order; and they're willing to engage in the hard work of retracing their steps and revising their work because they can see when they've taken the wrong path. And all this exploring, fussing, and revising that's associated with uncertainty makes them strong writers.

Forget about writer's block

It also makes them completely immune to **writer's block**. In fact, they dismiss writer's block as a myth. Here's what the American writer Ann Patchett has to say about the matter: *"[A]s far as I'm concerned, writer's block is a myth."*[6]

Ann Patchett is nothing if not direct.

She's also a good writer. Consider the reason she thinks it's a myth:

> ... if it were a complicated math proof you were wrestling with, instead of, say, the unknowable ending of Chapter 7, would you consider yourself "blocked" if you couldn't figure it out right away, or would you think that the proof was difficult and required more consideration?....
>
> Even if I don't believe in writer's block, I certainly believe in procrastination. Writing can be frustrating and demoralizing, and so it's only natural that we try to put it off. But don't give "putting it off" a magic label. Writer's block is out of our control, like a blocked kidney. We are not responsible. We are, however, entirely responsible for procrastination and, in the best of all possible worlds, should also be responsible for being honest with ourselves about what's really going on.[7]

Note what Patchett just did:

- Presented her thesis in a direct, concise statement: "writer's block is a myth."
- Supported her thesis in a way her readers could easily understand (and probably relate to): math can be just as difficult as writing.
- Engaged her readers by
    - Prompting them to think, so that they reach the conclusion she's guiding them toward: no one blames their difficulties in solving, say, quadratic equations on "mathematician's block," so why should

---

6. Ann Patchett, *This Is the Story of a Happy Marriage* (New York: Harper, 2013), p. 51.
7. Ibid.

we treat the difficulty of writing an essay on "the supernatural in *Hamlet*" or a report on "Canadian cultural identity" any differently?
- Anticipating and addressing their possible objections: But if there's no such thing as writer's block, then why can't I write this paper? Answer: Because you're procrastinating.

In the process, Patchett takes a familiar topic – writer's block – and puts a different spin on it from what we're used to hearing. There's none of the usual commiserating with the reader about the trials of writer's block and offering advice on how to overcome it. Instead, she tackles the topic in a way that most readers probably hadn't encountered before: by denying the existence of it. And even though her approach might be tinged with a bit of schoolmarmish finger wagging, it still leaves the readers with an insight they likely didn't have before – an encouraging insight, at that, because it suggests a solution to a troublesome problem: how to keep writing when the going gets tough.

Know the goal

Patchett's excerpt models what good writers do: present thesis; support thesis; engage readers, and, ideally, enlighten readers by providing them with something they hadn't considered before – in this case, a different way of looking at the topic under discussion.

That's *what* good writers do, and that's your goal.

Now that we're unburdened by worries about being uncertain or by writer's block, the next step is to figure out *how* to achieve that goal, by getting something down on the blank screen or piece of paper.

In the spirit of the counterintuitive principle, here's how you start:

Seek inspiration in the boring and the ordinary

Don't wait until you're in the mood. That's like waiting for your muse or for a spark of divine inspiration to descend upon you, focusing your thoughts and choosing your words. It's waiting for something that may or may not show up. Instead of putting yourself completely at the mercy of some capricious outside force – because your paper does, after all, have a due date – try being your own muse and generating your own inspiration. Right now.

What follows is a two-part plan to help you achieve that.

1. Be willing to sit in your own boredom. Your willingness to sit down and start writing the paper even though you don't feel like it – even though

you feel bored or distracted – can yield unexpectedly inspiring results. Try it. Find a quiet place, away from people you might be tempted to talk with and away from digital distractions. It could be your bedroom, library carrel, office space, or even a corner table in a coffee shop after the lunch rush. Begin by typing – or handwriting, if you prefer – your topic. It could be as general as "Climate change" or as specific as "Yeats' symbolic use of mythology in 'Leda and the Swan.'" *And then just start writing anything at all that you've heard or researched or that you believe about the topic. Write anything that comes into your mind.*

2. As you write, honour the sound of relentless tapping on the keypad – or the feel of your hand moving nonstop across the page. I know. That sounds like some kind of New Age, touchy-feely advice, completely inappropriate in the academic world. In fact, the academic world is likely to greet that kind of advice with eye-rolling dismissiveness. That's why I don't want you to think about the academic world at this stage. In particular, don't think about your professor peering over your shoulder as you write, sometimes frowning and always **editing**. Don't be concerned about correct spelling or grammar. Don't fret over whether your writing is organized into proper paragraphs. Don't even be concerned about being logical.

That's the plan for you to get started: straightforward, simple, and entirely within your capability.

FURTHER INSTRUCTION FROM VARIOUS WRITERS, REAL AND FICTITIOUS

"Write your first draft with your heart"

In the Hollywood movie *Finding Forrester* the main character, an acclaimed author, instructs his teenaged protégé, "You must write your first draft with your heart; you rewrite with your head." We'll get to the rewrite part later. Right now, focus on the directive "write your first draft with your heart." At first glance, this advice seems anathema to the academic world where logic and intellect rule. But consider this: logic and intellect are strengthened when they stem from your heart's desire. So many essays, dissertations and books are either abandoned or done poorly because their writers lose interest or confidence. These losses are more apt to be restored (or avoided altogether) when the content holds a place in the writer's heart.

And if you're not convinced by a fictitious character in a Hollywood movie, I'll bring in the big guns: William Butler Yeats, one of the greatest poets – if not *the* greatest – of the last century, acknowledges the inspiration behind his poetry when he writes

> I must lie down where all ladders start
> In the foul rag and bone shop of the heart.[8]

This advice, by the way, is not permission to base your final draft on emotions, unsubstantiated opinions, or stream of consciousness musings from the heart. Rather, it's intended to get you engaged in the paper by helping you discover why the topic is worth getting excited about. It's intended to help you get something down on the page that you can work with.

Therefore, if you're feeling particularly hesitant about this exercise, try starting with a "heart-based" question, "How do I feel about this topic?" You might, for example, care nothing at all about climate change. Write that down, and see where that thought leads. Or you might feel "Leda and the Swan," with all its mythological references, has no relevance to anyone's life today. Write that down, and see what thought it prompts next.

Avoid "editing yourself off the page"

Your task right now is to write nonstop without judging what you're writing – or imagining how someone else might judge what you're writing. All that judging can result in what Patchett calls "editing yourself off the page": deleting or crossing out your words until your writing is "down to a trickle, and then a drip."[9] Good writers, ironically enough, are often vulnerable to this self-defeating practice, their desire for perfection outracing their trust in the writing process.

That's why this stage of the process requires letting go of the need to ruthlessly edit anything that doesn't fit within the conventionally and rigorously logical academic mindset. Just write. Do not judge.

Write to discover what you know

There's value in seeing where tapping the keyboard or moving your hand across the paper will take you. And it will likely take you further than you expected. In fact, if you're seriously following this plan, it can't be otherwise because that's the nature of writing: to generate – and to order – ideas, insights, and perspectives you didn't know you had.

If you've ever encountered the advice, "write what you know", put it

---

8. W.B. Yeats, "The Circus Animals' Desertion," in *Yeats: Selected Poetry*, ed. A. Jeffares (London: Pan Books, 1990).
9. Patchett, *Story*, p. 26

aside in favour of "write in order *to discover* what you know." Writing is a process of discovery. That's why journal writing can be so useful. People write in journals for different reasons, but usually to record events, dreams, or problems. No one would make this effort if there weren't a benefit – and the benefit is suggested in the term itself: "journal" is related to the word "journey." Metaphorically, the act of writing in a journal takes you on a journey. It transports you from where you are right now to a place further along the path, one that allows you a different view or a clearer understanding.

Part of that new perspective or clarity comes from the fact that writing orders your thoughts. Most of us are susceptible to "monkey mind," that habitual – and frequently stressful – habit of jumping from one disconnected, random thought to another. Sustained writing replaces "monkey mind" with focused, coherent thoughts. That's why writing in a journal can be healing. The two-part plan described here, a kind of "academic journal writing," can be similarly useful: it's impossible to write uninterrupted for any extended length of time without generating new perspectives that add order or clarity to your topic.

This kind of writing is sometimes referred to as **free writing**, meaning it's free of the conventional writing constraints: rules about grammar, spelling, punctuation, paragraphing and focus do not apply.

Find "your voice"

In addition to helping you generate ideas for your paper, free writing may also help you find what writing guru Peter Elbow refers to as your "**voice**." In case you hadn't noticed, academic (and business) writing not infrequently lacks energy or enthusiasm. At times it may seem as if the paper weren't actually written by a living, breathing human being but by an automaton or, at best, someone who is "bored and sleepy and devoid of energy."[10] One reason may be that the writing lacks the author's voice – a nebulous concept that's hard to pin down, but discernible when encountered. And you've probably encountered it if you've ever read – or written – a document full of phrases like "In today's society ..." or "Thus, it can be seen that...." Certainly, you encounter lack of voice in this excerpt from an essay on education:

> Tests should reflect changes in learned behavior; the normal utilization of reliability estimates must be revised since it is assumed

---

10. Peter Elbow, *Writing with Power*, 2nd edition (New York: Oxford University Press, 1998), p. 308.

that we are not measuring a trait or innate mental capacity but rather an acquired skill or concept which can be measured incrementally. Thus scores should reflect changes from one administration to the next.[11]

Figure 2.1. Find your voice

In an effort to maintain objectivity, and perhaps to convey a scholarly manner, the writer ends up standing aloof not just from the material, but also from the reader and, ultimately, from himself or herself. Lack of voice can make the words a chore to read – and more of a chore to write – even if the content is good.

Voice, in contrast, is a quality that makes the paper "readable," that attracts and retains the readers' attention because, every so often, we get a glimpse of the writer behind the words – witty, uncertain, fearful, optimistic, angry, hesitant, courteous.… That glimpse doesn't overpower the words, but it adds nuance and depth to them.

Voice no doubt played a role in making the following passage by Ernest Hemingway so well known – and so well loved. Read Hemingway's writing advice, from his memoir *A Moveable Feast,* and see if you can discern his voice:

> One true sentence. I would stand and look out over the roofs of Paris and think, "Do not worry. You have always written before and

---

11. Cited in Elbow, *Writing,* p. 288.

you will write now. All you have to do is write one true sentence. Write the truest sentence that you know." So finally I would write one true sentence, and then go on from there. It was easy then because there was always one true sentence that I knew or had seen or had heard someone say. If I started to write elaborately, or like someone introducing or presenting something, I found that I could cut that scrollwork or ornament out and throw it away and start with the first true simple declarative sentence I had written.

Voice alone doesn't guarantee your writing will be good. In fact, it's possible to overdo "voice", re-directing the reader's focus from what's being said to who's saying it. However, that doesn't mean it's not worth working on. It is. And one way to work on voice (as Peter Elbow suggests in *Writing with Power*) is through lots of free writing.

Remember, "things can only get better"

A bonus of free writing is the sense of relief you'll feel at having started the paper. As author Stephen King – yes, *that* Stephen King, of the horror fiction genre – explains, "the scariest moment (in writing) is always just before you start. After that, things can only get better" because you're breaking through that scary moment.[12] You've taken the first step toward writing the paper. You're now creating something that didn't exist before. That's a process to be honoured – and to feel inspired by.

Now begin writing: Two exercises (Exercises 2.1 and 2.2)

1. After reading the two-part plan above, along with its "further instruction," to make sure you understand what needs to be done and why, schedule 10 minutes to start an essay that you've been assigned in one of your classes or a document that you want or need to write. Follow the plan. (And if you *precisely* follow its instructions, you'll easily – and willingly – spend more than 10 minutes on this exercise).

2. Try a variation of the two-part plan: Take a sheet of paper, 8½" by 11" or, if you're feeling particularly optimistic, an even larger size. Smack in the middle write down your topic (either general or specific). Make it the sun around which revolves everything else you're about to write: anything you've read, heard, researched or believe about the topic – anything, in fact,

---

12. Stephen King, *On Writing: A Memoir of the Craft* (New York: Simon & Shuster, 2000), p. 269.

that enters your mind right now. Use arrows or colour coding to show how each entry is related to your topic or to subsets of your topic. (See Figure 2.2 on the facing page for an example).

Mind mapping – and the science behind it

"The Madman"

The previous exercise is often called **mind mapping**, but one author[13] refers to it as **"the Madman"** because it gives you license to write (or draw) whatever you like – words, phrases, pictures, even complete sentences – without regard for grammar, spelling or logic. It's diagrammatic brainstorming with arrows and perhaps colour. And it's completely nonlinear because writing seldom emerges in a linear, logical fashion. Its origins are often messy and chaotic, as illustrated in Figure 2.2.

The value of writing by hand

Aside from getting you started, mind mapping has another potential benefit: it requires that you **handwrite** (as opposed to type), an action that has been linked with increased neural activity in certain parts of the brain. Researcher Virginia Berninger at University of Washington has conducted functional MRI studies that compare typing with handwriting, using elementary school students. She found that these students "consistently produced more words more quickly" and "expressed more ideas" when they wrote by hand as opposed to typing on a keyboard.[14]

Her research offers intriguing possibilities for your own writing: when you're just starting the paper, or when you encounter a section of the paper that's giving you particular difficulty, try replacing the keyboard with a pen or pencil and pad of paper. Ideas might then flow more easily and with more subtlety.

Many writers intuitively know and practice this strategy already. The American novelist Robert Stone explained in an interview that he typed "until something (became) elusive". Then he wrote in longhand because the word processor "can rush something that shouldn't be rushed – you can lose nuance, richness, lucidity."[15] J.K. Rowling, author of the Harry Potter series, typically writes her first drafts using pen and paper, aided by a handwritten

---

13. B. Flowers, "Madman, Architect, Carpenter, Judge: Roles in the Writing Process." Retrieved from http://www.ut-ie.com/b/b_flowers.html.
14. M. Konnikova, "What's Lost as Handwriting Fades," *New York Times*, June 3, 2014.
15. Retrieved from http://www.theparisreview.org/interviews/2845/the-art-of-fiction-no-90-robert-stone.

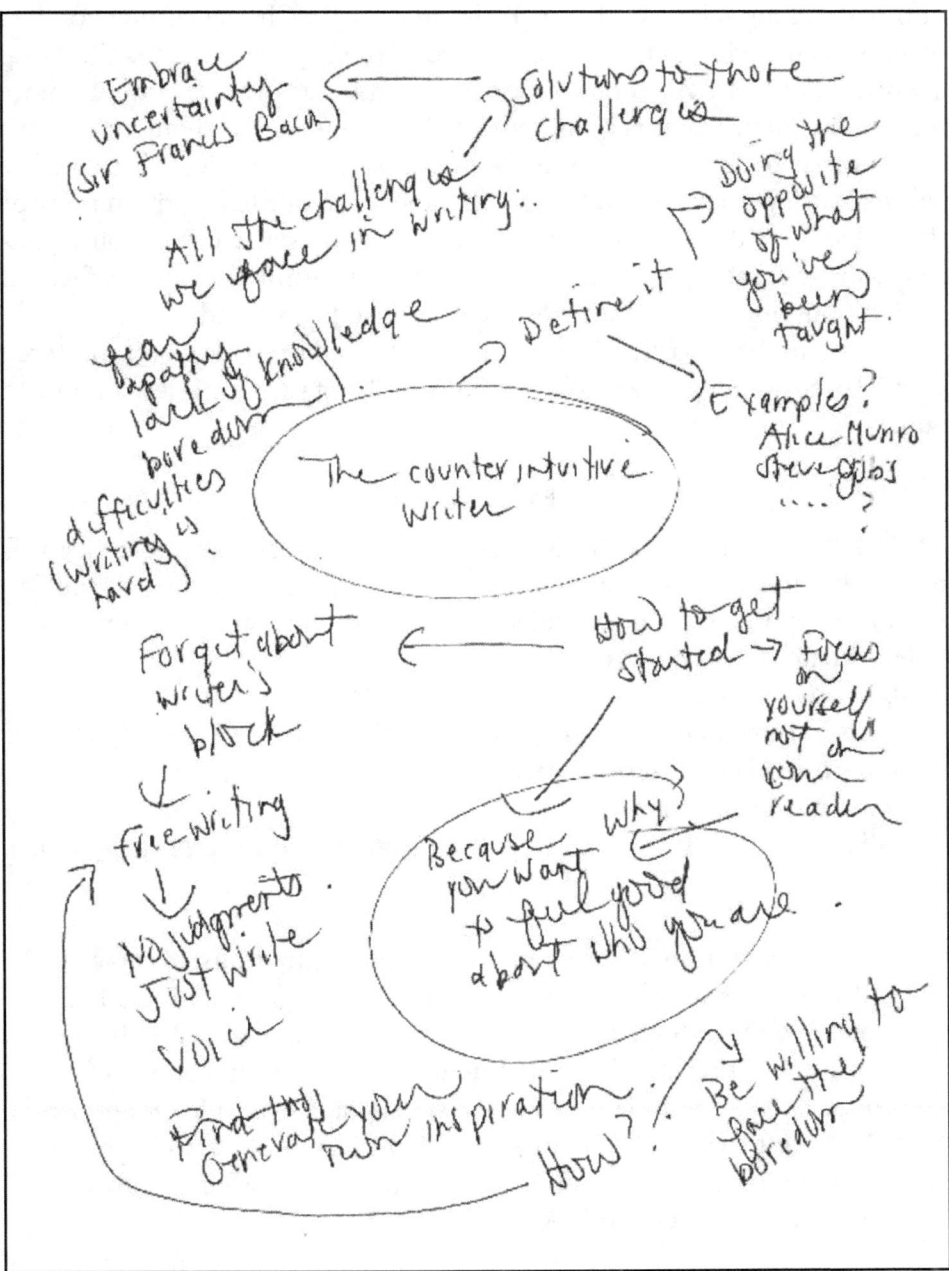

Figure 2.2: An alternative to "free writing"

organizational chart.[16] Poet and novelist Sylvia Plath also created detailed outlines in longhand. And *New York Times* critic Charles Simic wonders whether handwriting offers benefits beyond the keyboard because "writing a word out, letter by letter, is a more self-conscious process and one more likely to inspire further revisions and elaborations of that thought."[17]

Another benefit of handwriting, of course, is its physical presence: we can see, sitting on our desk, the pad of paper with our half-written essay or the notebook with our scribbled outline. Their presence can encourage us to complete a paper that otherwise might hide within a computer file, out of sight, out of mind, and unlikely, therefore, to be finished.[18]

For many, handwriting is becoming a bit of a dying – or never mastered – art. These are all good reasons to ensure that statement doesn't apply to you.

Exercise 2.3

Keeping in mind the discussion about voice, read the short passages below by Garrison Keillor and Rachel Toor (who prefers the word "soul" to voice). As you read each, consider these questions, making sure you provide evidence to support your answers:

Can you discern the author's voice (or soul)?
Does it strengthen the writing? How?
Does it weaken the writing in any way? How?
And, most importantly,
What lessons do you learn from all of this that you can apply to your own writing?

> My generation was secretive, brooding, ambitious, show-offy, and this generation is congenial. Totally. I imagine them walking around with GPS chips that notify them when a friend is in the vicinity, and their GPSes guide them to each other in clipped electronic lady voices and they sit down side by side in a coffee shop and text-message each other while checking their e-mail and hopping and skipping around Facebook to see who has posted pictures of their weekend. —*Garrison Keillor*[19]

---

16. Her chart can be seen online at http://blog.paperblanks.com/2013/05/j-k-rowling-book-outline/.
17. Retrieved from http://www.nybooks.com/blogs/nyrblog/2011/oct/12/take-care-your-little-notebook/.
18. Ibid.
19. Garrison Keillor, "My San Francisco Buzz," *Salon*, March 12, 2008.

Over the years many authors – including Bram Stoker (some of whose notes for his novel *Dracula* are reproduced at right), William Faulkner, Henry Miller, Joseph Heller, Norman Mailer, and Sylvia Plath – have used handwritten outlines to clarify their thoughts and sort out the structure of their works, whether novels, plays, or works of nonfiction. (See Emily Temple, "Famous Authors' Handwritten Outlines for Great Works of Literature," *Flavorwire*, May 13, 2013, at http://flavorwire.com/391173/famous-authors-handwritten-outlines-for-great-works-of-literature/3, for a number of interesting cases.)

One of the most poignant examples involves the American novelist, short-story writer, and poet Sylvia Plath (1932–1963) and her novel *The Bell Jar*. As an online British Library exhibit explains, the main character of the novel, like Plath herself, is a young woman struggling with mental illness and mid-twentieth-century views of women's place in society. The outline is written on pink Smith College stationery, and can be seen at https://www.bl.uk/collection-items/manuscript-outline-of-chapters-for-the-bell-jar-by-sylvia-plath.

Plath's work has come into greater prominence in the years since her death. Her *Collected Poems* won a posthumous Pulitzer Prize, and in 2018 to mark International Women's Day *The New York Times* published her obituary – 55 years after her passing – as part of a series of obituaries of women who had been overlooked by the newspaper at the time of their deaths.

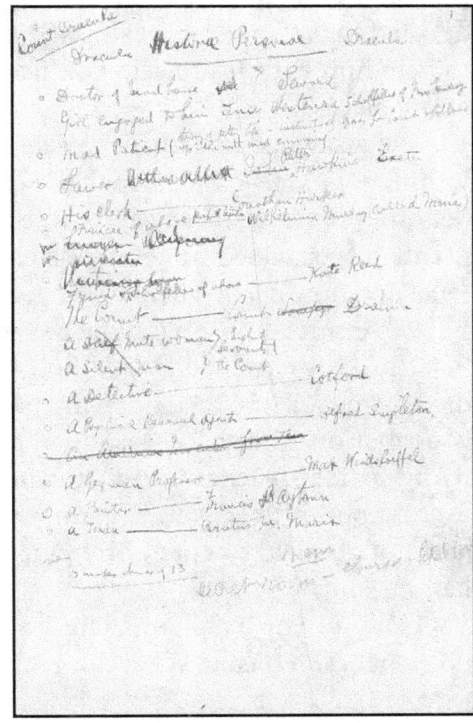

GIOVANNI GIOVANNETTI/GRAZIA NERI

Figure 2.3:
Handwritten outlines

Writing with Soul

Last fall I heard from a medical student who was trying to get a **personal essay** published in a prestigious journal that has a section devoted to first-person musings. The writer thought I might be able to help him with his revisions, since that journal had run a couple of my pieces.

His essay had already been rejected by the editor, who said his writing was "one-dimensional and dull" and lacked "soul." The student told me he had begged for a second chance and the editor had granted it, provided he revise the essay. He had completely rewritten it and now needed help putting, he said, the "final touches" on it.

When I read the revised piece I found it earnest and generic.

The draft I saw – dialogue-boosted and exclamation-point-riddled – smelled of effort, of trying to do right, of wanting to make a contribution. The genre was sad but familiar: The beautiful-heroic-dying-patient-teaches-the-doctor-in-training-about-life. The essay was supposed to make me care but didn't. Not about the patient, and not about the writer. The journal editor was right. The piece had no soul.

How do you help someone learn to write with "soul"? What does that even mean? What does it look like on the page?...

—*Rachel Toor*[20]

A final question to consider:
Do you agree that academic writing has no place for soul (or voice)?

FIND YOUR FOCUS

So far, we've discussed how to get something down on the computer screen or page through free writing and mind mapping. Our next step is to focus this material. In other words, now is the time to start figuring out what exactly you want to say. As you figure it out, be guided by two further pieces of counterintuitive advice:

1. Rein in your ambition.

I know. Parents and guidance counselors might disagree with this advice because it runs counter to all their hopes and dreams for your future. But probably none of them has to write a 1500-word essay on global warming. And 1500-word essays on global warming – or any topic, really – work better when they address a narrowed, specific focus as opposed to a broad,

---

[20] R. Toor, "Writing with Soul," *The Chronicle of Higher Education*, May 22, 2013,

overarching purpose. (In fact, that statement applies to essays of any length as well as to journal articles, dissertations and books.)

Keep in mind that "rein in your ambition" doesn't mean limit your aspirations or, in this case, the themes you pursue in your essays. It means keep them within your control – and your allotted word count.

2. Be readily influenced by others.

Those "others" are your readers. Think about their current knowledge, interests and expectations. Ask yourself how your paper could educate, enlighten and perhaps even entertain them. In other words, focus on an element that was downplayed earlier in the book: serving your readers' needs.

With those two pieces of advice in mind, consider again "global warming" as a topic.

A broad topic like "global warming" puts too great a burden on the writer and disregards the reader. No one writer can possibly research all the pertinent information on global warming – or understand it all. No one document can possibly explain in sufficient detail all the theories, causes, and effects of global warming. It's an overwhelming task that's likely to result in the writer resorting to superficial – and perhaps unsubstantiated – information culled from **Wikipedia** in a futile effort to cover all the bases. And superficial information means the essay skims the surface of the topic, providing information that the average reader already knows. Consequently, the average reader is likely to find your paper boring and not worth reading.

Compare the above topic with this one: "The impact of global warming on polar bear migration in the Canadian Arctic."

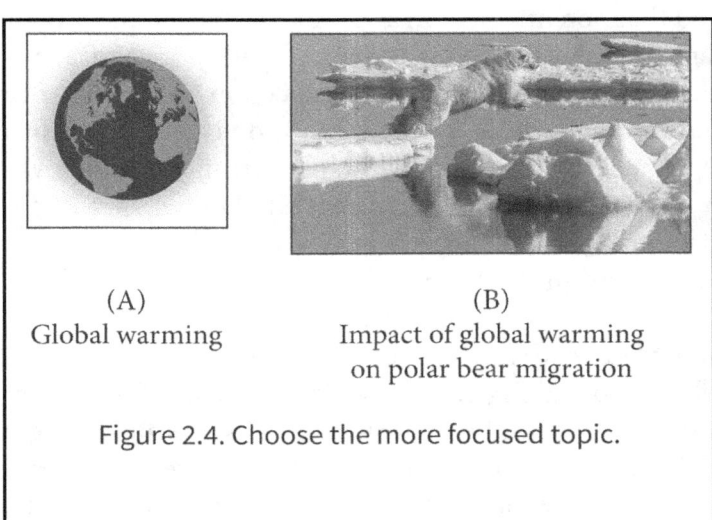

(A)
Global warming

(B)
Impact of global warming on polar bear migration

Figure 2.4. Choose the more focused topic.

The second topic makes the writer's job much easier, and it serves the reader's needs. With this specific topic, you can focus your research, more efficiently identifying only the most credible and suitable information sources. And because the topic is so narrowed, you have the space within your word allotment to delve into detail, providing your readers with new information – and therefore giving them an incentive to read your paper.

We gravitate toward general, all-encompassing topics for two reasons: (i) We haven't mastered the art of doing otherwise. We don't know how to take a broad topic and extract a specific focus from it. (ii) We have egos – and they tend to prefer the big and all-encompassing to the specific and focused.

Discover a spacious theme within a specific topic

Let's deal first with the more challenging of those two elements: the ego. This challenge isn't unique to you alone. It is, in fact, the bane of *every* writer. The ego prods us toward the all-encompassing topic because it's usually an important topic, perhaps one of universal importance. And writing about it gives us a chance to be associated with that importance. Hence, "Solutions to world hunger" may seem more substantive than "The role of community gardens in Halifax, Nova Scotia" or "Iconic female leaders" more compelling than "Adelaide Hoodless' impact on health care in Ontario."

Of course, it's perfectly reasonable to want your paper's topic to be important, substantive and compelling. That, after all, gives you the potential to think deeply and to develop insights that are important, substantive and compelling. But here's something to consider: it's possible to find those qualities and that potential within a specific, focused topic. In other words, go ahead and write about the big themes if that's your desire, but use your specific focus to ground those themes in a context your reader can understand. Even Michelangelo had to fit his grand vision within the ceiling of the Sistine Chapel. Do the same with your writing: fit what you want to say within the confines of a focused context. And when you do so, you'll intensify its impact.

Consider, for example, this passage:

> There is only so much air on the planet, and we must share it with all other breathing creatures. Now and since the beginning of breathing, we have all been breathing the same air, taking it into our bodies, transforming it and being transformed by it, using it to move through time, moment by moment, to be what we are. This

is intimacy: we take into our bodies the very air that others have breathed. Molecules of air that Buddha breathed, that Jesus breathed, that Plato, Hitler, Napoleon, Einstein, Shakespeare, the pope, the heavyweight champion of the world breathed; air breathed by men, women, and children, by heroes and murderers, by animals, plants, and insects, throughout time on earth – some of these same molecules have been inside of us.[21]

The author, Norman Fischer, has a big, universal message he wants to convey: the interconnectedness of all beings. A lesser writer might try to convey this message through a broad topic about peace, love, and the global community – leading to predictable generalizations that dilute the paper's impact and make the reader's eyes glaze over with boredom. Notice what Fischer does instead. He contains the discussion within a specific, focused topic: the fact that we all breathe the same air. It's a counterintuitive move, choosing the simple and the specific ("molecules of air") to convey a universally significant message. But it works because the author knows (like quite a few great writers before him) that it's possible to find a spacious theme within a narrowed topic.

That's what good writers do – and that's what the ego tries to prevent us from doing. The ego – the part of us that wants to assert how important we are – clamours for the reader's attention by grabbing hold of broad topics, and then skimming the surface of them. In the process, it overlooks entirely the potential and depth of the specific. The ego also preys on our insecurities, making us question whether we'll have enough to write (and meet the essay's assigned word count) if we choose a narrowed topic instead of a broad one. It lacks faith in our ability to find the spacious potential and depth within the specific.

The ego, in other words, is superficial, dimwitted, and a fearmonger. Don't let it choose your paper's topic.

A bit of mindful attention as you choose your essay's focus is the best prevention – or remedy – here. All it requires is asking yourself one question, and then giving yourself an honest answer to that question: "Why am I choosing this particular topic?" If the answer involves your desire to feel important or your anxiety about meeting the assigned word count, re-consider your choice because it's likely being guided by your ego and is, therefore, too broad and all encompassing. Instead, make the reader and your

---

21. N. Fischer, "Sailing Home," in *The Best Buddhist Writing 2009*, ed. Melvin McLeod (Boston: Shambhala Publications, 2009), p. 119.

message the guiding elements. When you do that, you serve your readers' needs by giving them a paper that has depth and accuracy. You also end up serving an important need of your own: your need to matter. Your paper is more likely to have an impact when it focuses on your reader and your message rather than on showcasing your importance or yielding to your fears about not having enough to say.

But this leads to the question, "What exactly is my message?" Answering that question is the function of the next section, which explains how to develop a thesis or purpose statement from your focused topic.

Develop your thesis or purpose statement

A **thesis statement** is the point of view or the specific argument you're going to present and support in an essay. If you're writing a report or proposal instead, the paper's focus may be referred to as the **purpose statement** rather than the thesis.

A thesis summarizes the paper's conclusions right at the start, usually in a sentence or two at the end of the introduction. A purpose statement may or may not directly disclose the paper's specific conclusions. Instead, it may simply describe the route the paper will take to arrive at its conclusions. Depending on the discipline and the type of document, a purpose statement may be the opening sentence or two of the document, or it may come at the end of the introduction. While it's not mandatory, the purpose statement is sometimes immediately identifiable by its preface: for example, "The purpose of this report is …" Here are some examples:

Thesis statement

"A well-written essay provides the student writer with the satisfaction of having accomplished a challenging task; insights that might otherwise have remained dormant; and the possibility of a good grade."

A detailed thesis statement, like the one above, will make the writing go more smoothly: your key points and the order in which they'll be presented are all contained within this statement. You've already put a fair bit of thought and perhaps research into your topic.

Those same advantages can also be found in a well-written purpose statement:

Purpose statement

"The purpose of this paper is to investigate three benefits of a well-written essay from the student writer's perspective."

This purpose statement identifies the paper's focus, but not its conclusions. Its opening – "The purpose of this paper is ..." – explicitly directs both writer and reader. There's no mistaking the sentence's intent or its important function in the paper. Compare it with the second purpose statement below:

"This paper investigates three benefits of a well-written essay from the student writer's perspective: personal satisfaction; new insights; and the possibility of a good grade."

With this version, the paper's three-part structure is embedded within the purpose statement. It's a combination of purpose and thesis statement.

Imagine you're assigned an essay on the general topic "digital technology and writing." As instructed earlier, begin by generating ideas and content for your general topic through either free writing or mind mapping. Next, scrutinize the material you've just produced, looking for connections and recurring themes. Sometimes this is enough: a narrowed purpose statement or thesis announces itself. Sometimes, though, you need to help it along with an additional three-part strategy:

1. *Ask questions*: What is digital technology? Does digital technology help or hinder writing? What evidence supports this impact? Why does this matter?

2. *Add modifiers to the key words:* Academic writing? Creative writing? Business writing? Student writers? Novelists? First graders? Undergraduate student writing? Web 2.0 technology? Social media technology? Answering questions and adding modifiers might lead to more free writing or mind mapping. Or the answers and the modifiers might be found within the free writing and mind mapping you've already done. In any case, this strategy may lead you to something interesting:

"Too much time spent communicating via Web 2.0 technology, such as texting, Twitter and Facebook, can weaken undergraduate student writing"

or

"This paper discusses the negative impacts of Web 2.0 technology such as texting, Twitter and Facebook on undergraduate writing."

Now that you have the start of a focused thesis or purpose statement, consider a third strategy to help further refine it.

3. Picture your bored, reluctant reader: Your professor may view reading and grading a batch of essays as an avocation to be embraced. He or she may be dedicated to fostering your intellectual growth through carefully reading every sentence and adding thoughtful notations in the margins. Chances are, however, your professor is also mightily bored with reading and commenting on student essays. After a while, even the most dedicated instructors balk at the prospect of reading yet one more paper.

©CANSTOCK PHOTO/JALEPHOTO

And they're not alone in feeling that way. Much of the population these days, from adolescents onward, could be characterized as reluctant readers, easily bored by unremitting text. The Internet, with its vast, immediate stores of hyperlinked information, may be to blame. Research suggests that Internet users – a group that includes everyone you know – skim, rather than read, when they're online.[22] Over time, this habit of skimming becomes ingrained, strengthening certain neural pathways in the brain, such as the ability to quickly move from one hyperlink to another, but weakening others, such as the ability (and the motivation) to read lengthy text.

What does this mean for you, writing your essay? It means you need to convince your reluctant readers that your paper deserves attention. It contains information and insights that make exercising those weakened neural pathways worth the effort.

The most immediate way to convince them is through your thesis or purpose statement: Will it catch their attention? Does it evoke the unfamiliar and intriguing – or does it default to the predictable, well-worn path? Since you've gotten this far in the book, you must know the latter is never preferred. A reluctant reader needs a counterintuitive writer.

Consequently, you might revisit "negative impacts of Web 2.0 technology on undergraduate writing." It's a focused topic, certainly, but it might be

---

22. Nicholas Carr, "Is Google Making Us Stupid?" *The Atlantic*, July 2008, http://www.theatlantic.com/magazine/archive/2008/07/is-google-making-us-stupid/306868/.

a bit predictable from the perspective of your main reader – your professor – who can probably easily summon a number of arguments linking Facebook and texting to poor student writing. You might, therefore, experiment with the topic. Instead of arguing that Web 2.0 technology weakens student writing, consider the opposite stand: could it strengthen student writing? Could you, in fact, argue the opposite of your original thesis, so that you end up with something like the following?

"Web 2.0 technologies such as texting, Twitter and Facebook can strengthen undergraduate student writing: along with opportunities to practice writing, these technologies also provide readership and immediate feedback"

or

"This paper explains why Web 2.0 technologies such as texting, Twitter and Facebook have the potential to strengthen undergraduate student writing."

There is nothing inherently wrong with the original version, which focuses on the negative impact, and there's nothing inherently superior with the revised version, which focuses on the positive impact. Both are workable, and both could be well received by your reader. One, however, might be better received than the other because it leads to more intriguing, informative material, taking the reader down the "path less travelled." Of course, a path that diverges *too far* from the reader's familiar mindset could also have the opposite effect: it might alienate your reader right from the start. No exact science can help you determine which path to choose. You have to figure that out for yourself, ideally based on the strength of your arguments – but, realistically, also based on your understanding of your audience.

Here's a guide to help your choice:

- Any thesis or purpose, including a provocative/unexpected one, that lacks strong support will inevitably result in a poor essay.
- A predictable thesis or purpose that's accompanied by strong support lays the groundwork for a good essay. (Maybe that's a bit restrained. A predictable thesis or purpose [i.e., one that re-affirms long-standing or widely held beliefs] has its own value, but translating that value into an *excellent* essay – as opposed to a good essay – is challenging.)
- A provocative/unpredictable thesis or purpose that's accompanied by strong support lays the groundwork for an excellent essay. (That's good advice if you're confident your readers are objective

and open to new viewpoints. If you suspect otherwise, modify your thesis or purpose so that it's less provocative/unpredictable.)

Exercise 2.4

Using the instructions and the examples provided above as your guide, practice turning these broad topics into specific thesis or purpose statements.

Begin with your broad topic.	Ask questions. (This step may require a separate sheet for free writing or mind mapping.)	Add modifiers. (This step may also require a separate sheet for free writing or mind mapping.)	Develop a focused, specific thesis or purpose statement.	Picture your bored reader's reaction. How might he/she respond to this thesis or purpose statement?	Should you revise your thesis or purpose statement? How?
Challenges facing post-secondary students					
Impact of technology					
Sustainability as a business philosophy					
The value of travel					
Being a new Canadian					
An ideal career					
The perfect diet					
The relevance of poetry					
Music as therapy					
Reducing our carbon footprint					
Your own broad topic					

Three annoying truths about the above exercise

In the process of completing the above exercise, you may have discovered three annoying truths about developing a thesis or purpose statement:

1. It's messy. The boxes couldn't contain everything you wanted to write, and your entries started spilling beyond their neatly defined spaces, the whole table becoming one big mess. That's good. That's how it's supposed to be. Our thoughts don't typically unfold in a neatly logical, linear manner, and, it bears repeating, neither does good writing.

2. The broad topic is of limited help. You may have ended up with a thesis or purpose that bears little resemblance to the original broad topic. That may be fine. The broad topics were unfocused and held no particular promise of interest for the reader. There's no value to be had in sticking closely to those qualities.

3. "It takes a long time for something to emerge that allows you to keep your self-respect about the matter."[23] Yes. We're back to quoting Leonard Cohen again, because he knew the importance of perseverance. And Malcolm Gladwell quantified this importance in his book *Outliers*, when he explained that mastering a challenging skill – and writing is a challenging skill – takes 10,000 hours of practice. So if you felt frustrated by the amount of time it took to complete this exercise, and if, even then, you're still not completely satisfied with the result, know you're in good company and on the right path. And at this stage, it still *is* a path, not a destination.

REVISING YOUR THESIS OR PURPOSE STATEMENT

Tightly clenching anything is generally an unhealthy habit because it robs us of the ability to be flexible and open. From the writer's perspective, clenching too tightly to a thesis or purpose means we resist credible perspectives and compelling insights that don't fit our thesis or purpose.

At this point, we're still in the early stages of the writing process. As you think more deeply about your paper and delve further into the research, you may come across strong material that runs counter to your thesis or that's not relevant to your purpose.

If you're too attached to the thesis or purpose you've already developed, you'll resist these good ideas or ignore them altogether. And ignoring good ideas because they don't precisely fit your purpose or perhaps even contradict your thesis weakens your paper. Good writers don't get so attached to their own material that they can't revise it when new and better possibilities

---

23. Retrieved from http://www.leonardcohenfiles.com/news2.html.

present themselves. If that should happen, revise your thesis or purpose so that you can include the new material in your paper. The revision might be a slight modification only or a complete change. In either case, the result will be a better paper, one that's not restrained by a death-grip clench on a thesis or purpose that doesn't honour your full understanding of the topic.

SUMMARY

Good writers are often uncertain writers, saved from complacency and mediocrity by their need to fuss, question and revise. Good writers recognize that writer's block is simply procrastination. And good writers get something down on the page or computer screen by following a number of durable, straightforward principles: ideas and phrasing for the first draft come more easily when they're not subject to the relentless scrutiny of logic, grammar and spelling; the act of writing generates ideas the writer didn't know he/she had; a writer's "voice" can make the paper more pleasurable to write and to read; and significant, spacious themes are best presented within focused, specific topics.

Chapter 3
Structuring Your Paper

This chapter will help you structure your writing by ...

- Becoming familiar with six different organizational patterns
- Restricting your paper to three to five main sections
- Memorizing (and applying) the first half of a mantra: "predictable structure ..." (The second half follows in Chapter 4.)

THREE WAYS TO STRUCTURE YOUR PAPER

Memorize these three words: *Clock. Globe. Triangle.*

You've just memorized three ways of structuring your paper. Essay writing allows all kinds of opportunities for creativity and for forging your own path. Save that creative energy and path-finding for the content (which we'll discuss in the next section). For the structure, let someone else do the hard work. And luckily for us, someone else has. Keith Spicer devoted an entire book to eminently practical, easy-to-follow advice on structuring: *Think on Your Feet: How to Organize Ideas to Persuade Any Audience*.[24]

This section is largely based on his work, the beauty of which lies in its simplicity and broad applicability. You can use these structures to organize any document (or presentation.)

The clock plan structures your essay chronologically. The natural inclination of most people is to start with the past (or the present) and move forward from there. Therefore, an essay on, say, "Challenges facing university students" could begin by discussing

- current challenges; and then move to
- short term challenges, perhaps within the next year or so; and finally
- long-term challenges in the more distant future (e.g., within the next five years or however you define "long term").

In other words, the clock plan organizes the paper's content within blocks of time.

The globe plan structures the material in your essay spatially. This method is less commonly used than the

---

24. K. Spicer, *Think on Your Feet: How to Organize Ideas to Persuade Any Audience* (Toronto: Doubleday Canada, 1985).

other plans discussed here, but that element of difference could work in your favour. Because it's a different, less common structure, the globe plan can allow your paper to stand out, in a positive way, from everyone else's work. Applying the globe plan to "Challenges facing university students" might result in this organizational plan:
- challenges that university students face adjusting to *their residence or off-campus home*
- challenges that arise within *the classroom*
- challenges they face as they return for visits to *their family home.*

As illustrated, the globe plan organizes the paper's content according to place or geography – in this case, three different locations: their new residence; classroom; and family home.

The triangle plan is probably the most widely used of all the plans discussed here, deriving its name from the fact that each angle represents one key point of your paper. These points can take the form of particular aspects or perspectives of the topic. Here's an example of the same topic – challenges facing university students – organized according to the triangle plan:

A triangle structure based on aspects
- academic challenges
- financial challenges
- personal challenges

or

A triangle structure based on perspectives
- the students' perspective of the top challenges
- the professors' perspective of the top challenges
- the family's perspective of the top challenges

It isn't a coincidence that the clock, globe and triangle structures explained above all revolve around **three key points**. Spicer explains why three is a good number to work with:
- A three-part paper builds momentum that "move[s] an audience from A to B to C."
- The number three has long resonated with audiences as a recurring figure in folklore, mythology, religion, systems of logic, lit-

erature and, for North Americans, popular culture: "think of the Three Musketeers, three blind mice, three men in a tub, and hundreds of other folkloric and literary-religious examples." We are, on some level, 'tuned in' to the number three.[25]

And if those two reasons seem too abstract, consider a third:
- Restricting your main points to three (or four or five at the most) increases the likelihood your audience will remember them.

If you think the three-part structure can't possibly contain all the complexities of your paper, try breaking each of the three main parts into subsets of three to five. Your first point might be further subdivided into three parts, your second point into four parts, and so on. That way, you're maintaining the overall three-part structure, which makes it easier for you to write the paper and easier for your readers to follow it.

THE VALUE OF A PREDICTABLE STRUCTURE

If you also think that all this fuss over the paper's structure is highly prescriptive and simple, you're right. It is. But that's by design. You want your paper's structure to be so tightly controlled and obvious that your readers can immediately "see" its organization. They can, with very little effort, and almost right away, discern the paper's clock, globe or triangle pattern – which means their attention won't be distracted by their own efforts to order the material they're reading.

And they *will* try to order the material if they can't make sense of it immediately. There's something within your reader – within all of us, actually – that craves order. In writing, that order can take the form of a predictable structure. The loveliest example is Shakespeare's repeated use of iambic pentameter. Its predictable rhythm of "light/strong light/strong" is said to "echo the beating of the human heart"[26] – and thus structure helps connect the words to the reader. But if that's too esoteric for your tastes, consider another example from a different poet. In W. B. Yeats's poem "A Prayer for my Daughter," he asks that his daughter might one day marry and "be brought to a house where all's accustomed, ceremonious." Of all the wishes a parent might have for his or her child, this one seems at first glance uninspired, completely underwhelming. But it's completely in tune with Yeats' counterintuitive perspective. A lesser writer might have predictably dismissed custom and ceremony as outmoded vestiges of the

---

25. Spicer, pp. 38, 39.
26. Leslie O'Dell, *Shakespearean Language: A Guide for Actors and Students* (Westport, CT: Greenwood Publishing, 2002), p. 32.

past. Yeats, however, does the opposite: he invokes them because he knows there's something within us all that yearns for harmony and order.

In short, framing your writing within a tight structure satisfies your readers' inherent need for order, and it imbues your writing with meaning. Your good thoughts, after all, are not enough all by themselves. They need to be placed in a meaningful order. The clock, globe and triangle structures are all ways of achieving this order. Routinely depending on one of them, or a combination of them, means you can then dedicate most of your writing time to figuring out and expressing the actual ideas or content – and your readers can then dedicate all of their time to focusing on those good ideas and content.

FIGURING OUT THE STRUCTURE BEFORE THE THESIS OR PURPOSE

Writers of fiction understand this – no one more so than British novelist E.M. Forster whose words "How do I know what I think until I see what I say" aptly sum up the theme of this section. Put simply, sometimes writers – and if you're writing an essay that makes you, for the time being anyway, one of them – can't figure out their thesis or purpose until they've worked out the paper's structure.

Therefore, you may need to take the material you've come up with during your freewriting or mind mapping stage, and neatly, logically order it, using one, or a combination, of the structures discussed here. Based on that, you then develop your thesis or purpose. Sometimes it works that way. As odd as it may seem, sometimes you won't know what you think until you see what you say.

Exercise 3.1

Revisit the example structures given above for the general topic "Challenges facing university students." These examples illustrate the clock, globe and triangle structures well enough, but they ignore completely the earlier advice about being specific. No one can effectively discuss all the academic, financial and personal challenges of university students in one essay – especially when that essay probably has a word limit somewhere in the vicinity of 500 to 2500 words.

Make the topic more specific by focusing on only one challenge, say, academic challenges. Take that one challenge – academic – and focus it even more by breaking it up into three sub-challenges. Here's an example, using the triangle pattern:

Academic challenges faced by university students:
- large, anonymous classes – limited one-on-one contact with instructors
- high standards
- the need for independent and disciplined decision-making – choosing a major, attending classes regularly, etc.

Compare these three main points to the three points in the original example (academic, financial and personal). Do you see how the more narrowed focus in the revised version would lead to a paper that's easier to write and more intriguing to read?

Now develop a thesis or purpose statement that "fits" the narrowed focus of those three new points.

The other examples illustrating the triangle, clock and globe structures are similarly broad. Re-work them in the same way: maintain the triangle, clock or globe structure, but narrow the focus of the three main points. Once you've done that, develop a thesis or purpose statement for each.

THREE MORE STRUCTURES

This section could easily have been entitled "Eight or nine more structures" – but you probably need only these remaining three:
- Ping pong
- Block-by-block
- Problem-solution

They're the handiest ones. (And you probably wouldn't have remembered eight or nine more structures, anyway.)

The ping pong structure has a "back and forth" fluidity that lends itself to essays that involve comparing and contrasting; presenting strengths and weaknesses; or discussing advantages and disadvantages. For example, a strength would be immediately followed by its corresponding weakness, an advantage by its corresponding disadvantage, and so on, until all the strengths and weaknesses or advantages and disadvantages have been explained.

Think of **the block-by-block structure** as a more patient version of the ping-pong method, one that's minus the potentially frenetic "back and forth" movement. Hence, only after all the similar points are presented are the differences raised. Or the strengths or advantages are presented together, in one block, and then followed by the weaknesses or disadvantages. Or vice versa.

Problem-solution. Pay particular attention to this one. It works with so many essay topics – and it can also work in tandem with the ping-pong and block-by-block structures. The problem-solution structure encourages you to think and to dig deeply into the topic. You're going beyond identifying an existing problem. You're now developing a potential solution to that problem.

Here's an example of the problem-solution, ping-pong and triangle structures working together:

> *Academic challenges (or problems) facing university students:*
> **Challenge #1:** Large, anonymous classes – limited one-on-one contact with instructors.
> **Solution:** Explore the possibility of enrolling in a small, specialized first-year seminar.
> **Challenge #2:** High standards.
> **Solution:** Take advantage of university-sponsored study groups.
> **Challenge #3:** The need for independent and disciplined decision-making and behaviour: choosing a major, attending classes regularly, etc.
> **Solution:** Consult with academic advisors.

Alternatively, you could approach the same topic by integrating the problem solution, block-by-block and triangle structures:

> *Academic challenges (or problems) facing university students:*
> - large, anonymous classes – limited one-on-one contact with instructors
> - high standards
> - the need for independent and disciplined decision-making and behaviour: choosing a major, attending classes regularly, etc.
>
> *Solutions:*
> - explore the possibility of enrolling in a small, specialized first-year seminar
> - take advantage of university-sponsored study groups
> - consult with the academic counselors

As illustrated, essays often contain more than one structure. An essay may be organized around one overall structure, but within that main structure are various other sub-structures. Which structure – or combination of structures – you choose depends on your thesis or purpose, your material and, to a certain extent, happenstance. A sudden insight or fleeting perception helps shape how the material gets ordered.

And that was an indirect way of saying that no rigorous formula exists for determining how to structure an essay. There is no one right way – only possibilities, of which half a dozen have been given here for you to consider.

REDUCE YOUR STRUCTURE TO ITS SIMPLEST TERMS

Some structures, though, may work better for your particular essay than others. In trying to figure out what structure or combination of structures works best for your essay, keep one word in mind: Simple. Let stark, unadorned, logical simplicity guide you in structuring your essay. Check out the sample structure below to see what I mean:

1. What is this paper about?
Academic challenges facing post-secondary students (large classes; high standards; independent decision-making) and solutions.

2. Why is this an important topic?
It affects an increasingly large segment of our population as post-secondary enrolment continues to increase (provide enrolment figures from two generations ago vs. one generation ago vs. today).

3. What are the challenges and possible solutions?
Discuss challenges in detail, using the structure or combination of structures already outlined above. Provide solutions.

4. What does all of this mean for future students?
Depends on where the students live: implications for students living in large urban areas; smaller cities and towns; rural areas.

Now, skim the **headings** without reading the rest. Can you easily "see" the logical flow from one section to another? That's what you want to aim for: it's a combination of ease and effort: the structure is easy to see, allowing you to now focus all your efforts on developing strong content. (Note: these aren't necessarily the headings that you'll use in the final paper. These are your "draft headings" that allow you to see the structure and to stay on track as you write the paper.)

Exercise 3.2
Figuring out the structure before the purpose or thesis

Below is material for an essay. Keeping in mind the six structures described above, order this material into a coherent essay structure – and then identify which structure or, more likely, combination of structures, have emerged.

Once you've done that, develop a thesis or purpose statement for the outlined paper.

Compare your results with the published essay ("A New Curriculum for Real-World Success" by Cathy Davidson[27]), which is available online. What are the strengths and weaknesses of your version and of the published version?

> To get us thinking about the possibilities of educational reform, I propose a Start-Up Core Curriculum for Entrepreneurship, Service and Society (SUCCESS).
>
> The opposition of "liberal arts" and "vocational education" carries with it a lot of residual 19th-century class snobbery as well as 20th-century quantitative bias. In the real world of the 21st century, though, there aren't "two cultures" – the arts and the sciences. We need both.
>
> Skills acquisition is no substitute for a degree. Just ask companies like Google and Apple: They may pick the cream of the online-educated crop for outsourced jobs that come without benefits or security, but typically they do not consider these students as corporate leaders of the future.
>
> Nearly 50 per cent of postsecondary students in the United States end up leaving without a degree. The data suggest that they drop out because of a shortage of funds or a lack of interest – but also because

---

27. C. Davidson, "A New Curriculum for Real-World Success," *The Globe and Mail*, October 13, 2012. The essay, which remains available at https://www.theglobeandmail.com/news/national/time-to-lead/a-new-curriculum-for-real-world-success/article4610483/, is a slightly modified version of Davidson's earlier essay for *Fast Company*, July 2012; that essay is available at https://www.fastcompany.com/2680124/a-core-curriculum-to-create-engaged-entrepreneurs).

they do not see real-world relevance.

Some argue that online courses (including those offered free by universities such as the Massachusetts Institute of Technology and Harvard) are the answer. If well-constructed, they work exceptionally well in certain fields, especially technical ones suited to individualized, challenge-based learning.

U.S. surveys of employers reveal, over and over, that what they prize most in future managers are excellence in written and spoken communication, critical and creative thinking, an ability to collaborate across distances and cultural differences, breadth of knowledge and experience that takes students out of localism and provincialism, basic technical skills, quantitative literacy, and an ability to be flexible and take risks in changing environments.

As a cartoon circulating on Facebook would have it, "Science can tell you how to clone a Tyrannosaurus rex. Humanities can tell you why this might be a bad idea."

As award-winning journalist Thomas Friedman recently suggested, "Big breakthroughs happen when what is suddenly possible meets what is desperately necessary."

SUCCESS, admittedly, would be expensive.

SUCCESS is not just about content mastery, but about putting deep knowledge into practice to address real-world global problems.

As for the subject focus of SUCCESS, even if a student were not to go into one of the many fields related to global health, such a foundational first year and experiential second year would show how the "wisdom of the ages" can help us deconstruct some of the cant of our era. After all, the "real world" itself demands serious, critical thinking – including how we might redesign the siloed, hierarchical, pre-professional research university that arose in the late 19th century. With a backlash against higher education in full swing, what better time than now to take up this challenge?

The second part of the program would then take students off campus for an eye-opening year of entrepreneurial, service-oriented, practical work.

Seminars would be devoted to the great books, from Socrates to Amartya Sen. But from there, students would be challenged to investigate how these thinkers would contribute to issues of general social health and welfare and tie their work into business and management frameworks.

SUCCESS would take up two years, with the first devoted to a thematic cluster of problem-based courses. For example, if the liberal-arts topic were "global health disparities," interdisciplinary, team-taught courses would touch on health but also humanities, the arts, social sciences and computational and biological sciences. Weekly meetings with all faculty and students would help to connect the intellectual dots.

To save costs, a SUCCESS program might include a mix of large lectures and online courses (in areas such as introductory statistics, foreign language or HTML). Both formats would be supplemented by small group meetings with peers, teachers, teaching assistants and sometimes guest experts.

Simultaneously contributing to the world, and learning from it, an engaged practicum would address the very real issue of "sophomore slump" (when the dropout potential runs highest). It would also be a targeted alternative to the typical year-abroad experience, which, even for the lucky 14 per cent of U.S. graduates now able to afford it, is often not linked to coursework or future careers.

Students do not need to go abroad to learn how to participate in and contribute to diverse cultures and populations, given the gap between rich and poor in North America. Many, if not most, colleges and universities are located with radical income and health disparities a few kilometres, if not blocks, away.

For their practicum, students could be placed in non-profits, community organizations, small businesses and after-school programs. They would lend their new expertise, deep thinking and skills in communication, leadership and collaboration to organizations desperate for help in financially strapped times. In turn, students would learn more about the urgencies of deep and broad knowledge, the importance of general and specialized education, the necessity for computational and social networking skills and the imperative for hard work and true dedication – not all of it well rewarded – than any classroom could begin to instill.

Exercise 3.3
Figuring out the thesis and then the structure

Keeping in mind the six structures described above, figure out an essay structure for the thesis or purpose statements that you developed in Exercise 3.1. Identify which structure – or combination of structures – emerges.

NOW THAT YOU KNOW THE RULES ...

Break them, now and again. The structures explained above, with their emphasis on three main points, provide you with a solid foundation. Once you've clearly mastered that foundation, however, don't be restricted by it. When your material requires it, modify these structures and deviate from the "rule of three". Always make sure, though, the reader can easily follow your structure.

SUMMARY

Readers want the structure of any academic paper to be so clear that they can discern it quickly and easily. You can provide that clear structure by following one or a combination of the following organizational patterns: clock, globe, triangle, ping pong, block-by-block, and problem-solution. However, once you become proficient in applying these structures, you may start to feel constrained by them. That's your signal to begin experimenting with another way to organize your paper. But all the while, remember this key principle: the structure should be simple and predictable.

Chapter 4
Developing Your Content

This chapter will help you figure out what to write by ...

- Focusing on the second half of the mantra: "predictable structure, **unpredictable content**"
- Understanding the value of "unpredictable content" for both writer and reader
- Becoming familiar with four strategies to generate unpredictable content
- Using detail to support your points and engage your readers
- Ensuring your arguments are logically developed.

WHY UNPREDICTABLE CONTENT WORKS FOR THE READER ...

The best essays contain some unpredictable content: a logical but unfamiliar perspective; a connection between facts or ideas that, at first glance, seem to have nothing in common; an argument that surprises while it convinces. In short, the best essays suggest, at least a little, that the writer has a different way of looking at things.

That "different way" can attract your readers' attention by throwing them off-balance.

A 10-second exercise (Exercise 4.1)

Stand beside a wall or within easy reach of a sturdy table or chair, so you'll have something close by to grab for support, if needed. Shift your weight onto one foot. Lift the other foot six or seven inches off the ground. Close your eyes. Spend the next 10 seconds trying to maintain (or re-gain) your balance.

Now consider this. You just spent 10 seconds in a state of intense focus, aiming for one goal: to be balanced. Maintaining (or regaining) our balance is dearly important to all of us. Without it, we feel shaky and vulnerable. That's why when we're feeling off-balanced we'll focus very hard to regain balance.

Similarly, if you want your readers' focus, throw them off-balance by giving them unpredictable content – content that rocks, even if it's just slightly, their stable foundation of all that's familiar, expected and certain.

That's akin to asking them to stand on one foot with their eyes closed. You'll have their complete attention as they try to regain their balance by making sense of the unpredictable content.

There's only one caveat to this advice: the readers' complete attention will be short-lived if they don't regain their balance quickly. Readers generally won't work hard to fathom unfamiliar material. Too many hours spent surfing and skimming the Internet have trained us to expect "understanding on demand." Make sure, then, your unpredictable content makes sense without making the reader work too long or too hard.

... AND FOR THE WRITER

What applies to the reader also applies to the writer. There's value to be had in throwing ourselves off-balance, figuratively speaking, by loosening our reliance on the known – all those conclusions that have been loudly proclaimed and repeated by many others – and exploring instead the unknown depths of our own, perhaps untested, thoughts.

In this excerpt from his 1784 essay "What is Enlightenment?"[28] philosopher Immanuel Kant spells out the nature of that value:

> Enlightenment is man's emergence from his self-incurred immaturity. Immaturity is the inability to use one's own understanding without the guidance of another. This immaturity is self-incurred if its cause is not lack of understanding, but lack of resolution and courage to use it without the guidance of another. The motto of enlightenment is therefore: *Sapere aude!* Have courage to use your own understanding!
>
> Laziness and cowardice are the reasons why such a large proportion of men, even when nature has long emancipated them from alien guidance, nevertheless gladly remain immature for life. For the same reasons, it is all too easy for others to set themselves up as their guardians. It is so convenient to be immature! If I have a book to have understanding in place of me, a spiritual adviser to have a conscience for me, a doctor to judge my diet for me, and so on, I need not make any efforts at all. I need not think, so long as I can pay; others will soon enough take the tiresome job over for me.

The tone is a bit harsh, but the message is compelling – and relevant:

---

28. Immanuel Kant, "What is Enlightenment?" as cited in Kant, *Political Writings*, 2nd edition, ed. H. Reiss (Cambridge: Cambridge University Press), p. 54.

when we habitually look to someone else to tell us what to think, we dishonour our own capabilities and potential for growth. Rather than moving toward enlightenment, we remain stuck.

This problem is typically not an issue for counterintuitive writers. They avoid simply restating conclusions that others have drawn. True, they research those conclusions, consider them, and cite them, when appropriate. And in the process of doing so, they're working in safe, familiar territory: repeating what credible sources – professors; reports; articles – have to say about the topic. However, it's also crowded territory: a lot of other writers are citing those same credible sources and repeating those same conclusions. That's why counterintuitive writers move on. They might, for example, take a conclusion from one of their credible sources and question it by pointing out a weakness; reinforce it by adding new support; develop it by integrating another perspective; or praise it by pointing out an unexpected insight.

Taking these extra steps toward independent thinking by incorporating your own views into the essay may initially feel like moving into unstable, perhaps even risky territory. But we've already established that feeling a bit off-balanced can heighten your concentration and result in a well-supported, thoughtful (perhaps even enlightened) perspective.

STRATEGIES TO GENERATE "UNPREDICTABLE CONTENT"
Pay attention to your title

- "Margaret Atwood returns from the future, to this moment"
- "7 famous foreigners for whom Canada proved fatal"
- "Our emotional relationship with clothes"
- "Of poison pens and profs"

Google "Maclean's Magazine" and you'll arrive at dozens more titles like the ones above – titles designed to attract attention and readership to serious articles written by good writers. If it works for *Maclean's* (or any number of other publications), it can also work for you – and this despite the dearth of creative titles in academic writing, generally. You've probably noticed that as you've conducted research, reading (or, more likely, skimming) scholarly articles in peer-reviewed journals. Journal editors and scholars don't often embrace witty titles. Some think it undermines the dignity or credibility of academic writing,[29] and some want to avoid misinterpretations. Humour, topical references or idioms may be misunderstood by readers from differ-

---

29. I. Sagi and E Yechiam, "Amusing Titles in Scientific Journals and Article Citation," *Journal of Information Science*, 34: 5 (2008): 680–687.

ent cultures. They're points to consider as you craft a title that will get your readers' attention.

And here's another point to consider. A creative title can be more than a means of attracting the readers' attention. A creative title can signal to you, as the essay's writer, that your paper will go beyond a dry recitation of facts, figures and other people's conclusions. It can affirm to you that you have the creativity to dig deep in this essay and present your own ideas, making it stand apart, in a positive way, from everyone else's. That's why I like to develop a creative title – a working one anyway – right from the start. It can motivate me to try harder.

Exercise 4.2

Develop a creative title for each of the essay topics you worked with in Exercise 3.1.

And then assure the reader (and yourself) that you know how to be conventional when convention's called for: place a **colon** after your creative title and write a conventional, informative subtitle (e.g., "Of poison pens and profs: 'RateMyProfessor' evaluations as a form of cyberbullying")

Read poetry

… or science or history or philosophy, or anything that's well written in any discipline, really. Because if it's well written, it probably invokes, at some point, a metaphor – the unlikely pairing of elements, scenarios or beliefs. And becoming well versed with metaphors makes us more likely to connect dots that no one else would think to connect. Newton's apple, Donne's compass, Porter's vertical mosaic, the American melting pot – all enduring metaphors that arose out of someone's ability to see things in a different way. That's also the essence of – and the reason for – unpredictable content: it claims the reader's attention and a place in their memory.

The title of Mark Kingwell's book *Catch and Release: Trout Fishing and the Meaning of Life* shows his affinity for metaphor. The following excerpt doesn't directly illustrate this affinity. It contains no sustained metaphors. It does, though, illustrate the product of a mind that likes reading and that doesn't shy away from drawing unexpected conclusions. As you read it, notice the unexpected conclusions he draws, the moments where his words take you by surprise and, in doing so, compel you to think.

> If you're like most people, there may be a tendency to wallow in your grief. "Some men, like bats or owls, have better eyes for the

darkness than for the light," said Dickens. And indeed it is easy to see the shadows of life now, to seek them out. But it is more complicated than mere disposition (the eyes you have) or even brain chemistry (the serotonin levels you register). You find that grief is stealthy. It works by ambush: a song, a sight, a sound. The crush of feeling, once started, does not want to abate.

And so you spiral down. The past is gone; it won't come back. That, after all, is what the past does – that's how it works. That scene of your comfort will not return. You have forever lost that moment of happiness. Real or imagined, it doesn't matter. For surely (you reason) that comfort was in reality more complicated than it seems in retrospect, scored with irritation and boredom and trivial worries about getting the bus back or having enough money to pay for lunch. Yes. And yet, it just doesn't matter much because – well, because she is gone. Or because they are dead. Or because he is right now making moments with another, not you. That's what has happened. And you can't change any of it.

But here is the part you wonder at and maybe frown over. It feels good, in its own twisted way, to think these thoughts and have these wrenching feelings – to have the tears leak out of you even as you try, childishly, to push them back in. Yes, it feels oddly good, and this is something you find hard to defend rationally but nevertheless appreciate as also part of your humanness, your need for connection, your sense of shared vulnerability. The pain is real yet exquisite, the longing sharp and unwelcome, yet also, like all longing, stimulating and … wise. Admit it: somehow, giving way to mourning is a pleasure. You know this is true.

This is not masochism, though your friends and your therapist may want to argue. It is wallowing, and that is something else. Schopenhauer, that great pessimist, the connoisseur of all things boring and depressing, saw this very clearly. Pain, he said, is always pleasure, and the perverse pleasure of mourning is one of the most interesting we know. If nothing else, it gives us a role to inhabit, a space of emergent meaning, a way of being in the world when the world seems – when the world is – drained of colour. It teaches us about the web of connection we have no choice but to inhabit, for reward and risk alike.

It can also, for the record, lead to art. The problem is, it doesn't have to; worse than that, it can lead to bad art just as easily as good.

This is a risk for everybody. Put your pencils away. Avoid the keyboard. Mourning becomes Electra, but it doesn't become most of us: we simply don't have the talent.

—Mark Kingwell[30]

Reflect on your own life

You've probably been told by at least one instructor not to use first person ("I") in your essays. He or she wanted you to focus on the issue being discussed in the paper and not on yourself. That makes sense – except when it doesn't.

Here's an excerpt by Ann Patchett that makes liberal use of first-person **pronouns**. Before you read it, though, do a quick exercise: jot down all the reasons people say they *don't* like Christmas.

Once you've done that, read on.

> I have never liked Christmas. In my family, there were happy Thanksgivings and tolerable Easters, but Christmas was a holiday we failed at with real vigor. I blame this on my parents' divorce. I was nearly six when my mother and sister and I left our home and my father in Los Angeles. The man my mother had been seeing in Los Angeles had moved to Nashville, and so we moved to Nashville as well. A year or so later they were married. My stepfather's four children still lived in Los Angeles with their mother. My stepfather's children spent their Christmases on a plane so that they could open presents in the morning with their mother in California and then open a second set of presents at night with their father in Tennessee. Thinking about this now, I realize how impossibly young they were to make a trip like that alone – a stepbrother and stepsister slightly older than I, a stepsister and stepbrother slightly younger. We were strangers but we had the world in common: they had betrayed their mother by leaving her alone on Christmas Day, just as my sister and I betrayed our father by staying in Tennessee.
>
> —Ann Patchett[31]

Now compare what you jotted down with the point made by Ann Patchett. I'm guessing "betrayal" is not on your list. She takes a familiar

---

30. Mark Kingwell, *Catch and Release: Trout Fishing and the Meaning of Life* (Toronto: Penguin Canada, 2003).
31. Patchett, *Story*, p. 11.

theme – Christmas is not a happy season for some people – and adds her own, unexpected reason for being disappointed with the holiday. It's a safe bet to say she could only have uncovered this reason by reflecting on her own life story.

Consider another piece that mines personal experiences for broader truths, Steve Jobs' commencement address at Stanford University, an excerpt from which is presented below. As you read it, think about the impact of Jobs' personal stories in supporting the themes they illustrate. Consider, too, the extent to which he incorporated "unpredictable" material into his address.

> I am honored to be with you today at your commencement from one of the finest universities in the world. I never graduated from college. Truth be told, this is the closest I've ever gotten to a college graduation. Today I want to tell you three stories from my life. That's it. No big deal. Just three stories.
>
> The first story is about connecting the dots.
>
> I dropped out of Reed College after the first 6 months, but then stayed around as a drop-in for another 18 months or so before I really quit. So why did I drop out?
>
> It started before I was born. My biological mother was a young, unwed college graduate student, and she decided to put me up for adoption. She felt very strongly that I should be adopted by college graduates, so everything was all set for me to be adopted at birth by a lawyer and his wife. Except that when I popped out they decided at the last minute that they really wanted a girl. So my parents, who were on a waiting list, got a call in the middle of the night asking: "We have an unexpected baby boy; do you want him?" They said: "Of course." My biological mother later found out that my mother had never graduated from college and that my father had never graduated from high school. She refused to sign the final adoption papers. She only relented a few months later when my parents promised that I would someday go to college.
>
> And 17 years later I did go to college. But I naively chose a college that was almost as expensive as Stanford, and all of my working-class parents' savings were being spent on my college tuition…
>
> —*Steve Jobs*[32]

---

32. Retrieved from http://news.stanford.edu/news/2005/june15/jobs-061505.html. The speech can be viewed on YouTube in its entirety.

The themes in Jobs' convocation address are the same as those presented at graduation ceremonies all over the world: trust in life; do what you love; follow your heart. In someone else's words, they might be dismissed as platitudes and easily forgotten. But Google the phrase "inspiring convocation addresses," and Jobs' name will appear. Watch his address on Youtube and you'll join over 20 million past viewers. What distinguishes Jobs' words? The powerful personal stories he uses to support his themes. Because they're his stories, and his alone, they're new to the audience. No one else has told them. Chances are, therefore, your eyes didn't glaze over with boredom as you read the excerpt – because the story's outcome isn't predictable. Unpredictable material has the potential to seize hold of the audience's attention like that. And a personal example has the potential to "connect" with the readers because they can relate to the circumstances or emotion underlying that personal story.

Consider whether an example from your own personal experience can similarly illustrate a point you want to convey in your paper. Make sure, however, that your focus remains on the point to be illustrated and that your personal example functions as supporting evidence only, not as the highlight of the paper. In other words, don't give that instructor who warned you not to use "I" the satisfaction of being right.

Write simply and concisely

Of all the advice in this book, this will be the hardest for some readers. Write simply and concisely. It goes against a need deeply ingrained within the academic world: the need to prove our intellect and therefore our worth. Equating intellect with worth is a common mistake among students and academics – and misjudging convoluted writing as a measure of both is equally common.

Fortunately, there's a remedy, the opening paragraph of a paper entitled "Molecular Structure of Nucleic Acids" (1953):

> We wish to suggest a structure for the salt of deoxyribose nucleic acid (D.N.A.) This structure has novel features which are of considerable biological interest.[33]

The authors, James Watson and Francis Crick, wrote this as the introduction to their paper, which was published in the prestigious journal *Nature*.

---

33. J.D. Watson and F.H. Crick, "Molecular Structure of Nucleic Acids: A Structure for Deoxyribose Nucleic Acid," *Nature* 171: 4356 (April 25, 1953): 737–738.

They did it in 25 words, two sentences and the **active voice**. The rest, all 818 words of it, models the same conciseness. This article went on to become, and still remains, one of the most important pieces of scholarship in the world.

Another 10-second exercise (Exercise 4.3)

When you feel the need to prove your cleverness, your education or your worth through big words or multisyllabic sentences, repeat Watson and Crick's opening two sentences.

Do this as often as necessary (i.e., until emulating their writing style becomes second nature to you).

And ironically, when you emulate their writing style, you'll find your own. That's the grace of embracing a simple, straightforward style: it leads us to our own voice, encouraging us to know what exactly we think and who, therefore, we are.

That's quite a claim to make about the power of simple, direct language, but consider this: when we write simply and concisely, there's no place to hide – no big words or convoluted phrasing to obscure our meaning or to act as a barrier between us and our readers. Our thoughts (or lack of them) are all clearly displayed. For example, when Watson and Crick write the second paragraph of their article in the same simple style as the first, we – even the non-chemists among us – can follow, if not all the details, the overall logical organization and sense:

> A structure for nucleic acid has already been proposed by Pauling and Corey. They kindly made their manuscript available to us in advance of publication. Their model consists of three inter-twined chains, with the phosphates near the fibre axis, and the bases on the outside. In our opinion, this structure is unsatisfactory for two reasons: (1) We believe that the material which gives the x-ray diagrams is the salt, not the free acid. Without the acidic hydrogen atoms it is not clear what forces would hold the structure together, especially as the negatively charged phosphates near the axis will repel each other. (2) Some of the van der Waals distances appear to be too small.

We now know the writers' view of their counterparts' work and the reasons for that view. It's clear.

Now read an excerpt about another scientist's view of his counterparts' work, from an article entitled "Transgressing the Boundaries: A Hermeneutic View of Quantum Gravity":

> It has thus become increasingly apparent that physical "reality," no less than social "reality," is at bottom a social and linguistic construct; that scientific "knowledge," far from being objective, reflects and encodes the dominant ideologies and power relations of the culture that produced it; that the truth claims of science are inherently theory-laden and self-referential; and consequently, that the discourse of the scientific community, for all its undeniable value, cannot assert a privileged epistemological status with respect to counter-hegemonic narratives emanating from dissident or marginalized communities.[34]

If you had trouble deciphering this passage, blame the writing, not yourself. The author, physicist Alan Sokal, submitted it as an experiment: he wanted to know if an article "liberally salted with nonsense"[35] could get published. And if you were impressed – or perhaps intimidated – by the writing, don't berate yourself. You're not the only reader apparently willing to accept that physical reality is really only a "social or linguistic construct." A leading North American journal of cultural studies published the article.

Sokal used this experiment to highlight "the apparent decline in the standards of intellectual rigor"[36] within the academic world. One measure of this decline is inflated language that sounds impressive but lacks clarity, support and perhaps even common sense. This kind of language makes our ideas difficult to see: they're hidden within extra **clauses**, cumbersome phrasing or unnecessary jargon. The reader has to work harder to make sense of it and may simply give up – rejecting the paper outright or, as Sokal's editor did, accepting it without fully assessing its merit.

Sokal's experiment took place in the 1990s. However, the problem of inflated prose masquerading as depth still exists today. It's one reason Harvard professor Daniel Pinker wrote an article entitled "Why Academics Stink at Writing."[37] A surprising – disheartening – number of published ac-

---

34. Alan Sokal, "Transgressing the Boundaries: A Hermeneutic View of Quantum Gravity," *Social Text* 46/47 (1996): 217–252.
35. Alan Sokal, "A Physicist Experiments with Cultural Studies" (1996), http://www.physics.nyu.edu/sokal/lingua_franca_v4/lingua_franca_v4.html.
36. Ibid.
37. *The Chronicle of Higher Education*, September 26, 2014, http://chronicle.com/article/Why-Academics-Writing-Stinks/148989/.

ademic articles are difficult to understand because of convoluted, cluttered writing. Some of them may be on your reading lists and in your course manuals. You may feel tempted to imitate them as a way of asserting that you belong in the academic world. Resist that temptation. You'll create a barrier between you and your readers because they can't understand – or they're bored by – your writing. You may also end up deluding yourself into thinking that you're writing something of substance when in fact you're not. Mundane observations and faulty logic can be hard to detect when they're wrapped up in clutter. There's no place for them to hide, though, when the language is simple – so they're easier for you to detect and to remove from your final draft.

But most seriously of all, copying someone else's notion of what an academic should sound like will stifle your own voice – and your own unique way of looking at things. Helen Sword, author of *Stylish Academic Writing*, explains it this way: "Intellectual creativity thrives best in an atmosphere of experimentation rather than conformity."[38] Don't conform to a stereotyped notion of academic writing characterized by unnecessary big words and convoluted phrasing. Instead, commit to writing simply and concisely. That way, you're more likely to connect with your audience and with your own creativity.

And at least one study gives us hope that some people will then view you as more credible than your wordy counterparts:

> People who use complicated language when simple language would suffice are viewed as less intelligent than people who used more basic words.... Study author Daniel Openheimer asked students to read writing samples from graduate school applications, sociology dissertations and various translations of Descartes. The more unnecessarily complex the samples were, the worse the essays were rated. But, Mr. Oppenheimer added, "it's important to point out that this study is not about problems with using long words—it's about problems with using long words needlessly."[39]

Ten Tips for Writing Simply and Concisely

Here are some tips[40] on how to write simply and concisely:

---

38. H. Sword, *Stylish Academic Writing* (Cambridge, MA: Harvard University Press, 2012), p. vii.
39. *The Globe and Mail*, March 30, 2003.
40. This section is taken directly from the *School of Hospitality, Food and Tourism Undergraduate Style Guide*, University of Guelph.

1. Avoid beginning sentences with "It is …" or "There are …"

    ✗   ~~It is~~ the purpose of this report to discuss …

    ✓   This report discusses …

2. Eliminate chains of "which" and "that" clauses.

    ✗   The recommendations ~~that are~~ most important …

    ✓   The most important recommendations …

3. Reduce the number of **prepositional phrases.**

    ✗   The introduction ~~of~~ an employment equity program ~~by~~ the company will result in …

    ✓   The company's new employment equity program will result in …

4. Don't directly address the reader as "you."

    ✗   As soon as ~~you~~ enter the restaurant, ~~you~~ notice the décor, which is comfortable and rustic.

    ✓   The décor is rustic, yet comfortable.
              or
    ✓   Entering the restaurant, guests immediately notice the rustic, yet comfortable décor.

5. Use the active rather than passive voice.

    ✗   The following sources were utilized in this paper: …

    ✓   This paper is based on the following sources …
              or
    ✓   We used the following sources of information: …

6. Choose direct, simple language whenever possible.

✗ It is inconsequential to arrive at a feasible solution if it cannot be implemented.

✓ Solutions must be practical.

7. Replace the "to be" **verb** whenever possible.

✗ I ~~was responsible for~~ the co-ordination ~~of~~ the different work units.

✓ I co-ordinated the different work units.

8. Convert **nouns** that end with "ion" and "ent" into verbs.

See example above.

9. Eliminate the "**rubber stamps**": those words, phrases and perhaps complete sentences you didn't actually make up yourself. They came to you immediately, with no effort at all, because you've seen them written so often by so many other writers. If you've ever instructed a reader to "Please find enclosed …" or felt the need to insert "I would argue …" before stating your argument, you know what a rubber stamp is. The following exercise will give you practice in identifying – and eliminating – rubber stamps.

Exercise 4.4

You probably have at least fourteen years of formal schooling. Put that schooling to good use by rewriting the following sentences, substituting the rubber stamps with your own words and phrasing:

(a) First and foremost, I would like to express my appreciation for your assistance with this assignment.

(b) It has been brought to my attention that I am submitting my paper two days late.

(c) Please find attached my completed essay. As per your request, it is double-spaced.

(d) Last but not least, please do not hesitate to contact me if you have any further questions.

10. Make sure you're actually saying something.

This final tip sounds obvious, but it's easy to pad your writing with phrases and sentences that sound important at first glance, but that are empty of any real meaning.

EXAMPLE: *The subject of waste management is considered to be one of importance to the lodging industry at the present time.*

By following the previous tips, you can edit this sentence so that it's more straightforward and concise:

~~The subject of~~ Waste management is ~~considered to be one~~ of importance to the lodging industry ~~at the present time~~.
or
Waste management is an important issue for the lodging industry.

The first editing step brings the content into sharper focus, so that it's easier to read and evaluate. The second step is to ask if you're actually saying something. If the answer is "no" or "not very much" (as is the case here – it's a fairly general statement that most people would agree with), then work on adding more depth to the statement. The latter almost always entails being more specific:

Waste management raises important financial, legal, and ethical issues for the lodging industry.

The result isn't just a shorter sentence (from 20 words in the original to 13 words in the final version), but also a more focused statement that guides both reader and writer.

Exercise 4.5

Use the above guidelines to rewrite the following sentences:

(a) It was during this time that I was provided with the opportunity to work independently and also collectively in a team environment.

(b) Upon completion of this project, I had the unique opportunity of being involved in the development and implementation of the University's strategic plan.

(c) There are two areas that are particularly important.

(d) There are many corporations that have become active in community and service work.

(e) The reason why I am writing this paper is to discuss the impact of domestic tourism on Toronto's economy.

(f) The library has made available to us a variety of sources that will be very helpful for this assignment.

When can you ignore the above ten tips?

"Rarely" is best answer to that question, opening the possibility that on some – infrequent – occasions, you might deliberately add an extra word, phrase or clause to strengthen your writing.

Consider, for example, the opening line of Jane Austen's *Pride and Prejudice*:

> It is a truth universally acknowledged, that a single man in possession of a good fortune, must be in want of a wife.

Try applying the rules for simplicity and conciseness to that sentence, and you'll end up with something like "A rich man needs a wife." You'll end up, in other words, with something lost from the original: a hint of the writer's wit, a suggestion that what follows will touch on some larger social issues, or perhaps just a stylistic flourish that makes you smile as you read the sentence. Those are all good reasons to occasionally ignore some of the above ten tips.

But, of course, you need to know, really well, how to apply these tips before you can judge whether or not to ignore them.

SUPPORTING DETAIL

Secretly imagine your readers as slightly dimwitted

I know. We've already characterized readers as bored, and now this. It seems disrespectful. But that's why I added the qualifiers "secretly" and "imagine." The goal is not to paint a picture of readers who are so lacking that your writing takes on a condescending tone. The goal is to paint a picture. Period.

A 10-second exercise (Exercise 4.6)

Fill in the blank with as many answers as you can think of in the next ten seconds:

So much depends upon _____.

Now compare what you've written to the original answer, from the poem by W.C. Williams. (The text has been turned upside down, so you wouldn't inadvertently see it before giving your own answer).

Unless you were already familiar with this poem, "wheel barrow", "rain water" and "white chickens" probably didn't make your list. Words like "health", "love", "money", "family", "friendship", and "jobs" probably did. They're good words but predictable choices. And while they might conjure up specific images and details that you connect with, they're likely to evoke nothing more than vague, easily dismissed generalities in the reader's mind. They don't paint a picture that he or she can clearly see, the way a red wheelbarrow sitting in the rain does.

> chickens
>
> beside the white
>
> water
>
> glazed with rain
>
> barrow
>
> a red wheel
>
> upon
>
> So much depends

Painting a picture in your readers' minds means you've engaged them – and you need specific detail to do that.

You also need specific detail to support the points you're trying to get across. And this is where the average writer tends to get lazy. The average writer figures the point is so clear in his or her own mind that the readers will immediately see it with that same clarity. "Why do I have to go through the time-consuming, tedious business of spelling out what anyone with average intelligence can clearly see for themselves?" argues the average writer. This is such a common perspective – particularly among academic writers – that there's a name for it: the curse of knowledge. Harvard professor and author Steven Pinker explains why it's a problem:

> The curse of knowledge is a major reason that good scholars write bad prose. It simply doesn't occur to them that their readers don't know what they know – that those readers haven't mastered the patois or can't divine the missing steps that seem too obvious to mention or have no way to visualize an event that to the writer is as clear as day. And so they don't bother to explain the jargon or spell out the logic or supply the necessary detail.[41]

---

41. Pinker, "Why Academics Stink," p. 7.

Luckily, you're not the average writer. You understand that the reader is not you. "My readers are slightly dimwitted," you explain to yourself, in a completely respectful tone. "They can't 'see' what's in my mind unless I paint an exactingly detailed picture of it. And so that's what I'll do. I'll spell it all out clearly, leading them by the hand to the points I want to make in this paper." (And, in an ironic twist of events, you may now realize that the label "dimwitted" belongs not to the readers but to those academic writers beset by the "curse of knowledge.")

Lead your readers by the hand

Logic is the ruling principle here. Even when you're trying to evoke an emotional response from your readers, logic is still the foundation. The Greek philosopher Aristotle established how to build this foundation when he categorized three – yes, there's that magic number again – approaches to presenting an argument: **logos**, **pathos**, and **ethos**.

Logos refers to an argument based on reason. You're appealing to your readers' need for things to make sense. You can satisfy that need in the following ways:

1. By quantifying.

Whenever you make a statement that's not considered self-evident or **common knowledge**, see if you can support it with a quantifiable fact, such as an amount, number, statistic, or percentage.

Example: Undergraduate tuition is expensive in Canada.

Support needed? Yes. The term "expensive" is relative, after all. The readers' income, background, philosophical stance and political perspective can all influence their perception of what's expensive and what's not. Your supporting detail here could take various forms: examples of undergraduate tuition fees for different programs in Canada; the range of undergraduate tuition fees; the average undergraduate tuition fee per semester. Fortunately, quantifiable evidence to support a general statement tends to be relatively straightforward to research.

Exercise 4.7

What other quantifiable evidence would help you support the above statement?

2. By clarifying.

Now we're getting a bit more complicated. Whenever you make a statement that's not considered self-evident or common knowledge *or* a statement that may be contentious, follow it up with detail that illustrates, adds more depth, provides context or explains your reasoning. Depending on the statement to be supported, this detail might also include a definition, quotation, narrative, or an example. In other words, don't assume your readers will agree with or even understand the statement. Spell out your reasoning for them.

EXAMPLE: Undergraduate education should be free.

First, remembering all the lessons you learned earlier about being focused and specific, rewrite this broad statement. You might end up with something like, "Undergraduate education in Canada should be free because it serves our social interests to have well-educated citizens."

Support needed? Definitely yes. For some, this is a highly debatable point – and for those who already agree with the statement, clarifying detail is welcome, even gratifying, because it confirms their own views. You might start, for example, by defining "undergraduate education." Are you referring to both college and university programs? What do you mean by "social interests"? Can you cite examples of other countries that offer free undergraduate education? Or that are considering it? Why? What are the "social" benefits they've experienced? Or what "social" benefits do they anticipate?

Exercise 4.8

What other clarifying detail would help support the above statement?

Inserting clarifying detail into your paper is more of an art than inserting quantifiable evidence, but one form of support is not necessarily better than the other. The support you choose to provide – quantifying vs. clarifying –depends to a certain extent on the statement. Some statements lend themselves naturally to one type of support – but perhaps not as much as you think.

3. By providing a balanced approach.

A balanced approach is always best. Relying only on quantifiable evidence may result in a dry, robotic tone to your writing, where the readers lose sight of your argument – and your voice – as they're hit by an onslaught of numbers. Conversely, a sole reliance on clarifying detail such as examples and narrative may lead to some readers dismissing your paper as "anecdotal" and lacking scholarly clout. The latter response might be unfair, prompted more by the reader's personal preferences than quality of content. (Some disciplines – and some temperaments – gravitate more toward quantifying evidence than clarifying; and vice versa). In any case, the best way to avoid that sort of response is to provide an appropriate balance of quantifying and clarifying support. It will strengthen your writing.

Exercise 4.9

Test the validity of that last statement: Read the following excerpt and then go back and re-read it, circling all the quantifying support and underlining all the clarifying support.

> ##### Obama's Plan Focuses Where It Should— on Our Neediest Students
>
> With average annual full-time tuition and fees of $3,347 for 2014-15, community colleges may appear relatively inexpensive to policy makers and the media. But paying for community college remains a steep challenge for millions of students and families. I see this each fall at Montgomery County Community College, where before the start of the fall 2014 semester nearly 1,500 students were deregistered for nonpayment. Most of these students built full-time schedules. They took time to meet with an adviser. Many persevered through the college's placement-testing processes. Yet, they were unable to pay their tuition. We witness these dynamics all the time. Changes in tuition and fees, of just a couple hundred dollars, can directly influence enrollment decisions.
>
> Tuition is only the beginning of the cost of higher education, which includes books, equipment, transportation, and living expenses. To highlight this, a student at Montgomery once told me that retention to her meant coming to class tomorrow, not coming to class from one semester to the next. She spoke of her worry each week about having the money to pay for gas to get to class ....
>
> Early estimates are that [a] program [to make post-secondary education universally affordable] would cost the federal government about $6-billion a year. That represents less than one-tenth of the Education Department's annual budget, and the Education

Department's budget in turn accounts for less than 3 percent of all federal spending.

—*Karen A. Stout*[42]

Pathos refers to an argument based on emotion. You're appealing to your readers' hearts, perhaps by addressing important values or beliefs or by sharing personal stories that remind them of our shared humanity. This kind of emotional appeal can help you forge a personal connection with your readers. It can have a powerful impact. But it can also run the risk of sentimentality, diverting attention from the essay's central objective argument – and undermining your academic credibility.

That's why you need to remember that your reader has a head as well as a heart. Make sure any emotional appeals *logically* support your central argument.

Read the excerpt below to see if you agree with those last three statements. And while you're reading, remember W.C. Williams' poem and its lesson: note the writer's use of specific detail to paint a picture.

What I Learned at Law School: The Poor Need Not Apply

"I'm sorry, Eric, but there is nothing we can do for you." Sharp pain and anger grew in my chest as I stared across the large wooden desk. I could feel the tears welling up in my eyes.

"Are you going to be okay? Let me know if I can do anything." The words of the associate dean were meaningless, a performance dictated by institutional etiquette.

"You mean I have to drop out of law school, in my third year?" Absurd, a comedy. I wanted to laugh and cry.

"We can make arrangements so that you can take an academic leave of absence for up to two years."

It sounded like I would be planning the funeral of my academic career. As I walked away from the student service offices at the University of Ottawa, I felt I had reached the end of a long journey – a journey around an oval track, carrying a boulder on my back. The boulder was poverty, and its grinding physical and psychological strain had finally brought me to my knees.

The university shrugged its shoulders as the "hard work equals

---

42. K. Stout, "Obama's Plan Focuses Where It Should—On Our Neediest Students," *The Chronicle of Higher Education*, January 19, 2015. Retrieved from https://www.chronicle.com/blogs/conversation/2015/01/11/obamas-plan-focuses-where-it-should-on-our-neediest-students/.

success" myth dissolved in front of me. Don't come to law school if you are poor, was the message. Don't try to become a lawyer if you are poor.

I was dropping out because I couldn't afford to continue. Tuition for the year was $15,000 and the government's cap on student loans for me was $12,000. I was denied a line of credit by five commercial banks because I had a low credit score and no one to co-sign. I had no one to co-sign because my mother made $19,000 last year.

What is it to be "poor"? For me it was being raised by a single mother on disability; public housing; the food bank; parcels from the Salvation Army at Christmas; seeing my brother stabbed nearly to death, police take my mother to a psychiatric hospital and Children's Aid take my four-year-old niece. And not being able to do anything about any of this.

What does poverty look like? There's the day to day: You open the fridge and there's a mustard or mayo sandwich for dinner. Then the month to month: You wait for your bus, are buzzed like cattle into an Ontario Works cubicle to get your cheque, hang your head as a smiling volunteer hands you a box of food. You carry your box home on the bus, wearily eyeing the canned string beans and cranberry jelly from someone's Thanksgiving.

You can use these images to tell a story, but what does poverty feel like? Usually it starts with anger. You are angry at yourself, your family, and the indifferent forces that eventually grind you down. You push against these feelings because you don't have the luxury – you have to keep on. You feel vulnerable. You teeter between risks not taken because the difference between failure and success is homelessness. Or you take stupid risks because you have nothing to lose.

I learned early on that anger and envy will paralyze you. You need to deal with it somehow. My mother had prayer and Jesus Christ; my brother turned to drugs. I did what I was told and became what is known as a member of the "respectable poor." To be in this group you study hard, stay out of trouble, respect your scummy restaurant bosses and borrow on your Visa card at 25 per cent interest. Most importantly, you buy into the myth "where there's a will there's a way."

My generation has reluctantly accepted the myth amid "austerity" and a new type of poverty. We're entering the work force just as employers, governments and unions are hedging themselves against falling pensions, benefits, pay and jobs. Two years ago we said "enough" and occupied parks across the world. Our neighbours eventually got annoyed and gave police and politicians the nod to push us back to our Starbucks jobs, where we exist between the dreams of our parents, our useless degrees and the reality of minimum-wage jobs. We make your lattes to the tune of our own contempt.

For those who have made it out of this youth unemployment crisis, there is a sense you are either lucky or connected. We also feed the myth. We need it. Why else would we borrow $50,000 for an education?

Meanwhile, school administrators, politicians, employers and bureaucrats prune away to make that education inaccessible. The law school adds an extra box to a scholarship application that puts it out of reach, or raises tuition another $1,000.

I faced a phalanx of administrators at the University of Ottawa, each pushing me along with a version of "No, we can't help you until you pay your tuition." When I got to the top of the authority chain I felt like I was meeting the all-powerful Wizard of Oz. But unlike the wizard, the associate deans weren't incompetent – they just didn't care. I gave them a short story of my life and current circumstances and they told me my only recourse was to apply for an "emergency bursary." But since my financial hardship was "foreseen" I didn't qualify.

I am by far not the only one who's faced this crisis. Since I opened up to my peers, many have told me they are in the same boat. This is why there are so few working-class lawyers.

Fortunately for me, my own story has a happy ending. This summer, when I'd accepted I would have to drop out, a friend offered to co-sign a loan. Knowing I would graduate on time meant I could apply for articling positions, which led to an offer that I hope will be my one-way ticket out of poverty. I know I got lucky.

—*Eric C. Girard*[43]

Exercise 4.10

The above essay is written in a journalistic style, so the tone and struc-

---

43. Eric C. Girard, "What I Learned at Law School: The Poor Need Not Apply," *The Globe and Mail*, November 17, 2013. Retrieved from www.theglobeandmail.com/life/facts-and-arguments/what-i-learned-at-law-school-the-poor-need-not-apply.

ture are less formal than that of an academic essay. If you were to re-write it in a conventional academic style, what would the thesis and supporting arguments be? (Don't worry too much about the wording. You're not actually rewriting this paper; point form here is fine). The essay clearly uses pathos or emotional appeal. Is this approach adequately supported by quantifying and clarifying support?

Be a constructive pessimist[44]

Here's a strategy to make sure your own essay has strong support: be a **constructive pessimist**.

This advice runs counter to the conventional wisdom of "think positive." But try the opposite of what convention dictates. Look at your work in progress with a jaundiced, pessimistic eye. Be wary and questioning of everything you've written. In particular, scrutinize any sentences that begin with "I think" or "I feel." Aside from the redundancy problem – it's your paper; of course, the sentences indicate what you "think" or "feel" – these might be indicators that you're drifting away from strong supporting evidence and relying on your own opinions. Your opinions, however, carry no weight if they're not supported.

Being a pessimist will prompt you to identify all the weaknesses and gaps in the writing and to anticipate all the objections that your reader may have to your argument. You can then constructively address those weaknesses, gaps and objections – a process that will involve adding more supporting detail.

The **ethos** approach depends on the reader perceiving you as credible, as someone whose opinion and judgment can be trusted. And one of the best ways to cultivate that perception is by doing the opposite of what your natural inclination might be. That is, focus less on what you think and more on what your readers think. Get inside your readers' heads, understand their views – particularly those that run counter to yours – and then make sure your writing reflects that understanding. Being a constructive pessimist is helpful here. Constructive pessimists are willing to acknowledge views contrary to their own. They're even willing to modify their own views when they encounter those that are stronger. Constructive pessimists, in other words, are thoughtful, insightful and open-minded – all attributes that increase a writer's credibility and that usually indicate the writer has thoroughly thought about, read about and researched his or her topic.

How else, besides being a constructive pessimist, might you signal to

---

44. I don't know the origin of this term, only that it has a useful application to writing.

the reader that you have these attributes and that you are, therefore, a credible writer? Think about that question as you read the essay excerpt below by Malcolm Gladwell.

Complexity and the Ten-Thousand-Hour Rule

Forty years ago, in a paper in *American Scientist*, Herbert Simon and William Chase drew one of the most famous conclusions in the study of expertise: "There are no instant experts in chess—certainly no instant masters or grandmasters. There appears not to be on record any case (including Bobby Fischer) where a person reached grandmaster level with less than about a decade's intense preoccupation with the game. We would estimate, very roughly, that a master has spent perhaps 10,000 to 50,000 hours staring at chess positions...."

In the years that followed, an entire field within psychology grew up devoted to elaborating on Simon and Chase's observation—and researchers, time and again, reached the same conclusion: it takes *a lot* of practice to be good at complex tasks....

This is the scholarly tradition I was referring to in my book *Outliers*, when I wrote about the "ten-thousand-hour rule." No one succeeds at a high level without innate talent, I wrote.... But the ten-thousand-hour research reminds us that ... [i]n cognitively demanding fields, there are no naturals. Nobody walks into an operating room, straight out of a surgical rotation, and does world-class neurosurgery. And second ... the amount of practice necessary for exceptional performance is so extensive that people who end up on top need help. They invariably have access to lucky breaks or privileges or conditions that make all those years of practice possible. As examples, I focussed on the countless hours the Beatles spent playing strip clubs in Hamburg and the privileged, early access Bill Gates and Bill Joy got to computers in the nineteen-seventies.

—*Malcolm Gladwell*[45]

Exercise 4.11

List all the ways in which Gladwell establishes his credibility (i.e., uses ethos appeal) in the above passage.

---

45. M. Gladwell, "Complexity and the Ten-Thousand Hour Rule," *The New Yorker*, August 21, 2013, http://gladwell.com/complexity-and-the-ten-thousand-hour-rule/.

Exercise 4.12

As you read each of the following statements, decide first whether or not it needs further support. Justify your answer. And if the answer is "yes," give an example or two of how you might support that statement. As you craft your example(s) consider this question: Does your example fall under "logos," "pathos" or "ethos" – or is it a combination?

STATEMENT: "People who are interrupted while writing end up producing lower-quality essays than writers who are allowed to work undisturbed."[46]

STATEMENT: "Many ... writers have discovered a deep, intuitive connection between walking, thinking, and writing."[47]

STATEMENT: "...the process of creativity, whatever it is, is essentially the same in all its branches and varieties, so that the evolution of a new art form, a new gadget, a new scientific principle, all involve common factors."[48]

STATEMENT: "Few students get through university without some encounter with depression, anxiety, panic, hysteria, anorexia, bulimia, loneliness, heartbreak, acute crises of identity or even suicidal thoughts."[49]

STATEMENT: "Many thoughtful and eloquent academics have defended the use of jargon in appropriate contexts."[50]

STATEMENT: "A book or article weighed down by awkwardly placed **parenthetical citations** and ponderous footnotes will probably be less readable, less engaging, and ultimately less persuasive than a piece of writing that wears its scholarly apparatus lightly."[51]

STATEMENT: "Recent research illustrates how writing by hand engages

---

46. A. Robb, "Interruptions Are Even Worse Than We Thought: That Gchat Is Definitely Hurting Your Work," *The New Republic*, July 16, 2014, http://www.newrepublic.com/article/118714/interruptions-work-make-you-way-less-productive.
47. F. Jabr, "Why Walking Helps Us Think," *The New Yorker*, September 3, 2014.
48. I. Asimov, in MIT Technology Review, October 20, 2014, http://www.technologyreview.com/view/531911/isaac-asimov-asks-how-do-people-get-new-ideas/.
49. M. Wente, "University's Not Meant to be Easy," *The Globe and Mail*, December 4, 2012.
50. H. Sword, "Inoculating against Jargonitis," *The Chronicle of Higher Education*, June 8, 2012.
51. H. Sword, *Stylish Academic Writing*, p. 135.

the brain in learning."[52]

STATEMENT: "It's no accident that so much attention is paid to grammar in the teaching of writing. Grammar is the one part of writing that can be straightforwardly taught."[53]

SUMMARY

"Predictable structure. Unpredictable content." Four strategies for applying the second half of this mantra are as follows:

1. Experiment early in the process with a creative title, a reminder as you write that creativity will play a central role in your paper.
2. Read widely. Anything that's well written in any discipline will introduce you to unfamiliar perspectives.
3. Reflect on the connection between your own life and your paper's topic.
4. Write simply. Straightforward, concise writing gives you a better chance of connecting with your own voice and your own thoughts. Because they're yours alone, they'll help your paper stand apart in a unique and unpredictable way.

None of the above matters, however, without strong support. Let logic be the guiding principle as you support your general statements using one or a combination of three approaches: logos, pathos, ethos.

---

52. G. Bounds, "How Handwriting Trains the Brain," *The Wall Street Journal*, October 5, 2010.
53. Elbow, *Writing*, p. 138.

Chapter 5
Avoiding the Common Pitfalls that Weaken Your Paper's Content

This chapter will help you strengthen your essay's content by ...

- Understanding and avoiding three common errors in logic
- Ensuring your Internet-based research is credible
- Avoiding unintentional **plagiarism**
- Developing your own ideas through a 4-step synthesis guide.

FAULTY LOGIC

It bears repeating: the best writing is logical. This statement holds true no matter what your topic is. It applies equally to a reflection paper on why the Romantic poets resonate within your deep heart's core as it does to a dissertation on fruit fly propagation. But being logical is challenging because it requires you to think hard, to focus and perhaps to rise above and see beyond any long established, comfortable biases you might have. Here's a quick guide[54] to help you meet those challenges – and write a good paper.

Unsupported generalizations

After having read the previous section on logos and done its exercises, you should be an expert on avoiding this problem. But you're probably not, not yet. Few writers are. That's because broad, simplistic statements are so easy to make. Try it: "a university degree has less value today than it did before"; "the liberal arts are impractical"; "business majors are mostly interested in making money"; "community colleges have less status than universities" ...

Notice that each of those statements has an easy familiarity. You've probably heard or said, believed or dismissed one or all of them before, without thinking too much about them. But "not thinking" is anathema to logic – and to good writing. Reconsider any broad statement that comes easily to you, without your having to think much about it. This kind of statement is probably a generalization: a conclusion that lacks evidence. It needs to be

---

54. The following list doesn't cover all the examples of faulty logic. That would require a far lengthier list. Explained here, instead, are the most common pitfalls.

immediately followed with support, explanation or clarification – or abandoned completely. Some generalizations cannot be reasonably supported.

Exercise 5.1

Revisit each of the generalizations above and figure out what kind of follow-up supporting detail would transform it from a generalization to a reasonable conclusion. (As you do so, keep in mind the earlier discussion on logos and the three ways in which you can satisfy your reader's need for things to make sense: quantifying; clarifying; and balancing). Conversely, identify any instance where this transformation just isn't possible – and the statement should therefore be discarded.

Circular reasoning

This one's tricky. It hides under the guise of offering reasonable evidence.

EXAMPLE: Writing should be taught at the postsecondary level because it's an important skill. Consequently, more undergraduate writing courses should be offered.

Deconstruct the sentences, and you'll see the problem: "Writing should be taught at the postsecondary level because … it's important … Therefore it's important to offer more undergraduate writing courses."

There's no evidence to support the conclusion that writing is important. Consequently, you're not furthering your argument. Instead, you're just going around in an endless circle, repeating the same thing. There's no progression of thought.

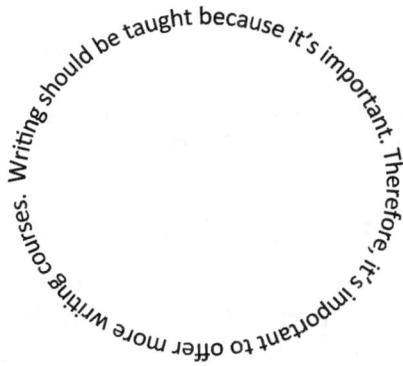

Figure 5.1: Circular reasoning doesn't advance your argument

Exercise 5.2

Correct the circular reasoning above by adding specific evidence.

EXAMPLE: Writing should be taught at the postsecondary level because it reinforces critical thinking skills.
 … helps the writer project a professional image
 … _____
 … _____
 … _____
Consequently, more undergraduate writing courses should be offered.

Add two or three more entries to the list above. It's good practice. Relevant specific detail adds depth, strengthening and expanding your argument. If it helps, think of your argument as a spiral, its evidence and explanation serving to expand its original premise. (See Figure 5.2.)

Figure 5.2: Visualize your argument as a spiral, with movement and depth

Post hoc, ergo propter hoc

I was trying to avoid this – using Latin rather than English phrasing – on the grounds that the best writing uses familiar language. But sometimes that rule needs to be broken. This well-known Latin phrase literally translates as "after this, therefore because of this," referring to the mistaken notion that if one event follows another, the first event inevitably caused the second one. In other words, if B follows A, then A must have caused B. (You see why "*post hoc, ergo propter hoc*" is a useful shortcut to explain this weak reasoning).

As with the other two examples of faulty logic – unsupported generalizations and circular reasoning – we're prone toward making this kind of error because it's easy. It allows us to arrive at a quick, straightforward conclusion without having to think deeply. That's an attractive prospect for most of us. The problem, however, is that those "quick, straightforward" conclusions don't allow for the possibility of nuance and ambiguity – two attributes which tend to characterize our world. And all of this is an indirect way of saying something that resonates with the counterintuitive writer: a multi-faceted – or even inconclusive – conclusion that reflects the complexity of a situation is more impressive than one that falsely paints a black and white picture. You're more likely to arrive at the former if you pay attention to the logic of your argument.

Consider, for example, the following. A sociology essay concludes that Canada's policy of allowing more immigrants into the country has led to increased unemployment. A reflection paper blames a course's poor attendance rate on the instructor's policy of "no texting, no cell phones, no laptops." A business report argues that lack of social interaction among employees has resulted in an operation's high turnover rate.

In all three examples, one event follows another: increased unemployment rate follows increased numbers of immigrants; poor class attendance follows a ban on technology in the classroom; and a high turnover rate follows lack of socializing among employees. But arguing for causation on the basis of timing is akin to arguing on the basis of superstition: I wore my purple sweater today, and I passed my exam; therefore my purple sweater caused me to pass my exam.

And while there's no shortage of successful writers who rely on superstitious rituals to help them write (a favourite pen, a particular coffee mug – and maybe even a purple sweater), they don't base their writing on superstitious causality. The link between cause and effect is usually more complicated than one event following another. Successful writers know this, and so they dig deeper.

Exercise 5.3

For each of the three examples given above, dig deeper. Brainstorm alternative possible causes of each outcome: increased unemployment rate, poor class attendance, high employee turnover. Making this list doesn't discount the first cause that was cited (immigration; ban on technology; and lack of socialization). It just prompts you to think more about your evidence – or lack of it – and to consider that a particular event might have more than one cause. It prompts you, in other words, to develop a more nuanced, complex argument.

Any writing assignment can be vulnerable to the faulty logic issues explained above. Research papers, though, come with some additional challenges:

FLIMSY INTERNET-BASED EVIDENCE
ADD (Author, Date, Depth and Detail)

I've been repeating the word "evidence" quite a bit, as if it's a panacea to all academic writing problems. It's not. Not all evidence is created equal. An example of flimsy evidence that's more likely to weaken than support your document includes any content acquired from questionable Internet sources.

How do you know if your Internet source is questionable? A University of Guelph librarian offers this acronym as a guide: "ADD."[55]

Author. Determine whether or not the website author is knowledgeable about the issue by examining his or her credentials. Are they provided on the website? Is there any indication that the author has a particular bias or perspective that might influence the content's credibility? Here, the "About" page can be particularly helpful, giving you a glimpse of the author's purpose in creating this site. Can you get in touch with the author – or is it an anonymous posting?

Date. Is the information current? Has it been revised or updated? Are all the links working? ("Dead" links indicate a poor source). Keep in mind, though, that currency of information is more important for some topics than for others. For example, an essay on technology requires up-to-date information because technology progresses and changes at such a rapid pace. However, an essay on, say, ethics might credibly draw upon older content because matters of ideology, philosophy or values may not change over time. In these cases, a good paper written twenty years ago might be just as credible – or more – than a recently published paper.

Depth and Detail. Does the source offer relevant and sufficient detail? Consider the amount and type of quantifying and clarifying information.

---

55. ADD was the acronym used by a University of Guelph librarian during a research workshop for an undergraduate communications class (Fall 2014).

Where does the information come from? What evidence is used to back up claims? Can any claims be verified by another source? Pay particular attention to articles that consist of a string of short paragraphs (i.e., fewer than three sentences) or bulleted lists of abbreviated entries – these may indicate shallow content.

ADD "Q"

And because I'm a writing instructor, I'll add one more criterion to the list above:

Quality of writing. Spelling, grammar and punctuation errors, typos, and weak or non-existent paragraphing (e.g., a tendency toward paragraphs that are either very short or very long) are all legitimate reasons to question a website's credibility. After all, if a writer hasn't taken the time to proofread for and avoid remedial errors like these, he or she probably hasn't taken the time to proofread for and avoid the more complex errors of content. Check also for these latter errors, in particular, unsupported generalizations, circular reasoning and faulty cause and effect relationships.

Lack of **referencing**, either through footnotes, endnotes or links that lead to related material might also indicate lack of credibility. Has the author relied solely on his or her own views – or is there evidence of research?

Wikipedia?

The academic world tends to distrust Wikipedia. Your instructors may warn you against citing it, cautioning that it's not a credible source of information. And there may be some truth to that: anyone, after all, can write an article for Wikipedia; no one automatically oversees the accuracy, objectivity and correctness of the writing. Your instructors may also be weary of reading papers that derive their material solely from this source. As the fifth most consulted website in the world,[56] Wikipedia has a reputation for being the primary – and sometimes only – source that students turn to when researching their papers. Any research paper based on one source, particularly one that's perceived as questionable, is bound to be weak. Those are good reasons for your instructors to warn against it.

But there might also be some academic snobbery at play here. Wikipedia offers over 20 billion pages of information written by 14,000 new editors per month.[57] Dismissing outright all that information and all those

---

56. "Wikimedia Report Card," Wikimedia Foundation, August 2014, http://reportcard.wmflabs.org/.
57. "Wikimedia Report Card," Wikimedia Foundation, February 2015, http://reportcard.wmflabs.org/#.

editors isn't reasonable. There's nothing inherently wrong with turning to Wikipedia as your first source of information – as long as you don't use it indiscriminately and as your only source. Apply as much of the ADD Q rule to the Wikipedia site as possible. In particular, pay attention to the references cited. They may be the best part of the Wikipedia entry, allowing you to bypass Wikipedia as your formal reference and use instead any credible references it provides.

In short, Wikipedia can be a helpful starting place, to give you a general orientation to the subject matter, to identify relevant trends, and to point you in the direction of some good sources that will allow you to delve more deeply into your topic. And those are the best sources to cite, as opposed to the Wikipedia entry itself.

GOOGLING ... ONLY?

You're probably using "**Google**" as a verb, as in "I'll Google some information for my research paper". Try creating – and using – two new verbs to help you find better information more quickly: "Google Scholar" and "database."

Now, "better information" and "more quickly" suggest that Google is not the most effective and efficient way to research an academic paper. Here's the evidence to support that statement: Google (or any similar public search engine, such as Bing or Yahoo) will lead you to
- Newspaper and magazine articles about your subject that aren't written by a subject specialist and that target a broad audience. Consequently, they may lack important quantifying and clarifying detail.
- Personal websites and blogs about your subject that could be written by anyone at all and that could contain any number of inaccurate facts and statements.
- Corporate or business sites pertaining to your subject that are biased or whose primary goal is to sell you something.

In other words, Google can lead you to sources that aren't useful because they're written by people who lack expertise in your subject and a vested interest in providing current, complete and accurate information about that subject.

To be fair, Google can also lead you to informative, well-written articles, including those that are **peer-reviewed**, the gold standard for research paper citations. "Peer-reviewed" means the article has been critiqued for its scholarly value and reliability by specialists in the field. However, when you're relying only on Google, you'll have to sift through a number of questionable sources before you get to those articles that are informative and well written and those that are peer-reviewed. And if Google does lead you to a peer-reviewed article, you'll probably be given access to the paper's **abstract** only. As a rule, subscription–based journals (which publish peer-reviewed articles) don't give away their articles free of charge.[58]

Think of **Google Scholar** (scholar.google.ca) as a shortcut. As its name suggests, it's a specialized version of Google, searching out only scholarly or academically credible information. In the case of peer-reviewed articles, you still won't be able to access the entire article, but you'll have saved considerable time finding promising titles and abstracts.

You can then find and access the entire text of these articles through another means: your university or college library's **databases**. Databases are huge repositories of subject-based information. Libraries subscribe to them, allowing their users free access to all the information they contain. Your librarians can identify your discipline's relevant databases and explain how to use them to access articles you've already identified through Google Scholar and to find other focused, scholarly sources of information for your **research essay**.

These databases also offer another benefit: many of them allow you to organize your bibliographic information, formatting it into the style requested by your instructor, such as **MLA** or **APA**. Don't discount the value of this benefit: keeping track of your sources throughout the research process is much preferred to the time-consuming, frustrating alternative: trying to identify and compile your sources after the paper has been written, so that you can properly reference them – and avoid any hint of plagiarism (an issue discussed shortly).

· · · · ·

If you're like most students (and most writers, generally), "Googling" is your first course of action when you start researching your paper. It shouldn't be discounted as a useful research strategy. However, it does have limitations. Consider "Googling" as akin to taking the scenic route home: it's going to be a winding path, sometimes leading to interesting sites, but perhaps just as often to dead ends and detours that bypass sites you need to see. And it's going to take longer than the more direct, focused route offered by Google Scholar and your library's databases.

In short, go ahead and "Google," but know when it's time to exit this

---

58. The exception is open access journals. As their name indicates, these kinds of journals provide free access to their articles over the Internet.

scenic route and get on the superhighway that Google Scholar and your library's databases represent.

Plagiarism ... unintentional or otherwise

In some ways, the above distinction doesn't matter. Whether intentional or not, plagiarizing jeopardizes your credibility – and the worth of your writing. It also jeopardizes something else: your sense of self-worth. Knowing that you cheated or that you can be perceived as cheating means you're not going to feel good about yourself.

And plagiarism *is* cheating. That's not a debatable point in the classroom. Others may argue about the "grey zones" of plagiarism. They may point out that students have grown up believing that everything on the Internet is part of the public domain and therefore free to be copied, pasted and downloaded without a second thought about attribution or citation. They may even see a connection between plagiarism and creativity.[59] Your professors, however, are not among those. When faced with a suspected or confirmed case of plagiarism, they're not likely to engage the student in a philosophical discussion. They're more likely to penalize – and to remember. In the academic world, plagiarism is a high crime not easily forgotten.

Here's a definition of that crime:

> In academic writing, it is considered plagiarism to draw any idea or any language from someone else without adequately crediting that source in your paper. It doesn't matter whether the source is a published author, another student, a Web site without clear authorship, a Web site that sells academic papers, or any other person: Taking credit for anyone else's work is stealing, and it is unacceptable in all academic situations, whether you do it intentionally or by accident.[60]

And here's a test to help you *really* understand that definition:

1. **Paraphrasing** an analysis or conclusion from an article is fine provided you meet two conditions: you cite the source immediately after the paraphrased text and in the References or Bibliography at the end of the paper. TRUE *or* FALSE

---

59. For an interesting article on this topic, see Malcolm Gladwell's "Something Borrowed: Should a Charge of Plagiarism Ruin Your Life?" *The New Yorker,* November 22, 2004.
60. Retrieved from http://isites.harvard.edu/icb/icb.do?keyword=k70847&pageid=icb.page342054.

2. Copying someone else's work word-for-word is acceptable as long as you enclose the copied passage in quotation marks or, if it's more than 40 words, in a freestanding block of text. TRUE or FALSE

3. Any material taken from another source needs to be referenced. TRUE or FALSE

4. A citation at the end of the paragraph lets the reader know that the entire paragraph is based on that particular source. TRUE or FALSE

5. In your paper, you present an idea that you've arrived at independently. Before submitting the paper, you read an article that states the same idea. You do not need to reference this article. TRUE or FALSE

6. Your essay includes information that your professor covered during a lecture. You are required to include the source of this information within your paper and at the end of your paper, in the References or Bibliography. TRUE or FALSE

7. Your research topic is the same (or similar) to a paper you wrote and submitted previously for another course. You may use this paper – or large sections of it – again, since you are the author. TRUE or FALSE

8. English isn't your first language, so you routinely enlist someone's help in looking over your essay drafts. This is not considered plagiarism. TRUE or FALSE

ANSWERS: Check the question numbers. They're listed in reverse numerical order to prevent you from having inadvertently seen the answer before you completed the test.

8. The answer depends on what you mean by "help." Having someone proofread your writing for spelling, grammar and punctuation errors isn't plagiarism. Neither is discussing the thesis, organization or supporting evidence. In fact, discussing your ideas with others is a useful habit. It can broaden your perspective and strengthen your material. The key modifier in that last sentence, however, is "your." Consult with others, but make sure the paper's ideas and wording remain yours alone. If they're not, you're guilty of plagiarism. The lesson here? Let your obliging friend, academi-

cally gifted sibling or helpful parent know that they may not develop your thesis, figure out how to present your evidence, or actually write parts of your essay. That's cheating.

7. FALSE. Writing assignments are generally intended to strengthen your thinking skills. They're meant to challenge you. There's no strengthening and no challenging when you submit in one course an essay that you've already written for another course. Now, re-working that essay is a different story. For example, you might use a previously submitted paper on, say, "A defense of Canada's universal health care system" as the basis for a new paper entitled, "A comparison of Canada's health care system with the American model." Here, you're moving forward with the second essay by exploring new ideas, even though you're likely borrowing material from your first essay. And in the interests of complete transparency, you would need to discuss this strategy with your instructor.

6. FALSE. You need to reference the instructor's lecture material in the body of the essay only. Entries in the References or Bibliography section at the end of the paper are reserved for those that can be retrieved. Unless your instructor's lecture was preserved on, say, YouTube for anyone to look up, it can't be retrieved. The same applies to a conversation, an interview or e-mail. (i.e., you may have saved the e-mail and recorded the interview, but they still can't be publicly retrieved).

5. This is a grey idea. Referencing an article that presents the same idea you independently developed would be a nice – but not mandatory – touch. You could present the idea so that it's evident you arrived at it independently, but then acknowledge that you're not alone in this belief by citing your reference.

EXAMPLE: "A tatoo both connects and separates us from others – a conclusion that also resonates with Jamison in her *New York Times* article 'Mark My Words. Maybe.' "

In this case, citing the Jamison article affirms the thoroughness of your research and perhaps also the strength of your idea. At least one published writer from a credible source shares your view on tatoos. If there's strength in numbers, you just reinforced your view.

Here's a good rule of the thumb: if you're uncertain, reference the source. Far better to over-reference than to omit a necessary reference and make yourself vulnerable to a charge of plagiarism.

4. FALSE. The reader is likely to assume that a citation at the end of the paragraph covers only the last sentence in the paragraph. The other sentences in the paragraph would need to be referenced individually. If

so many references interfere with the paper's readability, try another tactic: credit your source at the start of the paragraph with an introductory sentence such as "The following analysis, taken from MacLean and Miller (2018), illustrates some key concepts."

3. FALSE. If the material is already familiar to the general public or to readers within your discipline, then it's considered "common knowledge" and its source doesn't need to be identified. Sometimes it's going to be a judgment call, but here are some examples of common knowledge: the temperature at which water freezes, the first African-American president of the United States, or the author of the "to be or not to be" soliloquy. If I'm setting the bar too low here, it's to make a point: don't assume too readily that something is common knowledge and doesn't need to be referenced. Once again, it's better to over-reference than to risk an accusation of plagiarism.

2. FALSE. Quoting word-for-word requires two citations: one immediately after the quotation and one within the References or Bibliography section. The quotation marks or the indented block of text lets the reader know that these are not your words. It doesn't, however, credit the specific author(s). That's the function of the citation immediately following the quotation. The citation in the References or Bibliography allows the reader to look up the quotation in the original source.

1. FALSE. The two conditions cited here are true: when you borrow someone else's idea you need to acknowledge the source within the text and within the References or Bibliography. However, there's also a third condition: you need to use your own words when paraphrasing. If your paraphrasing follows too closely the original, you're plagiarizing even though you've referenced the information.

A 4-step guide to paraphrasing

To a certain extent, "too closely" is a judgment call. University of Guelph's Academic Integrity website defines it as "more than three consecutive words of an original text."[61] That might be too restrictive. After all, some terms and phrases are so commonly used that they're beyond anyone's claim of ownership. But it does signal the academic world's serious stance on this issue. Here's a guide to complying with that stance – and maintaining your credibility as a writer.

STEP 1: *Understand what paraphrase means.* It means restating your

---

61. Academic integrity at the University of Guelph. Retrieved from http://www.academicintegrity.uoguelph.ca/plagiarism_quiz.cfm.

source's material, retaining the same amount of detail but using your own words and sentence structure. (Summarizing, by the way, serves a similar function, but has a more limited scope. A **summary** briefly states the source's key points only and is much shorter than the original.)

Exercise 5.4

Read the following source material and then the paraphrase. Is the paraphrase acceptable or is it plagiarism?

SOURCE: In academic writing, it is considered plagiarism to draw any idea or any language from someone else without adequately crediting that source in your paper. It doesn't matter whether the source is a published author, another student, a Web site without clear authorship, a Web site that sells academic papers, or any other person: Taking credit for anyone else's work is stealing, and it is unacceptable in all academic situations, whether you do it intentionally or by accident.[62]

PARAPHRASE: In the academic world, drawing ideas or language from someone else without giving that person credit is plagiarism. It doesn't matter what the source is: a published article, another student, a Web site without clear authorship or one that sells essays. Whether it's done deliberately or accidentally, taking work from these sources or from any other person without acknowledgment is stealing and therefore unacceptable in any academic situation.[63]

ANSWER: *The paraphrase would be considered plagiarism, even though it's referenced, for two reasons: it closely imitates the sentence structure of the original, changing only an occasional word or clause; and it repeats verbatim some of the language of the original – including wording that doesn't fall within the category of "so commonly used that [it's] beyond anyone's claim of ownership."*

With those two reasons in mind, re-read the paraphrase, circling or underlining those parts of it that indicate plagiarism.

STEP 2: *Copy and paste to compile your research notes.* As you research

---

[62]. http://isites.harvard.edu/icb/icb.do?keyword=k70847&pageid=icb.page342054.
[63]. Ibid.

your topic, copy and paste any particularly relevant or useful information from the source articles into your research notes.

I know. It's probably the opposite of what you expected. "Copy and paste" is cited later in this chapter as a pitfall of good writing because of its association with plagiarism. But in this case it's being used to help you compile accurate and complete research notes, not to copy material directly from a source into your research paper.

STEP 3: *Include your reference information.* Reference information consists of the four W's: who; when; what; and where.[64]

EXAMPLE:
WHO **WHEN** **WHAT**
Norris, M. (2015, February 23). *Holy writ: Learning to love the house style.* New Yorker Magazine. Retrieved from http://www.newyorker.com/magazine/2015/02/23/holy-writ. **WHERE**

Make sure that any copy and paste material in your research notes is enclosed in quotation marks and accompanied by its reference information – a good reminder that these are someone else's words; and a good habit to save you the time of looking up the reference material later on.

STEP 4: *Visualize and paraphrase.* Sometimes we're so fearful of getting it wrong that we cling tightly to the source material – its wording, sentence structure and organization. But clinging tightly to the source material isn't paraphrasing. It's plagiarizing.

To overcome this fear and reduce the possibility of plagiarizing, try the following strategy. Visualize yourself talking to someone outside of class about some research material you'd like to include in your paper. (Make that person someone who's just *slightly* smarter than you are and whom you respect.) You're not in the classroom, so there's no fear of performance anxiety or the instructor's judgment – only the opportunity to express yourself, to be challenged, and to feel that you belong here, in the academic world.

Now write down the words you're saying. Compare them to the original source material to ensure that you've accurately captured its meaning and then make any necessary revisions. That's your paraphrase.

---

64. S. Ryan, Teaching Prof Conference handout, 2008, p. 14.

Exercise 5.5

Re-read the Kant excerpt on page 43. Following Step 4 of the plan outlined above, paraphrase it.

Now do the same for paragraph 3 of the Gladwell essay on page 65.

THE COPY AND PASTE HABIT TAKEN TO AN EXTREME

Consider these scenarios:

1. At some point while writing your research paper, you become fixated on two numbers: the number of words you've written vs. the number of words you've been assigned to write.

2. At some point while writing your research paper, perhaps right from the start, you assume your ideas are inferior to those that have been written – and published – by someone else. If it's been published, you say to yourself, it must be better than anything I could write.

As distinct as they appear, these two scenarios are actually related insofar as they can lead to the same outcome: a copy and paste habit. You've experienced this habit if your written work revolves around material from published articles in the form of direct quotations, summaries and paraphrases.

The key words in that last sentence are "revolve around." Quoting, summarizing and paraphrasing all play important roles in the research paper – but they're supporting roles. The starring role should be reserved for your own words and ideas. Otherwise, as discussed in Chapter 4, your research paper is simply a mouthpiece for other people's views, lacking any spark of originality – and therefore reducing the chances of you (and your reader) becoming truly excited about it. A paper that simply repeats what's already been written and published treads down a well-worn, familiar path. That's not a path that beckons the counterintuitive writer.

Why would any writer feel compelled to elevate someone else's words and ideas from supporting to starring role – and what's the remedy for it? The two scenarios above give us a clue.

For those who are fixated on word count, quoting broad swathes of text from published articles allows their own paper to be "padded" with someone else's words, so that it meets, with relative ease, the assigned word count. The remedy for kicking this habit begins with a disclosure: assigned word counts are somewhat arbitrary. They exist to answer the frequently asked question, "How long should the paper be?" but more importantly to indicate how in-depth and comprehensive your research is expected to be. A 5,000-word assignment carries heavier expectations than a 1,500-word assignment. So fixating on word count alone focuses your energy in the wrong place. Pay attention instead to what's implied by the word count, which is the expected level of detail, depth and coverage. That's the important factor, not whether your paper contains the exact number of words requested.

For those who assume that someone else's ideas carry more weight than their own, then emphasizing someone else's ideas makes perfect sense. Except for the faulty logic of that statement. Did you catch it? What evidence suggests that your words and ideas are inferior?

Chances are, you're basing this assumption less on concrete evidence and more on lack of confidence and the subsequent desire to play it safe. Lack of confidence means we dismiss our potential to write well and consequently don't even try, opting to repeat instead what someone else has written. When we do that, we stay within the safe territory of what has already been judged worthy. It wouldn't have been published if it weren't good, right? And so we base our writing on words and ideas that have been published by someone else rather than take the risk of falling short with our own.

Here's an exercise to help address that fear of taking a risk and of crafting, therefore, your own good words and ideas.

A two-minute writing exercise (Exercise 5.6) (which may take longer, but you won't mind)[65]

Write for at least two minutes on a personal topic of your own choosing. It can be anything at all (e.g., family, academic, work-related; serious or lighthearted.) The only rule is this: Make sure your piece logically ends with this sentence, "At that moment I knew I was at my best."

Re-read what you've just written, several times if you like and perhaps even aloud.

Now circle the modifiers that best describe you, based on what you just wrote:

- Intelligent
- Creative
- Brave
- Wise
- Funny

---

65. This is a modified version of a public speaking exercise that I heard about at a Teaching Professor conference. I don't know who should be credited for that exercise.

- Resilient
- Strong
- Patient
- Resourceful
- ...
- ...
- ....

Add and circle any other appropriate modifiers.

Anne Frank said it best in her famous *Diary*:

Everyone has inside of him a piece of good news. The good news is that you don't know how great you can be....What you can accomplish! And what your potential is!

In other words, you're more than you realize. Within you – within every person, actually – is a deep reservoir of talent and insight and capability. It's the best part of who you are, and it never leaves you. The problem, though, is that you may have forgotten about it. This exercise was your reminder. Use it as a catalyst to create your own words and ideas when you're writing – especially when there's a voice in your head telling you that you lack the capability.

Paraphrasing or Summarizing vs. Synthesizing

Understanding how paraphrasing or summarizing differs from **synthesizing** can help you start creating your own words and ideas.

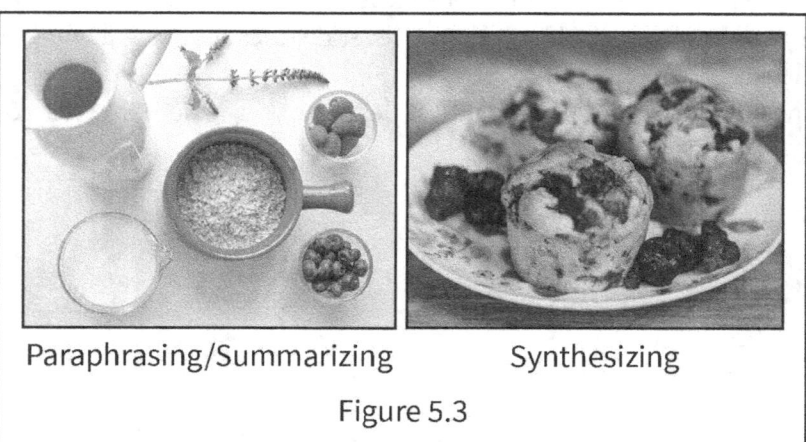

Paraphrasing/Summarizing   Synthesizing

Figure 5.3

PARAPHRASING OR SUMMARIZING: presenting someone else's work. It showcases your understanding of what someone else has written. No new ideas are created.

SYNTHESIZING: combining information or ideas from your research sources to point out a connection, illustrate a relationship or introduce a new perspective. It showcases not just your understanding of someone else's work, but also your ability to expand upon it.

If a culinary analogy helps, think of paraphrasing or summarizing as setting out on the counter all the ingredients you need to bake something. Synthesizing is what you get after you mix and bake all those ingredients. It's creating something that didn't exist before. (If a picture helps, see Figure 5.3).

And if neither the analogy nor the picture helped much, try reading the following two passages.[66] As you read, ask yourself which passage illustrates summarizing and which illustrates synthesizing.

PASSAGE #1

Since at least the time of peripatetic Greek philosophers, ... writers have discovered a deep, intuitive connection between walking, thinking, and writing.... "How vain it is to sit down to write when you have not stood up to live!" Henry David Thoreau penned in his journal. "Methinks that the moment my legs begin to move, my thoughts begin to flow." Thomas DeQuincey has calculated that William Wordsworth – whose poetry is filled with tramps up mountains, through forests, and along public roads – walked as many as a hundred and eighty thousand miles in his lifetime, which comes to an average of six and a half miles a day starting from age five.

What is it about walking ... that makes it so amenable to thinking and writing? The answer begins with changes to our chemistry. When we go for a walk, the heart pumps faster, circulating more blood and oxygen not just to the muscles but to all the organs – including the brain. Many experiments have shown that after or during exercise, even very mild exertion, people perform better on tests of memory and attention. Walking on a regular basis also promotes new connections between brain cells, staves off the usual

---

66. Passage #1 is excerpted from F. Jabr, "Why Walking Helps Us Think," *The New Yorker*, September 3, 2014; retrieved from http://www.newyorker.com/tech/elements/walking-helps-us-think. Passage #2 is excerpted from D. Beres, "How Does the Brain-Body Connection Affect Creativity?", *Big Think*, May 17, 2017; retrieved from http://bigthink.com/21st-century-spirituality/walking-and-creativity. Note that neither of these excerpts includes proper academic referencing.

withering of brain tissue that comes with age, increases the volume of the hippocampus (a brain region crucial for memory), and elevates levels of molecules that both stimulate the growth of new neurons and transmit messages between them.

Passage #2

Stanford researchers Marily Oppezzo and Daniel L. Schwartz wanted to know if the brain-body connection offered by walking alone is enough to kickstart creative juices. Their answer is yes.

The team conducted four experiments to better understand how walking affects creative thinking....

In the first experiment participants completed the two tests while seated and then while walking on a treadmill (to factor for environmental influence). In the next they were tested while seated and then walking, walking and then seated, and seated twice. In the third experiment they walked outdoors, and in the fourth a variety of situations were tested: sitting inside, walking on a treadmill, walking outside, or being rolled around on a wheelchair outdoors....

[The researchers'] assessment? Walking encourages creativity. In three of the alternate uses studies the numbers were profound: 81%, 88%, and 100% of participants were more creative walking than sitting, including on the treadmill....

How could walking at a regulated pace on a machine while facing a white wall promote creativity? The researchers believe that a "complex causal pathway" exists between the physiology of walking and proximal cognitive processes....

They admit that environment does matter in certain situations, however. Novelty is important both as inspiration and distraction. Where you walk influences creative potential ...

In Passage #1, the author relates the work of other writers to one theme: the existence of "a deep, intuitive connection between walking, thinking, and writing." Thoreau directly refers to this connection himself, and the author simply points out that fact. With Wordsworth, however, the author infers that the poet must have believed in the connection between walking, thinking, and writing because "his poetry is filled with tramps up mountains, through forests, and along public roads." Identifying a common thread that runs through the works of writers since the days of the Greek philosophers onward is an example of synthesis – and a fairly straightforward example, at that.

A more subtle example of synthesis occurs in the passage's next paragraph. Here the author extends the common thread established in the first paragraph to a completely different genre of writing: science. Evidence from the realms of cardiovascular health and neurology is linked to each other and to the "walking, thinking, and writing" theme embraced by the writers discussed earlier.

In Passage #1, the author used synthesis to call attention to a similar, perhaps unstated, theme found throughout diverse readings. Sometimes, however, synthesis leads the writer to develop his or her own theme. Consider this excerpt from Nicholas Carr's "Is Google Making Us Stupid?"[67]:

> For me, as for others, the Net is … the conduit for most of the information that flows … into my mind. The advantages of having immediate access to such an incredibly rich store of information are many, and they've been widely described and duly applauded. "The perfect recall of silicon memory," *Wired*'s Clive Thompson has written, "can be an enormous boon to thinking." But that boon comes at a price. As the media theorist Marshall McLuhan pointed out in the 1960s, media are not just passive channels of information. They supply the stuff of thought, but they also shape the process of thought. And what the Net seems to be doing is chipping away my capacity for concentration and contemplation… Once I was a scuba diver in the sea of words. Now I zip along the surface like a guy on a Jet Ski.

Synthesis doesn't have to be complicated – but it can be thought-provoking. In fact, that's usually its intent. In the straightforward, three-step synthesis above, Carr cites one writer who praises the Internet as "an enormous boon to thinking." He then contrasts that view with Marshall McLuhan's (pre-Internet) theory, concluding that the Internet can "shape the process of thought." Having pointing out the different views of these two writers, he presents his own thesis: "the Net seems to be … chipping away my capacity for concentration and contemplation."

The art of cohesively integrating your sources – and perhaps using that

---

[67]. N. Carr, "Is Google Making Us Stupid?: What the Internet Is Doing to Our Brains," *The Atlantic*, July/August 2008; retrieved from http://www.theatlantic.com/magazine/archive/2008/07/is-google-making-us-stupid/306868/.

as a springboard to present an entirely new idea – is called **synthesis**. And if synthesizing is an art – indeed a high art when the combined elements come from completely different, even unexpected, realms – then summarizing is a craft, as illustrated by Passage #2. Here, the writer simply explains in his own words the purpose of the cited research and its major findings or conclusions. Nothing more.

You may be assigned essays at the postsecondary level that ask you to do nothing more than summarize your research sources. (Summarizing has its place, and it's discussed in more detail later in the book.) But it's more likely your instructor will expect you to synthesize those sources because it calls on higher order thinking skills.

A 3-step guide to synthesizing your research material

Step #1

Compile relevant material from your research sources. As mentioned earlier, copying and pasting can be a good habit in this instance because it ensures your research notes are accurate and complete.

Make sure you enclose any "copy and paste excerpts" in quotation marks and note their bibliographic information, including page numbers. If it's an unpaginated Internet source, note which paragraph contained the excerpt.

Example

Reference information:

(a) Harvard Health Publications Newsletter (2011, October 11). Writing about emotions may ease stress and trauma. Harvard Medical School. Retrieved from http://www.health.harvard.edu/healthbeat/writing-about-emotions-may-ease-stress-and-trauma.

Relevant material from this article:

"Writing about thoughts and feelings that arise from a traumatic or stressful life experience – called expressive writing – may help some people cope with the emotional fallout of such events. But it's not a cure-all, and it won't work for everyone. Expressive writing appears to be more effective for people who are not also struggling with ongoing or severe mental health challenges, such as major depression or post-traumatic stress disorder." (paragraph 1)

"…writing helps people to organize thoughts and give meaning to a traumatic experience." (paragraph 8)

"It's also possible that writing ... fosters an intellectual process – the act of constructing a story about a traumatic event – that helps someone break free of the endless mental cycling more typical of brooding or rumination." (paragraph 9)

"When people open up privately about a traumatic event, they are more likely to talk with others about it – suggesting that writing leads indirectly to reaching out for social support that can aid healing." (paragraph 10)

"A few studies have found that people who write about a traumatic event immediately after it occurs may actually feel worse after expressive writing, possibly because they are not yet ready to face it." (paragraph 11)

Reference information:
(b) Baikie, K.A. & Wilhelm, K. (2005). Emotional and physical health benefits of expressive writing. *Advances in Psychiatric Treatment*. Vol. 11 , pp. 338–46, http://apt.rcpsych.org/content/11/5/338.

Relevant material from this article:
"Writing about traumatic, stressful or emotional events has been found to result in improvements in both physical and psychological health, in non-clinical and clinical populations. In the expressive writing paradigm, participants are asked to write about such events for 15–20 minutes on 3–5 occasions. Those who do so generally have significantly better physical and psychological outcomes compared with those who write about neutral topics." (p. 338)

"Some studies found that patients with cancer reported benefits such as better physical health, reduced pain and reduced need to use healthcare services (Rosenberg et al., 2002; Stanton & Danoff-Burg, 2002), although others failed to find any benefits (Walker et al., 1999; de Moor et al., 2002)." (p. 340)

"Our review of the literature shows that psychological health benefits tend to be more often found when participants' traumas and/or symptoms are clinically more severe, although results are inconsistent." (p. 340)

"Overall, studies examining expressive writing demonstrate some beneficial effects in physical and/or psychological health. Although the empirical findings are at times equivocal and further research is required to clarify populations for whom writing is clearly effective, there is sufficient evidence for clinicians to begin applying expressive writing in therapeutic settings with caution." (p. 341)

Reference information:
(c) Pennebaker, J. (1997). Writing about emotional experiences as a therapeutic process. *Psychological Science*, vol 8, no. 3, pp. 162-166. Retrieved from http://gruberpeplab.com/teaching/psych131_fall2013/documents/13.1_Pennebaker1997_Writingemotionalexperiences.pdf.

Relevant material from this article:
"The mere act of disclosure is a powerful therapeutic agent that may account for a substantial percentage of the variance in the healing process." (p. 162)

"the writing paradigm" (p. 162)

"Students who write about emotional topics show improvements in grades in the months following the study." (p. 162)

"… we found … the more that individuals used positive emotion words, the better their subsequent health." (p. 165)

"Most studies that have been conducted have not examined individuals with major emotional or physical health problems or substance abuse problems One obvious question is the degree to which writing can serve as a supplement to—or even substitute for—some medical and psychological treatments." (p. 165)

STEP #2

In the second step, scrutinize your material to identify common themes or topics.

Example

	Common theme: Benefits of writing
Harvard Health Publications (2011)	"…writing helps people to organize thoughts and give meaning to a traumatic experience"
Baikie, K.A. & Wilhelm, K. (2005)	"writing about traumatic, stressful or emotional events has been found to result in improvements in both physical and psychological health, in non-clinical and clinical populations. In the expressive writing paradigm, participants are asked to write about such events for 15–20 minutes on 3–5 occasions. Those who do so generally have significantly better physical and psychological outcomes compared with those who write about neutral topics." (p. 338)
Pennebaker, J. (1997)	"Students who write about emotional topics show improvements in grades in the months following the study." (p. 162)

Step #3

This is the challenging step: synthesize your material. There's no one right answer –and that's why you might end developing some intriguing, unpredictable content.

Example

The psychological and physical benefits of writing about emotional, stressful or traumatizing subjects are well documented. One study suggests this kind of writing may even help students improve their grades. Therefore, journal-writing assignments might be an appropriate addition to post-secondary writing courses.[68]

An additional benefit of synthesizing your research material? It allows you to shape the essay to fit your own interests and background. That's gratifying and enjoyable – and that's why I concluded my own example of synthesis above with a reference to journal writing.

Exercise 5.7

Follow the previous example to create your own synthesis, using the research material provided above (i.e., start with Step #2 and then move on to Step #3).

---

68. This example lacks proper referencing. For now, focus on developing your content.

	Common theme: _____
Harvard Health Publications (2011)	
Baikie, K.A. & Wilhelm, K. (2005)	
Pennebaker, J. (1997)	

Your synthesis:

....

....

SUMMARY

Some common pitfalls that undermine the strength and credibility of student essays are as follows:

- Faulty logic that stems from lack of supporting evidence;
- Weak Internet-based research practices, which overlook the potential of Google Scholar and library databases in favour of Wikipedia and public search engines like Google;
- Plagiarism, whether deliberate or unintentional;
- An overdependence on source material.

The first three problems all come with fairly straightforward remedies: generate more and better evidence; develop more effective and efficient research strategies; and become more aware of what constitutes plagiarism and why it's considered an academic crime. However, the last one, which suggests a reluctance to develop and present your own, independent ideas, is more challenging to address. It requires drawing on your confidence as a writer who has something of value to say and your skill in synthesizing your source material to craft those valuable thoughts.

Chapter 6
Writing the Introduction

This chapter will help you write your introduction by ...

- Identifying four challenges that prevent you from starting – and four strategies to address those challenges
- Recommending a new approach to structuring your introduction that's designed to capture your reader's attention
- Explaining the deductive and inductive approaches to writing and how to structure your introduction to fit each approach
- Providing sample essay introductions with commentary on their strengths and weaknesses.

Introductions are hard to start writing. They carry the weight of all your expectations – good, bad, and indifferent. For example, you might be feeling pressured to produce the perfect essay; anxious about the prospect of failing; or completely uninterested in the entire project. And as you start writing the introduction, those expectations are going to be put to the test. Are you actually writing the perfect paper? Are you failing? Or, perhaps most vexing of all, does your indifference persist? The answers matter because they reveal whether or not those burdensome expectations have disappeared and, consequently, whether or not you feel good about yourself. And that's one (probably completely unexpected) reason that introductions are challenging to write.

This next section delves a bit deeper into those and other challenges and offers strategies to address them

FOUR CHALLENGES IN WRITING THE INTRODUCTION – AND FOUR REMEDIES

CHALLENGE #1: *The pressure to produce a perfect paper prevents me from starting the paper.*

Consider this scenario: "In my mind, I can see my essay: insightful, beautifully phrased, astonishing in its depth yet not without some touches of wit. An A++ paper. Now, though, I'm afraid to start writing the paper because I'm afraid the reality won't match what I've imagined. I'm afraid I'll disappoint myself."

Really good writers and really good students often fall prey to this kind of thinking.

REMEDY: "Don't let the perfect be the enemy of the good."[69]

Perfection is often misunderstood as an original state rather than an outcome. As if perfect prose could emerge whole, clear and beautiful from the depths of someone's mind, waiting to be typed or written on the blank screen or piece of paper in front of them. That's not usually, if ever, the case. More typically the road to that outcome is littered with draft after draft, not a little of which contains some grievously embarrassing writing. That's the nature of writing, and that's why it's important not to get discouraged by your first attempts at the introduction. Perfection takes a while, and even after a while – which is to say after multiple drafts – it may still not make an appearance. That's when you decide that good writing is good enough. You move on, write the introduction and all the rest. And as you do so, you're strengthening your craft, making it more likely that perfection will show up when you write the next essay's introduction.

CHALLENGE #2: *Writing the introduction will only confirm what I already know: I'm not a good writer. It's demoralizing to have that evidence presented to me in the form of a poor introduction.*

REMEDY: When you're feeling this way, read bad prose.

We have Stephen King, the successful – and prolific – American writer to thank for this particular piece of counterintuitive advice. Here's how he explains it:

> What could be more encouraging to the struggling writer than to realize his/her work is unquestionably better than that of someone who actually got paid for his/her stuff?[70]

Reading something that got published even though it's a mediocre or badly written piece can light a fire under a demoralized writer, prompting the realization, "If this got published, then my writing isn't as bad as I feared." And sometimes that's enough motivation to get you started – and to persist – writing your introduction.

You can find bad writing easily enough in certain newspapers and magazines and sometimes (actually, more often than you'd think) in academic journals. In fact, the latter supplied most of the entries in the Bad Writing Contest, which ran from 1995 to 1998 for the purpose of "[celebrating] the most stylistically lamentable passages found in scholarly books and arti-

---

69. Possibly an Italian proverb, but often attributed to Voltaire.
70. King, *On Writing*.

cles."[71] The winning entry for 1998 was published in the scholarly journal *Diacritics*. It consists of one sentence:

> The move from a structuralist account in which capital is understood to structure social relations in relatively homologous ways to a view of hegemony in which power relations are subject to repetition, convergence, and rearticulation brought the question of temporality into the thinking of structure, and marked a shift from a form of Althusserian theory that takes structural totalities as theoretical objects to one in which the insights into the contingent possibility of structure inaugurate a renewed conception of hegemony as bound up with the contingent sites and strategies of the rearticulation of power.[72]

Compare this sentence to a sample of your own writing when you need some reassurance that you're capable of composing a clear, straightforward introduction. Your own work is bound to look good by comparison – and that might be the encouragement you need to start your essay.

CHALLENGE #3: *The idea of writing this paper is overwhelming. I don't know where to begin.*
REMEDY: Begin in the middle.
If writing the introduction continues to be daunting for you, consider starting somewhere in the body. You can then write the introduction afterwards. An additional benefit of this strategy is that it helps ensure your introduction matches what's been written in the body.

CHALLENGE #4: *I have no interest in this topic. Writing about it makes me feel both bored and boring. Those are conditions I prefer to avoid.*
REMEDY: Rethink the inverted triangle.
The inverted triangle (see Figure 6.1) is the conventional writing advice to structure an introduction: organize your thoughts and information so that they move from the general to the specific; or from the familiar to the unknown.
However, this advice may inadvertently conflict with another rule about writing the introduction: grab the reader's attention immediately.
Do you see the contradiction? How can you grab the readers' attention

---

71. Retrieved from http://denisdutton.com/bad_writing.htm.
72. Ibid.

if you're starting off with what they already know? Years of being in the classroom, where reading is mandatory, may have blinded us to a truth about readers: increasing numbers of them don't actually like to read. They'll look for reasons not to read what you've written. And if the first few sentences of your essay offer general statements they're already familiar with, or could have guessed, you've given them a reason to judge your essay as boring. You've given them a reason not to continue reading.

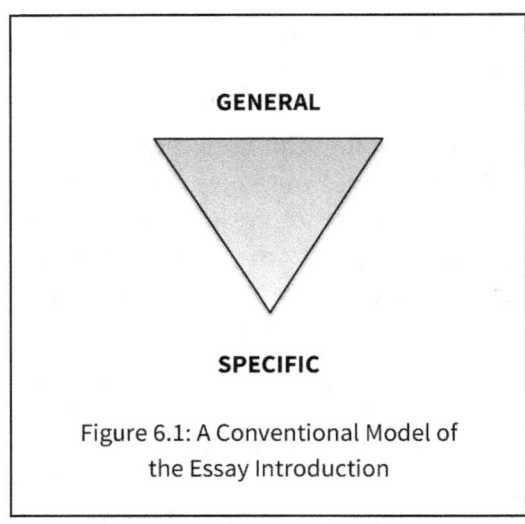

Figure 6.1: A Conventional Model of the Essay Introduction

Consider, for example, these opening statements:

"*Hamlet is considered one of the greatest dramas in the English language.*"

"*Women have tried for years to achieve equality in the workforce.*"

"*Childhood obesity is a growing problem in North American society.*"

They're typical of what you might encounter in a college or university-level essay. But would you describe them as "attention-grabbing" openings? Probably not. None of them says anything that the average reader doesn't already know and hasn't already heard. And therefore the average reader would likely perceive all of them as boring.

To figure out if your own introductory statement is attention-grabbing, ask a simple question: "Could a reasonably-educated person easily come up with what I've just written?" If the answer is yes, you're wasting your readers' time (and inadvertently labeling yourself as boring) by writing it. Give your readers something they don't already know.

To help you achieve that goal, modify the inverted triangle model (see Figure 6.2). By structuring your introduction to move from "specific" to "very specific," you could re-write the above opening lines:

FROM "Hamlet is considered one of the greatest dramas in the English language."

TO "*Hamlet continues to be firmly entrenched within our 11th-grade English curriculum, its themes of love lost, betrayal, and madness apparently finding a particular resonance with 16-year-olds.*"

FROM ~~"Women have tried for years to achieve equality in the workforce."~~

TO "The most powerful person in the world today is a woman …"

FROM ~~"Childhood obesity is a growing problem in North American society."~~

TO "The average boy in Canada consumes 123 pounds of sugar a year."

Get specific immediately. You're more likely to craft an attention-grabbing opening that way, one that saves your introduction (and you) from being judged "boring." A specific opening also sets the stage for an introduction of substance, signaling to your readers that they're about to encounter content that's new and intriguing.

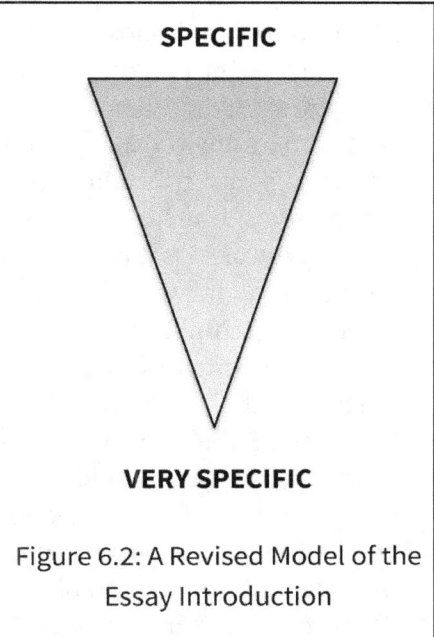

Figure 6.2: A Revised Model of the Essay Introduction

How to grab the reader's attention in the first line

Being specific and giving readers something they don't already know are the two broad principles. You can apply those principles by starting your paper with any of the following:

- An intriguing or provocative quotation that's relevant to your topic. (Note: If there's a good chance the reader has heard a particular quotation many times, it's probably no longer intriguing or provocative.)
- A brief story or anecdote. Brevity is key here. Make sure your story supports or illustrates a broader point you want to make. It can be personal, real-life or fictitious.
- A surprising statistic.
- A question that is *just* beyond the reader's ability to answer accurately. A "big" question such as "What is truth?" is probably far beyond the reader's ability to answer – so it gets eliminated as an engaging opening line. "Does Facebook distort the truth about people's lives?" offers a better possibility.
- A teaser. Defined as "[a] device intended to arouse interest or curiosity

especially in something to follow,"[73] a teaser encourages you to continue reading because of intriguing information it leaves out but implicitly promises to disclose further on. (For an example, see the opening statement at the end of this section – the one that begins "Good scientific writing is …")

- A statement that challenges conventional beliefs. "Challenge" doesn't necessarily mean a combative, over-the-top statement. It could be something subdued: "Salt may not be the demon that dieticians once thought it was." Or it *could* be combative and over-the-top: "Dieticians have held us hostage for years with their war against salt." Be wary, though, of combative, over-the-top statements. They may suggest you're clenching too tightly—a grip you were warned against earlier.
- A statement that catches the reader off-guard with its directness or bluntness. Some topics are considered best handled at arm's length – as if it's indelicate to address them too directly. Matters such as sex, aging, and discrimination often fall into this category. Academics, in particular, tend to write as if directness were a scholarly shortcoming that makes them vulnerable to criticism, and so they cautiously qualify everything.[74] In a statement remarkable for not doing so, Stephen Pinker (2014) explains that

> Academics mindlessly cushion their prose with wads of fluff that imply they are not willing to stand behind what they say. Those include *almost, apparently, comparatively, fairly, in part, nearly, partially, predominantly, presumably, rather, relatively, seemingly, so to speak, somewhat, sort of, to a certain degree, to some extent* …. in the vain hope that it will get them off the hook … should a critic ever try to prove them wrong.[75]

But a carefully written opening is not the same as a cautiously written opening. When you avoid the latter and work on the former, you may end up with an opening like,

Good scientific writing is not a matter of life and death; it is much

---

73. Retrieved from http://www.merriam-webster.com/dictionary/teaser.
74. To be fair to academics, though, the peer-review process encourages this kind of writing. Publication in peer-reviewed journals might be denied if a reviewer strongly objects to what's been written – hence, the perceived need to tread cautiously, avoiding overly direct statements.
75. Pinker, "Why Academics Stink," p. 5.

more serious than that.[76]

Did that get your attention?

HOW TO STRUCTURE THE INTRODUCTION

Every reader, whether consciously aware of it or not, approaches the introduction with two questions: What is this essay about? Is it worth my time to read it?

Well-written introductions answer both questions clearly and unequivocally.

We've already dealt with how to address the first question – that's the function of the thesis or purpose statement. In the structure explained above, it's placed at the end of the introduction.

The second question gets addressed in the rest of the introduction. There's no template to guide you here. And there really shouldn't be. Templates present a "one size fits all" approach that may not consider your particular topic, the type of essay you're writing – reflection, opinion piece or research – or the discipline you're writing for. All these factors, together with your own unique voice and insights, would influence how to answer the second question. The best that can be offered are some suggestions, which follow below.

First, figure out *exactly* why your essay is worth the reader's time. There will probably be more than one reason or, more accurately, your reasons may overlap.

For example, your essay may be worth the reader's time because it

- Advances research already conducted or analyses already published
- Provides insight into an issue that's important to a particular community, interest group, region, industry, or individual (i.e., the reader)
- Offers an intellectually interesting discussion
- Presents strategies/recommendations
- Increases awareness of an issue.

And while it's not a priority – in fact, rarely even a concern – in academic writing, there's no rule against including "entertains the reader" as a secondary reason.

In short, a well-written essay gives the reader something of worth that

---

76. R. Day and B. Gastel, *How to Write and Publish a Scientific Paper*, 7th edition (Cambridge: Cambridge University Press, 2012), p. xv.

he or she didn't have before: new information, a different insight, a heightened awareness and, ideally, a sense that reading your essay is the best possible use of his or her time.

Second, figure out what specific content – beyond the opening, which has already been discussed – needs to be included in the introduction to achieve that goal. That content might include

- An overview of what's already been written or discussed about the topic
- Some background information that places the topic in perspective or context
- Key definition(s) to clarify what's being discussed.

Examples of Essay Introductions

As you read each sample introduction below, pay particular attention to the way in which it's structured.

Introduction #1[77]

Jane Austen, legend has it, was continually interrupted by visitors while she sat in her family's living room secretly writing the novels that would make her famous. Most of us, though, probably wouldn't do our best work in that setting.

Now it's a fact. A team of researchers at George Mason University has found that people who are interrupted while writing end up producing lower-quality essays than writers who are allowed to work undisturbed. Researchers have known for a while that interruptions inhibit our ability to carry out many tasks – from detecting traffic signals to performing surgery. This study is unique, though, in looking at – and quantifying – how distractions affect the caliber of creative work.[78]

Notes: The second sentence, which is part of the introduction's "attention-grabbing" opening, explicitly connects the reader to the topic and to the writer: "Most of us, though, probably wouldn't do our best work in that setting." Your instructor has a reason for cautioning you against habitually using a first person pronoun in your essay, as we discussed earlier. But its careful use can reduce the distance between reader and writer, reminding

---

77. Referencing information is not included in this excerpt.
78. Robb, "Interruptions."

the reader that a real person wrote this paper – in this case, one who links herself with the reader by referring to "we" and "us".

That hard-working second sentence accomplishes something else: it lets the reader know that this essay is worth reading, by implicitly promising to explain the setting we need to do our best work.

The theme "this essay is worth reading" is reinforced in the last sentence with its emphasis on "this study is unique".

Introduction #2

In 1921, the Olympia Veneer Company became the first worker-owned cooperative to produce plywood. By the early 1950s, nearly all of the plywood produced in the United States was manufactured by worker-owned cooperatives. Today, however, worker-owned cooperatives seem few and far between. Say "co-op" and most people think of Park Slope foodies or strictly guarded apartment buildings. Worker ownership may seem a relic of the past, but it could actually play a significant role in reviving the union movement, bolstering the green economy, and stemming the tide of de-industrialization.[79]

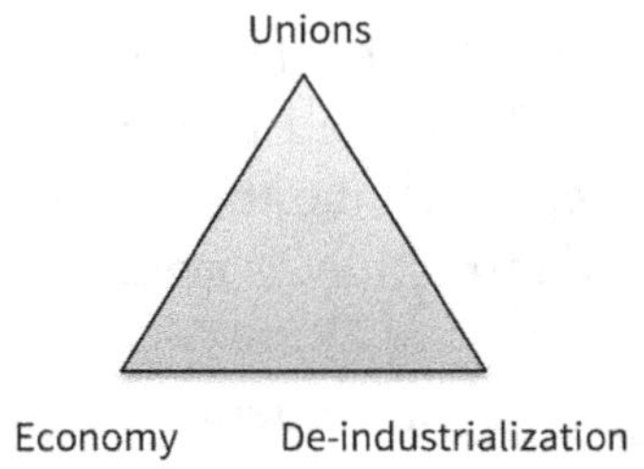

Notes: This introduction lacks an attention-grabbing opening. It is, though, a clear example of the clock plan as it moves from 1921 to "the early 1950s" to the present day. Right from the start, it promises the reader a straightforward, easy-to-follow structure.

Pay attention, also, to the thesis statement, the last sentence in the paragraph: it contains the entire structure of the essay – triangle plan – and therefore makes the writer's job easier. No need to wonder what to discuss first, second and third in the body of the essay. It's already been figured out and presented in the thesis. (See Figure 6.3.)

Figure 6.3: The Essay Structure Embedded within the Thesis Statement of Introduction #2

---

79. S. McElwee, "When Workers Own Their Companies, Everyone Wins: How a Very Old Economic Model Could Help the New Economy," *The New Republic*, August 1, 2014.

Introduction #3:

... women have regularly felt pressure to indulge in some form of artificial self-improvement. These conscious decisions to attract men may reflect subconscious, psychological perceptions of attraction woven throughout the course of evolution. One of these influential yet contradictory factors in sexual selection is height. Admired female models boasted in the media are generally taller than average female height (Pettijohn & Jungeberg, 2004; McDowell et al., 2008). However, studies show that men generally tend to prefer female partners who are relatively shorter (Pawlowski, 2003), which may be due to cultural and evolutionary norms in which men exhibit physical dominance over women (Buss, 1994; Fielding et al., 2008). A possible reason for this paradox may be the influence of the aesthetic and erotic quality of female legs, which contribute to the perception of height (Swami et al., 2006; Sorokowski et al., 2008). Existing studies argue over whether height or leg length is more influential in indicating health and fertility (Lawlor et al., 2002; Pawlowski et al., 2003; Lawlor et al., 2004; Swami et al., 2006; Fielding et al., 2008; Fraser et al., 2008, Helle et al., 2008; Sorokowski et al., 2008). Despite the evidence indicating both height and leg length are influential towards female attraction, I have found no current studies that find a compromise between the two components. Therefore I propose to demonstrate that the ideal female physique, which demonstrates the greatest potential of health, fertility and attraction, is average height with high leg-to-body ratio.[80]

Notes: This is a student research essay. The writer has done a good job of synthesis and of introducing herself as a thorough and serious researcher.

But does her handling of the references affect the introduction's readability? Helen Sword (2012), in *Stylish Academic Writing*, warns against "lengthy parenthetical citations" that "slow down the text's momentum" and prompt the question "how can you possibly tell a compelling research story if you have to stop and cough every few seconds?"[81]

To improve the paragraph's flow, the writer might have used **signal phrases** to accommodate some of her **in-text citations**.

Example: Rather than the parenthetical citation at the end of the sentence or clause, such as "men generally tend to prefer female partners who

---

80. R. Mei, "The Average Beauty," http://www.people.fas.harvard.edu/~expose/issues/issue_2010/mei.html.
81. Sword, *Stylish Academic Writing*, p. 144.

are relatively shorter (Pawlowski, 2003)," try instead a signal phrase that incorporates the citation within the sentence: "*According to Pawlowski (2003),* men generally tend to prefer female partners who are relatively shorter" or "*Pawlowski (2003) concludes* that men generally tend to prefer female partners who are relatively shorter."

Combining parenthetical citations with signal phrases reduces the likelihood of your reader having to "stop and cough every few seconds."

And finally consider the writer's use of first person ("I") in the last two sentences. The first instance ("I have found no current studies that find a compromise between the two components") illustrates another use of first person: to acknowledge the limitations of your statement. There's an important distinction between "I have found no current studies" and "No current studies exist." First person ensures greater accuracy. In the second instance, though, the use of "I" may be extraneous. Try rewriting the sentence without it.

Introduction #4

The problem is my age. It relentlessly advances while the faces staring back at me in the classroom remain the same, fixed between late adolescence and early adulthood. In short, I grow old while my students do not. And the increasing gap between our ages causes me some concern, pedagogically speaking.[82]

Notes: This introduction is the start of a reflective, personal essay. It illustrates a style that's appropriate for journal writing assignments, blogs, newsletters – or essentially any social media writing. The emphasis in these writing assignments is *engagement*. You want your readers to feel less as if they're being "lectured at" and more as if they're being directly engaged in a conversation. (Actually, there's an argument for cultivating that kind of style in academic writing, as well. But that's another story.) First person pronouns (e.g., "I", "you", "we"), personal examples and narratives all figure prominently in this kind of writing. The tone tends to be conversational and relaxed.

These characteristics mislead some people into thinking that the personal essay is easier to write than the conventional academic essay.

They're wrong. All the rules we've covered so far still apply. Check out, for example, the structure of this introduction:

---

[82]. J. Flaherty, "Millennial Students and Middle-Aged Faculty: A Learner-Centred Approach toward Bridging the Gap," *The Teaching Professor* 26: 2 (2012): 1, 3.

(i) "The problem is my age" – it's specific; it's a "teaser"; and it just may disarm the reader with its bluntness. All elements of an attention-grabbing opening.

(ii) The next two sentences in the introduction provide increasingly specific detail, following the revised model discussed in this chapter.

(iii) "And the increasing gap between our ages causes me some concern, pedagogically speaking." The last sentence of the introduction presents the paper's thesis. And note that the thesis targets not just the writer's concerns but also the readers': concerns about pedagogy (teaching and learning) are relevant to a broad audience.

A personal essay does not, in other words, give you license to ramble or to navel-gaze, focused on issues of no interest or relevance to anyone but you. In fact, the personal essay may be more challenging than a conventional academic essay to write because it requires balancing what academic writers often mistakenly see as incompatible: logic with emotion; professionalism with passion; and research with introspection.

But if your writing illustrates that balance, then chances are your paper contains depth and insight because it addresses what the famous economist E.F. Schumacher termed "the true problem of living … reconciling opposites."[83]

That's why you want to aim for balance in your writing.

DEDUCTIVE VS. INDUCTIVE

DEDUCTIVE: "If you don't know where you're going, you might end up someplace else."[84]

Re-read the last sentence of the four introductions above, and you'll see one common element: a thesis statement. That's a signal this essay takes a **deductive approach**: its conclusion (or thesis) is placed at the beginning; the rest of the paper provides support for that particular conclusion. This pattern, known as the deductive approach, is common in non-scientific academic papers. It helps the reader – and the writer – stay on track throughout the essay because both know where they're headed right from the start.

INDUCTIVE: "It is a capital mistake to theorize before you have all the evidence. It biases the judgment."[85]

Sometimes not knowing – not exactly, anyway – where you're headed at the start can lead you down an interesting path. And that's the benefit of the

---

83. E.F. Schumacher, *Small Is Beautiful: A Study of Economics as if People Mattered* (New York: Random House, 1973), p. 77.
84. Quotation from the well known American baseball player Yogi Berra.
85. Arthur Conan Doyle, *A Study in Scarlet,* Part 1, Chapter 3.

inductive approach. A writer using the inductive approach doesn't begin with a thesis. Instead, he or she begins by presenting the evidence and then analyzes it to see what it yields: what patterns, inferences, or conclusions can be drawn. This kind of essay doesn't provide a thesis statement in the introduction. It provides a purpose statement, a question or an hypothesis (an educated guess) that determines the kind of evidence to be examined in the rest of the paper. It's a common approach in scientific essays.

Figure 6.4 illustrates the two different approaches: deductive vs. inductive.[86]

Which is better?

Neither. They're simply two different approaches. Sometimes the decision to choose one over the other will have already been made by your instructor's preference or your discipline's tradition. And sometimes, for no clear reason, one approach just emerges as you start working on your paper.

The deductive approach provides you with a clear, straightforward task: present evidence that supports your thesis. It's the mainstay of all those five-paragraph essays[87] that you were probably taught to write in high school. And so it has the advantage of a familiar, predictable structure,

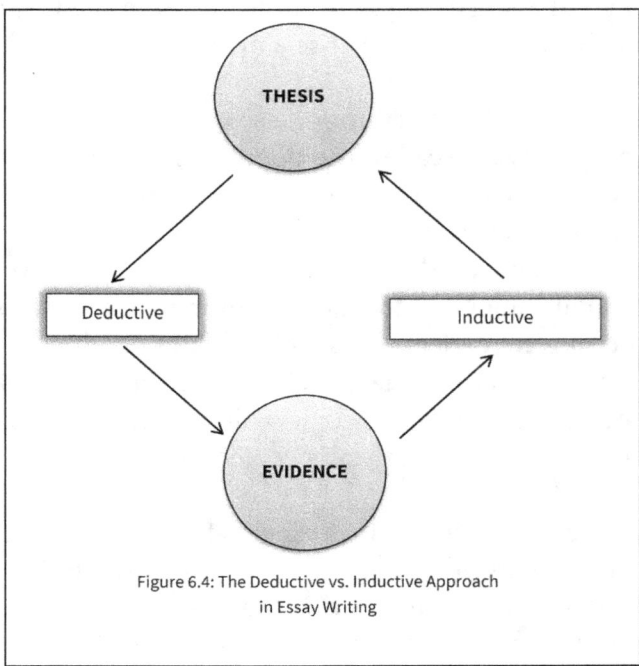

Figure 6.4: The Deductive vs. Inductive Approach in Essay Writing

---

86. This figure is a modified version of one presented on https://toknow-11.wikispaces.com/Deductive+and+Inductive+Reasoning.
87. If you're puzzled by this reference, see the sample outlines at the start of Chapter 3. They're examples of the five-paragraph essay model.

which then allows both you and the reader to focus on the content. Familiarity can breed boredom, though. Don't forget the importance of pairing your predicable essay structure with unpredictable content. (See Chapter 4 if you need a refresher on that.)

The inductive approach may make you feel like a detective: you need to analyze your evidence to build a thesis. This task allows you the chance to be flexible and even creative in fashioning your essay's structure – but it also offers more opportunities for your essay to veer off course.

The mantra "predictable structure, unpredictable content" applies equally to both approaches, but perhaps with a slightly different emphasis. If you're writing a deductive essay, pay particular attention to "unpredictable content"; if you're writing an inductive essay, to "predictable structure."

Introductions that signal an inductive approach

Your introduction should clearly indicate whether your essay is using a deductive or an inductive approach. Examples of introductions that signal a deductive approach have already been given. Examples of introductions that signal an inductive approach are given below.

Read them and ask "How are they different from the first set of examples? How are they alike? Do I prefer one over the other – and, if so, why?"

Introduction #1

For the past two decades, the population of Canada has been the subject of a vast and largely unnoticed experiment whose results have enormous relevance for the world.

The experiment used the entire adult population to test this question: Should higher education become nearly universal, with college and university degrees as widely held as high school diplomas? Given that postsecondary credentials have traditionally provided a large benefit to some people, will they continue to produce those benefits if held by nearly all people?[88]

NOTES: The rule of capturing the reader's attention still applies, whether you're using an inductive or deductive approach. And it's illustrated here, with this introduction's opening teaser. You need to read on to find out what this "unnoticed experiment" with "enormous relevance for the world" is all about. You also need to read the rest of the essay to find out the answers to the two questions posed at the end of the introduction. By posing

---

88. D. Saunders, "Why University Should Be Universal," *The Globe and Mail*, May 15, 2015.

those two questions in the introduction (as opposed to stating a thesis), the writer indicates he's taking an inductive approach.

INTRODUCTION #2

When faced with stressful life events, expressing one's deepest thoughts and feelings in writing, also known as "expressive writing" or "experimental disclosure," may be a useful tool.... (Frattaroli, 2006). Previous studies have shown that expressive writing delivers numerous benefits, including reductions in distress (Barry & Singer, 2001), [and] decreases in fatigue, tension, and upper respiratory symptoms (Lepore & Greenberg, 2002).... All of these factors, in turn, are likely to produce benefits for health and well-being....

Important exams are sources of significant stress and strain in the lives of students, as periods leading up to exams have been characterized by increases in cortisol (Lewis, Nikolova, Chang, & Weekes, 2008) and elevations in state anxiety and perceived stress (Lewis, Weekes, & Wang, 2007).

In a study by Lepore (1997), students ... who were assigned to write expressively about their upcoming exam showed significantly greater declines in depressive symptoms prior to their exam than those assigned to write about trivial topics.... However, it is unknown whether this experimental disclosure intervention affected students' performance ... as test scores were not collected....

The goals of the present study were twofold: first, to test whether exam performance can be improved by expressive writing, thereby extending Lepore's (1997) results; and second, to determine whether test anxiety, in addition to depression, can be reduced shortly before a graduate school entrance exam. We hypothesized that expressive writing would improve performance on entrance exams, and that depression and anxiety would mediate the relationship between writing and test outcomes.[89]

NOTES: While no hard and fast rules dictate how long the introduction should be, its length is typically proportionate to the length and complexity of the essay. Longer essays usually have longer introductions. The full version of this introduction,[90] at just over 550 words, represents about 10% of the entire paper. An essay assignment of, say, 2,000 words would prob-

---

89. J. Frattaroli, S. Lyubomirsky, and M. Thomas, "Opening Up in the Classroom: Effects of Expressive Writing on Graduate School Entrance Exam Performance," *Emotion*, 11: 3 (2011): 691–6.
90. As the ellipses indicate, only an abbreviated version of this introduction is presented here.

ably warrant an introduction of one-half to three-quarters of a typed, single-spaced page.

The purpose statement and hypotheses at the end indicate the essay's inductive approach.

I wrote earlier that I wasn't an advocate of **writing templates** – step-by-step guides on how to structure your writing – because they may inadvertently prompt you to slavishly follow their rules without assessing how well they fit your particular topic or paper. Templates, in other words, can undermine your originality – and, more importantly, your confidence to forge your own path.

That doesn't mean they're without merit, though. One that's particularly well known and frequently used in the natural and social sciences is **John Swales'**[91] **model** of how to structure a research essay introduction. Swales presented this model as an alternative to the popular problem-solution structure. In brief, it consists of four parts:

1. Explain why your research topic is important.
2. Summarize (selectively) research that's already been conducted on this topic.
3. Identify gap(s) in this research or questions that it raises.
4. Show how your paper addresses these gaps or questions.

Now re-read Introduction #2, identifying those parts that follow Swales' model and those that represent a new element, something that's not included in the model.

The point?

Perhaps I've been too hasty in dismissing writing templates. A good template, like Swales', can ensure your introduction stays on track, providing a logical flow from one point to the next. Using it for this purpose, however, doesn't mean surrendering your ability to think independently and, if it suits your purpose, to add material that doesn't fit the model.

Think about that last point as you read Introduction #3 below.

Introduction #3

If there is now a scientific consensus that global warming must be taken seriously, there is also a related political consensus: that the issue is Gloom City. In *An Inconvenient Truth*, Al Gore warns of sea

---

91. As cited in J. Swales and H. Najjar, "The Writing of Research Article Introductions," *Written Communication*, 4: 2 (1987): 175–91.

levels rising to engulf New York and San Francisco and implies that only wrenching lifestyle sacrifice can save us. The opposing view is just as glum. Even mild restrictions on greenhouse gases could "cripple our economy," Republican Senator Kit Bond of Missouri said in 2003. Other conservatives suggest that greenhouse-gas rules for Americans would be pointless anyway, owing to increased fossil-fuel use in China and India. When commentators hash this issue out, it's often a contest to see which side can sound more pessimistic.

Here's a different way of thinking about the greenhouse effect: that action to prevent runaway global warming may prove cheap, practical, effective, and totally consistent with economic growth. Which makes a body wonder: Why is such environmental optimism absent from American political debate?[92]

NOTES: You know this one's different from the others when its opening statement juxtaposes "scientific consensus" and "political consensus" with "the issue is Gloom City". And the closing question about the absence of "environmental optimism" in "American political debate" is introduced with a kind of folksy **sentence fragment**: "Which makes a body wonder."

You "hear" the writer's voice in that sort of incongruous phrasing. And you figure that anyone who uses the word "hash" as a verb – "When commentators hash this issue out" – is probably comfortable having his or her voice heard. (If you need your memory refreshed on the importance of voice, re-read the section entitled "Find 'your voice'" in Chapter 2.)

So that's another function of the introduction: it sets the tone of the essay. It lets the reader know that this writer has a sense of humour, irony, wit, playfulness – or not. Setting the tone or presenting the voice – I'm using those two terms interchangeably here – is an important, albeit often overlooked, function of the introduction. It can determine whether or not someone feels inclined to read your essay.

Besides tone or voice, two other elements make this introduction stand apart:

The thesis: "Here's a different way of thinking about the greenhouse effect …" This statement lets the readers know that they won't be asked to trudge down the same, well-worn path as all the other essays on the greenhouse effect. That's an enticing prospect for most readers.

The approach: The introduction's last paragraph contains both a the-

---

92. G. Easterbrook, "Some Convenient Truths," *The Atlantic Monthly*, September 2006.

sis statement (deductive approach) and a closing question (inductive approach), demonstrating that it's possible to use both approaches in the same essay.

The lesson? Don't be reluctant to add elements to your introduction that make it stand apart in a positive way from what others have written.

If you find yourself resisting this lesson because of the risk or extra effort it involves, here's some further instruction:

1. Minimize or eliminate entirely the risk of "being different" by following stringently the rules listed earlier in this chapter. It's possible to "be different," forging your own path in terms of style and content, while still respecting the rules.

2. Remember the one benefit that outweighs all others: how good you'll feel about yourself, knowing that your writing represents you, rather than your imitation of someone else.

SUMMARY

Three pieces of advice to boost your confidence and get you started writing the introduction:

1. A good introduction you've actually written is better than a perfect one you've only imagined.
2. Reading bad prose can be a morale booster – a reminder that your writing is better than many others'.
3. If writing the introduction is too daunting, start in the middle of the essay instead. You can always write the introduction later.

Two pictures to consider as you figure out what to include in the introduction, both repeated on the next page:

1. The revised triangle model.
2. Deductive vs. inductive approaches.

One thought to strengthen the style and content of your introduction:

Follow the rules, but at the same time make your introduction different, in a positive way, from everyone else's.

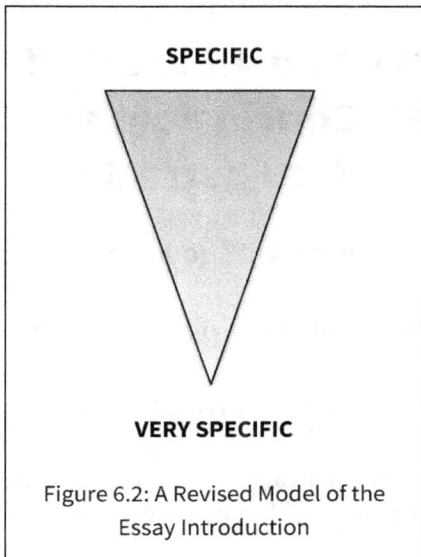

Figure 6.2: A Revised Model of the Essay Introduction

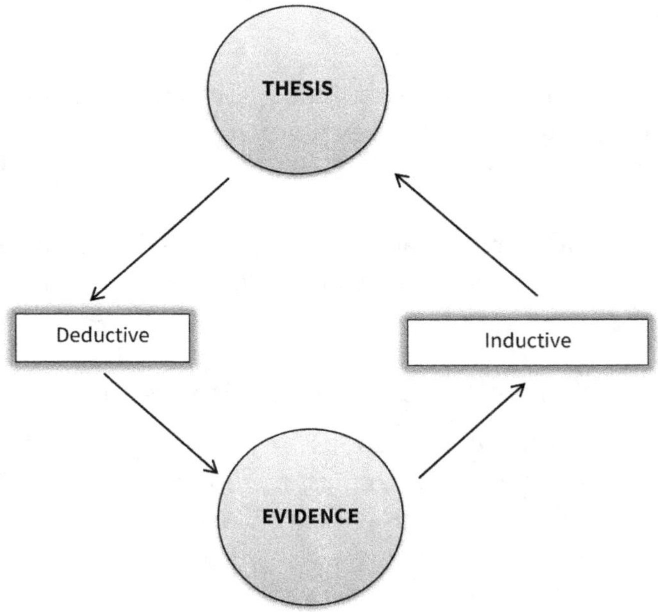

Figure 6.4: The Deductive vs. Inductive Approach in Essay Writing

Chapter 7
Writing All the Rest: Paragraphs, Conclusion, and Summary (or Abstract)

This chapter will show you how to ...

- Use one central principle to write the body paragraphs of your essay
- Develop a conclusion that connects with the reader (and, just as importantly, with yourself)
- Write a summary or abstract – a skill that's surprisingly useful, even when your papers don't require a summary or abstract

PARAGRAPHING

You've been writing paragraphs since grade school. You know these rules:

- Begin with a **topic sentence** that states the paragraph's main point.
- Limit each paragraph to one key point only.
- Use specific detail to illustrate or reinforce that one key point.

But there's another rule that most people have lost sight of. Take the timed exercise below to see if you're one of those people – or not.

Exercise 7.1: The invisible thread

PART A: Give yourself 10 seconds to memorize the following. Then close your eyes and repeat what you just memorized.

```
y                       n o                  c
             c           n                   l
n
              o                    e
                 t
```

PART B: Give yourself one second to memorize these two words: "Only connect."[93] Then close your eyes and repeat what you just memorized.

PART C: Compare your success at memorizing Part A to your success at memorizing Part B.

Consider the amount of effort you put into Part A as opposed to Part B.

Notice that both Part A and Part B asked you to memorize the same eleven letters – just arranged differently.

It's as if an invisible thread connected the letters in Part B to make complete sense when you read them – as opposed to the apparently haphazard arrangement of Part A. Consequently, Part B has "staying power" or more impact. The reader remembers what's been written – unlike Part A.

• • • • •

Now repeat one more time what you memorized in Part B. That's the invisible thread rule that most people overlook. "Only connect" means to achieve **coherence**. It requires taking the raw material of your paragraph – the ideas, data, or examples you want to present – and arranging them so they connect to each other, to your overall theme or topic and to your reader. By doing this, you can elevate a simple paragraph from something that's hard to decipher – and harder to remember – to something clear and memorable.

"Only connect" is the most challenging aspect of writing a paragraph – but it can make your paragraphs, and therefore your writing, stand apart from everyone else's.

I think the examples below are "only connect" paragraphs. Read them and decide for yourself.

EXAMPLE #1

Communications technologies are neither dehumanizing nor isolating when they provide social connectivity. When my phone beeps because my ninety-year-old grandmother in Istanbul is calling, it is anything but dehumanizing. When my high school classmates rally on Facebook to morally, physically, and, if necessary, financially support one of us during a major illness, it is anything but dehumanizing. On the contrary, without the Internet most of us would have disappeared from each other's communities and lives.

---

93. This two-word epigraph from E.M. Forster's novel *Howards End* is well-known in certain academic circles, where its meaning has been intricately discussed. For us, though, the meaning is simple. Read on to find out.

And it's profoundly humanizing when people first meet online and convert those relationships to face-to-face friendships, as about one in five people in North America have done.[94]

NOTES: The best way to determine if you're reading (and if you've written) an "only connect" paragraph is to judge how easily the sentences move from one point to the next. Is there a logical flow that allows you to keep reading without having to stop, go back and re-trace your steps because you've lost track of where you are or you can't fathom where any of this is headed? And if you do have to retrace your steps, perhaps because the material is unfamiliar and complex, or because you're feeling tired and distracted, are you frustrated or are you curious and motivated? How you feel as you read a paragraph is often the best indicator of whether or not it's an "only connect" paragraph.

Example #1 illustrates a few ways to achieve that logical flow:

- **A clear – and specific – topic sentence.** Think of the topic sentence as a mini thesis or purpose statement: "Communications technologies are neither dehumanizing nor isolating when they provide social connectivity." Its function is to let the reader know what the paragraph is about. There's no hard and fast rule that says you have to place the topic sentence at the start of the paragraph, as this one is, but if you're an inexperienced writer or if you're tackling a challenging point, starting with a topic sentence will help keep you on track. And if you're on track, your writing is more likely to flow logically from one point to the next, making it easier for the reader to follow.

- **A predictable structure.** The material in Example #1 is organized around two key tenets discussed earlier: the rule of three and the globe pattern. The three examples are organized spatially, moving in an outward, broadening circle that begins with the writer's personal life, moves to include his or her Facebook friends and ends with a reference to North Americans generally. When the structure makes sense like this, the reader moves easily from one statement to the next.

- **Parallelism.** It's a stylistic device that adds more than just style to a piece of writing. It also adds clarity and flow. Parallelism refers to sentences or phrases that have a similar or perhaps identical construction. This similarity links the sentences. It's the "invisible thread" that connects them to each other. Check out, for example, how the writer introduces each exam-

---

94. Z. Tufekci, "The Social Internet: Frustrating, Enriching, but Not Lonely." *Public Culture* 26: 72 (2014): 13–23.

ple: "When my phone beeps …"; "When my high school classmates rally …"; "… when people first meet online …" The repetitive sentence structure – "when" followed by a noun followed by a verb – signals to the reader that these sentences are all connected. They're all examples that reinforce the writer's main point.

Example #2

Psychoanalysts have concocted countless theories about why we fall in love with whom we do. Freud would have said your choice is influenced by the unrequited wish to bed your mother, if you're a boy, or your father, if you're a girl. Jung believed that passion is driven by some kind of collective unconscious. Today psychiatrists such as Thomas Lewis from the University of California at San Francisco's School of Medicine hypothesize that romantic love is rooted in our earliest infantile experiences with intimacy, how we felt at the breast, our mother's face, these things of pure unconflicted comfort that get engraved in our brain and that we ceaselessly try to recapture as adults. According to this theory we love whom we love not so much because of the future we hope to build but because of the past we hope to reclaim. Love is reactive, not proactive, it arches us backward, which may be why a certain person just "feels right." Or "feels familiar." He or she is familiar. He or she has a certain look or smell or sound or touch that activates buried memories.[95]

NOTES: Example #2 illustrates another way to achieve coherence:
- **Unity**: In an "only connect" paragraph, every sentence fits with the one that came before and the one that comes after. And they all connect back to the topic sentence – which connects back to the paper's main thesis or purpose. If we were to show these connections diagrammatically, the result would be something like Figure 7.1 on page 117.

• • • • •

Readers are on a journey into the unknown, but if they are provided with signposts and maps, they won't feel lost. —*Peter Elbow*[96]

- **Transitions**: Those "signposts and maps" are transitions: connect-

---

95. L. Slater, "Love" (2006). Retrieved from http://ngm.nationalgeographic.com/print/2006/02/true-love/slater-text.
96. Peter Elbow, "The Music of Form," *College Composition and Communication 2* (2006), p. 12, http://scholarworks.umass.edu/eng_faculty_pubs/2P.

ing words or phrases that show how the parts of your paragraph are related and where the paragraph is headed. Some transitions take the reader by the hand and explicitly show him or her how the sentences are connected. When you read "For example" at the start of a sentence, you know immediately you're about to get an example to illustrate a point that was just made. "However" prepares us for a different direction or perspective from the previous sentence. "Furthermore" signals an extension of the point already made. And "therefore" suggests that point is about to be wrapped up. Other transitions work more subtly. They might consist of synonyms, pronouns, or repetition. No matter what form they take, though, their job is the same: to strengthen the paragraph's **coherence** – or the flow from one part to another.

Exercise 7.2

The **highlighted** sections below from Watson and Crick's paper (which was cited in Chapter 4) are examples of subtle transitions.

Read them and figure out how they function as transitions. If it helps, insert arrows to show the connections, as in Figure 7.1 above. Don't worry if the result is messy. That's a sign that the paragraph "coheres."

A structure for nucleic acid has already been proposed by Pauling and Corey. **They** kindly made **their** manuscript available to us in advance of publication. **Their model** consists of three intertwined chains, with the **phosphates near the fibre axis**, and the bases on the outside. **In our opinion**, **this structure** is unsatisfactory for **two reasons**:

(1) We believe that the material which gives the X-ray diagrams is the salt, not the free acid. Without the acidic hydrogen atoms it is not clear what forces would hold the structure together, especially as the negatively charged **phosphates near the axis** will repel each other.

(2) Some of the van der Waals distances appear to be too small.

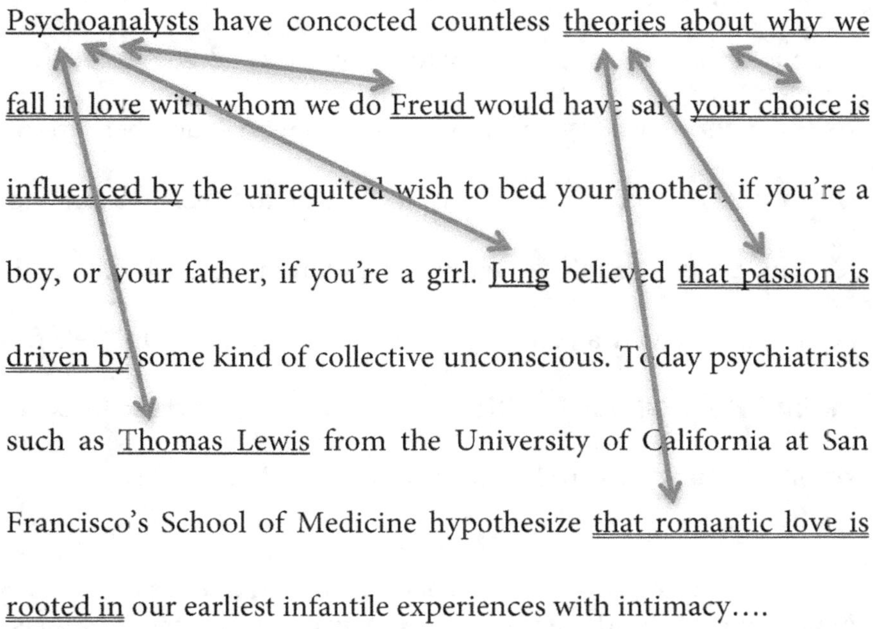

> Psychoanalysts have concocted countless theories about why we fall in love with whom we do Freud would have said your choice is influenced by the unrequited wish to bed your mother if you're a boy, or your father, if you're a girl. Jung believed that passion is driven by some kind of collective unconscious. Today psychiatrists such as Thomas Lewis from the University of California at San Francisco's School of Medicine hypothesize that romantic love is rooted in our earliest infantile experiences with intimacy....
>
> Figure 7.1: Paragraph unity means everything is related

Exercise 7.3

The **highlighted** sections below from Example #2 are yet more subtle examples of transitions.

1. Read them and figure out how they function as transitions. If it helps, insert arrows to show the connections, as in the figure earlier in the chapter. (Again, expect to make a mess.)
2. Highlight the examples of parallelism that also function as transitions.

> **Today** psychiatrists such as Thomas Lewis from the University of California at San Francisco's School of Medicine hypothesize that romantic love is rooted in our earliest infantile experiences with intimacy, **how we felt at the breast**, **our mother's face**, **these**

things of pure unconflicted comfort that get engraved in our brain and that we ceaselessly try to recapture as adults. **According to this theory** we **love** whom we **love** not so much because of **the future** we hope to build but because of **the past** we hope to reclaim. **Love** is **reactive**, not **proactive**, **it** arches us **backward, which** may be why a certain person just "feels right." Or "feels **familiar." He or she** is **familiar**. He or she has **a certain look or smell or sound or touch** that activates buried memories.

Example #3

The serial comma is the one before "and" in a series of three or more things. With the serial comma: My favorite cereals are Cheerios, Raisin Bran, and Shredded Wheat. Without the serial comma: I used to like Kix, Trix and Wheat Chex. Proponents of the serial comma say that it is preferable because it prevents ambiguity, and I'll go along with that…. But pressed to come up with an example of a series that was unambiguously ambiguous without the serial comma I couldn't think of a good one….

Fortunately, the Internet is busy with examples of series that are absurd without the serial comma:

"We invited the strippers, J.F.K. and Stalin." (This has been illustrated online, and formed the basis of a poll: which stripper had the better outfit, J.F.K. or Stalin.)

"This book is dedicated to my parents, Ayn Rand and God."

And there was the country-and-Western singer who was joined onstage by his two ex-wives, Kris Kristofferson and Waylon Jennings.[97]

Notes: "Only connect" applies to all writing, even cheeky journalism. In honouring that rule, the writer of the above piece used the following tools:
- **Ample supporting detail.** We've been over this before, but it bears

---

97. M. Norris, "Holy Writ: Learning to Love the House Style," *The New Yorker*, February 23 and March 2, 2015.

repeating: general statements typically need to be explained/illustrated/reinforced with specific supporting detail. The exception is self-evident statements or statements that are common knowledge – categories that probably don't include "Proponents of the serial comma say that it is preferable because it prevents ambiguity." Hence, supporting detail is needed. It connects the reader to the topic by clarifying the topic.

- **Paragraph length and layout.** Good journalism can teach us a lot about academic writing. For instance, the original paragraph in Example #3 was considerably longer than the shortened version that appears here, illustrating that paragraphs don't have to strictly follow the 3-to-5-sentence rule that's often presented as the traditional standard length. But neither should they go on interminably, as paragraphs in published academic papers often do.

Then how long should a paragraph be? Here's a test: after you've written a page or two, print off the paper, hold it at arm's length, and, without reading anything, just stare at the page. Does it *invite* you to read the paper? Does it *ask* to make a connection with you? You'll immediately know if the answer is "yes," tipped off by two clues: varying paragraph lengths and a layout that facilitates reading.

Varying paragraph lengths – as opposed to consecutive lengthy blocks of text or a series of very short paragraphs – makes your audience more receptive to reading your paper. Most readers view a block of lengthy paragraphs as intimidating and somewhat wearying. The prospect of having to plough through all that unremitting prose is discouraging. Conversely, a string of short paragraphs (three sentences or fewer) signals shallow content that's likely not worth the reader's time. And they're probably right. Extremely short paragraphs often mean a lack of necessary detail, just as habitually long paragraphs may suggest lack of unity – too much material crammed together that doesn't belong together.

Layout that facilitates reading includes white space, bulleted lists, headings and figures. These visual elements make the paper aesthetically pleasing – a quality not to be dismissed as shallow or unimportant. We're drawn to the aesthetically pleasing, after all, and more likely, therefore, to connect with what's written on that page.

Now, with that information in mind, revisit Example #3. Note that the differing paragraph lengths and the ample use of white space give the reader a break, some time to catch his or her breath and think about the material. That is, it gives the reader a chance to connect with the content.

Published academic papers can teach us a lesson in this regard. Although they typically pay little attention to layout, most of them use headings – ranging from the traditional, albeit generic, "**IMRAD**" (Introduction; Methods; Results; and Discussion) to more unique, **informative headings**. Some, recognizing the limitations of generic headings – they do nothing to distinguish one paper from another – use only the latter and some mix the two, combining generic major headings (e.g., "Background"; "Analysis"; "Conclusion") with more specific subheadings of the writer's own creation. In any case, good headings can reinforce the principle of "predictable structure" by alerting the reader as to what's coming up. Headings, particularly the non-generic ones, also allow the reader to ignore or skim those paragraphs of little interest and focus on those of greater interest. And they can also be a way keeping you on track as you write. They act as a visual reminder to keep your thoughts corralled within whatever that heading signifies.

Finally, informative headings that you develop yourself allow you to have some fun, experimenting with your own creativity. Here, for example, are headings from a chapter by writer Michael Pollan, entitled "The Industrialization of Eating."[98]

From Whole Foods to Refined
From Complexity to Simplicity
From Quality to Quantity
From Leaves to Seeds
From Food Culture to Food Science

Pollan doesn't allot each paragraph its own heading, of course. And you probably won't either, assuming your paper is of any significant length. Rather, each heading introduces a *section* of paragraphs, explicitly connecting them to each other and to the specific topic embedded in that heading.

This example illustrates something else: using parallelism to create headings. All five headings share a similar structure, which reminds the reader that all five sections of the chapter are connected.

Consider how you might use headings in your own writing. But keep in mind that some fields (e.g., the natural and social sciences) welcome headings more than others (e.g., the humanities).

- **Quotations**. First, let's get the terminology down correctly. "Quote" is a verb: "I quote a lot when I can't figure out what to say myself." "Quota-

---

98. M. Pollan, "The Industrialization of Eating," in *In Defense of Food: An Eater's Manifesto* (New York: Penguin Books, 2008), pp. 101–136.

tion" is the noun: "Writing a 1500-word essay is easy if I use a lot of quotations." At this point some readers will get irritated at the triviality of it all, pointing out that the language evolves, and most of the English-speaking population – at least those who have to write essays – probably use "quote" as a noun, as in "I don't get the fuss about using quotes in a paragraph."

They've got a point. But they may be missing another point: good writers are fussy, obsessive even, when it comes to choosing the right words. They don't quote liberally just to meet a word count, each paragraph part of a patchwork of someone else's words and thoughts. They quote because the quotation strengthens what they themselves want to say.

In short, you quote someone else because you want to

- discuss in greater detail what that person has written
- capitalize on that person's "star power" to highlight that your paper draws on the work of known authorities in the field
- harness the impact a particular quotation carries because of its conciseness, eloquence, insight or wit.

Ideally, the quotations in your paper will serve all three functions. But if they serve none, you're better off using your own words. (That advice, by the way, applies especially to the natural sciences, where quotations are used sparingly, if at all.)

Keep in mind, too, that quotations don't have to be lengthy. They can be one word, a phrase, a sentence, or one or more paragraphs. They do, though, have to be integrated into your work, not presented as freestanding and self-evident. Here are some ways of achieving that:

INCORPORATE THE QUOTATION INTO YOUR OWN SENTENCE.

According to the article "On the Death of the Phone Call" by Clive Thompson, published in *Wired* magazine in 2010, "the average number of mobile phone calls we make is dropping every year.... And our calls are getting shorter: in 2005 they averaged three minutes in length; now they're almost half that." Safe behind our screens, we let type do our talking for us – and leave others to conjure our lives by reading between the lines.[99]

Note how the writer has seamlessly integrated the quotation into his

---

99. T. Chatfield, "I Type, Therefore I Am," *Aeon*, May 27, 2013, http://aeon.co/magazine/technology/tom-chatfield-language-and-digital-identity/.

own sentence. The ellipsis (…) signifies that wording from the original has been omitted – either because it's not relevant in this context or it doesn't grammatically fit the sentence. And the statement following the quotation reminds the reader of the writer's presence: the quotation is not used to make its own freestanding point but to support a point the writer wishes to make.

Another example:

In his classic text *On Writing Well*, Zinsser described "the most important sentence in any article [as] the first one," its function being to "induce the reader to proceed to the second sentence."[100]

Here, the writer has inserted a word ("as") to make the sentence grammatically correct. Enclosing the word in square brackets indicates that it's not part of the original quotation.

Introduce the quotation with a colon.

Re-read the last paragraph in Example #3 to see how that's done. There's only one rule to remember here: whatever comes before the colon should be a complete sentence. Grammatically, the quotation following the colon can be anything at all – a word, phrase, complete sentence or whole paragraph.

The lesson here? Well-chosen quotations can add impact that helps you connect to the reader.

Exercise 7.4

Example #3 is journalism and contains elements that would not be appropriate in an academic essay. What are they? What do they add to the paper? And how could you achieve the same effect in your own academic writing without using these particular elements?

---

100. William Zinsser, *On Writing Well*, 7th edition (New York: Collins, 2006), p. 54.

Elements of an "only connect" paragraph: A recap

THE ELEMENTS   THE RECAP

*	Topic sentence	Your "mini-thesis": the paragraph's main point. Usually found near the start of the paragraph to focus both reader and writer. EXCEPTIONS: A topic sentence isn't needed if your paragraph is continuing the point made in the previous paragraph, or if you're relating a narrative or story.
**	Predictable structure	Every paragraph should be well structured. *Predictable* structure, though, is a bonus. Remember the essay mantra "Predictable structure. Unpredictable content"? It applies to individual paragraphs as well.
*	Unity	Focus on only one key point per paragraph – which is related to the paper's overall thesis or purpose.
*	Ample supporting detail	Every general statement supported by detail/evidence/explanation – which might come in the form of quotations. Exception: self-evident statements or common knowledge does not require supporting detail.
**	Transitions	Two types: direct; subtle. Try for both.
***	Parallelism	Some sentences or phrases – including headings – share a similar structure. Adds coherence, sense of style *and* clarity.
***	Varying paragraph lengths	Sends a message to the reader: I don't want to bore, intimidate or tire you.
***	Layout	White space; bulleted lists; headings; and figures. Sends a message to the reader: I want to make your reading as comfortable and easy as possible.

* The reader needs this to understand your point.
** The reader doesn't have to work so hard to understand your point because of this.
*** You've increased the likelihood that the reader will enjoy reading your paragraph because of this.

WRITING THE CONCLUSION

Consider your attitude

You're almost finished. Granted, you may be weary of writing this paper. You may be stressed about the imminent – or perhaps just past – deadline. You may long for this whole project to be completed and to go away. If so, one impulse will seem most compelling and natural to you right now: just write the conclusion in order to get this paper done.

Resist that impulse.

Of all the reasons to write (or to do anything, actually), "to get it done" is the weakest. That kind of motivation – the kind that lacks any trace of enthusiasm – may breed resentment. It will certainly encourage laziness, which means less care and depth than you'd normally strive for. And that result will demoralize you because it won't represent your best effort. Remember, you began this whole project with one goal only: to feel good about yourself. Don't jeopardize that now, as you write the conclusion.

Adjust, if necessary, your attitude

Adjusting your attitude is simpler than you think – but that doesn't mean it's easy. For most people, showing their vulnerability is not easy. However that's exactly what I'm recommending to help you shift your attitude, if attitude-shifting is needed, and to write a strong conclusion. Read on for details of how to accomplish that.

First, just for the time being, ignore the classic advice on how to structure a paper (or a speech): "Tell them what you're going to tell them. Tell them. And then tell them what you told them." Or more accurately, ignore the third sentence.

That sentence has resulted in too many essay conclusions that simply re-state, with dull predictability, the introduction. But the introduction and the conclusion are (or should be) completely different. In the introduction, you're dealing with an unknown audience. At this early stage, your readers are like bystanders, nodding politely as you present your thesis and its related material, but keeping their distance, all the same, because they really don't know you. You haven't yet told your story, provided your support, and proved your point. In other words, you haven't yet convinced the audience of your credibility as a writer of academic essays. That's why, in the introduction, you need to be on your best *scholarly* behaviour – and I mean "scholarly" in the conventional sense of the word: a bit detached and completely objective.

However, the conclusion is a different story. By now, your relationship with the reader has evolved. You've told your story, and, if you've followed the guidelines in this book, provided your support and proved your point. You've established your credibility as someone who can write clearly and convincingly. In other words, throughout the entire paper so far, you've flexed, for all to see, your academic muscle and shown your powers of logic. So now try relaxing, just for a bit, in the conclusion. And by "relaxing" I mean try giving the reader a fuller glimpse of who you are. Perhaps, for example, you're truly worried about the fate of the Arctic polar bears that you've been writing about. Directly tell the reader that. Maybe after having analyzed Hopkins' poem "The Windhover," you find that the poet has touched your own "heart in hiding" – or not. For a sentence or two in your conclusion, try letting the reader know how you *feel* – as opposed to what you think.

That simple action should help inject some energy into your mindset and into your writing. After all, to operate solely on the level of intellect and logic, which is what academic writing mostly involves, requires that we keep suppressing what's in our hearts. Too much of that, however, and we end up *disheartened,* falling into the "do it to get it done" trap.

The best academic writers avoid that trap. They're not afraid to give the reader a glimpse, in the conclusion, of how they *feel.* Read the following excerpts, all from conclusions, to see what I mean:

> It has not escaped our notice that the specific pairing we have postulated immediately suggests a possible copying mechanism for the genetic material.[101]

The authors, Watson and Crick, were immensely pleased with themselves. That fact – and that feeling – wouldn't have escaped the notice of any contemporary who read this sentence. The "possible copying mechanism" they're referring to would be the start of a scientific revolution. Prefacing it with the coy and understated "It has not escaped our notice" was their way of emphasizing, through contrast, the enormity of their discovery. In other words, they're gloating: quietly, subtly, but definitely gloating.

Getting a glimpse of that very human feeling underneath the scholarly façade makes the conclusion a bit more interesting to read – and, I'm guessing, a bit more enjoyable to write.

> Americans love challenges, and preventing artificial climate change is just the sort of technological and economic challenge at which this nation excels. It only remains for the right politician to recast the challenge in practical, optimistic tones. Gore seldom has, and Bush seems to have no interest in trying. But cheap and fast improvement is not a pipe dream; it is the pattern of previous efforts against air pollution. The only reason runaway global warming seems unstoppable is that we have not yet tried to stop it.[102]

---

101. Watson and Crick, "Molecular," 737–8.
102. Easterbrook, "Convenient."

"Bush seems to have no interest in trying." With this statement, journalist Gregg Easterbrook easily divulges his political leanings – and his impatience. Here, he's not just writing from his head, but also from his heart.

Read the paragraph aloud and see if you can also detect the sense of urgency he feels.

Actually, **reading your own work aloud** is a good practice generally. Listening to how the words sound can tell you something about the flow of your writing, the appropriateness of your word choice *and* the feeling you've conveyed.

In this next conclusion, writer **Nicholas Carr** is referring to the film *2001: A Space Odyssey*, directed by Stanley Kubrick. HAL is the name of a computer.

> I'm haunted by that scene in *2001*. What makes it so poignant ... is the computer's emotional response to the disassembly of its mind: its despair as one circuit after another goes dark, its childlike pleading with the astronaut – "I can feel it. I'm afraid" – ... HAL's outpouring of feeling contrasts with the emotionlessness that characterizes the human figures in the film, who go about their business with an almost robotic efficiency.... That's the essence of Kubrick's dark prophecy: as we come to rely on computers to mediate our understanding of the world, it is our own intelligence that flattens into artificial intelligence.[103]

There's a reason Carr writes "I'm haunted by that scene" instead of "That scene is haunting." He wants to show us how he feels as opposed to what he thinks. He wants us to know that the essay's objective analysis leads to a conclusion he finds personally distressing. In other words, he wants to connect with us. Nothing is more satisfying, or more "heartening," to a writer than to connect with the reader – and Carr does it through giving us a glimpse of his own vulnerability in one sentence in the conclusion.

He also accomplishes something else in that one sentence in the conclusion: he connects with himself. Two different aspects of who he is get acknowledged and integrated here – the analytical side and the personal side. Consequently, the writer connects with his whole self, which is probably a necessary precursor to connecting with the reader or with anyone else, for that matter.

I know. It's started to sound suspect again, like some sort of New Age

---

103. Carr, "Google."

nonsense and the antithesis, therefore, of what conventional academic writing is all about. But if you're this far along in the book you must know that convention isn't always enough. Peter Elbow echoes this sentiment when he explains "a general principle that students need to know."

> ... if you can demonstrate to readers that you can meet their conservative demands in the early pages of an essay, they often don't mind later features they would have objected to at the start.... The convention of a detached disinterested voice is supposed to serve the goal of objectivity, but do we really serve that goal when we hide our bias? When older scholars have accumulated more "academic capital," they often write stronger prose ... because they don't feel obliged to hide....[104]

Once you've established your "academic capital" in the introduction and in the body, try giving the reader a glimpse of another side of yourself – the side that has emotions, feelings, and, yes, even a bias. Don't overdo it, though. As illustrated in the above conclusions, one carefully written sentence or even one phrase could be enough to strengthen your connection with the reader – and stir up your own enthusiasm.

Experiment with that when you write your next conclusion, and see what happens.

Include the three "Rs"

Now, back to the nuts and bolts of writing a conclusion. Here's what your readers will expect you to do for them in the conclusion:

RESTATE YOUR THESIS OR YOUR PURPOSE.

Don't copy and paste the thesis or purpose statement from the introduction. You might, though, borrow one or two key words, maybe even a phrase, from the introduction. That kind of subtle repetition can bring the paper full circle to its original focus, reinforcing, and reminding the reader of the central point.

REMIND THE READER ALSO OF THE MAIN POINT(S) YOU'VE DISCUSSED ALONG THE WAY.

If the only way you can do this is by reciting one point at a time, each separately parceled in its own sentence, that's satisfactory. It probably won't

---

104. Elbow, "Music," pp. 31, 32–33.

make for riveting reading, but at least you've neatly packaged the paper's highlights, which will especially please those readers who depended on all being revealed in the conclusion and who therefore decided to skim rather than carefully read the body paragraphs. There's something to be said for that. Better yet, though, try applying the synthesis skills discussed in Chapter 5, to integrate your key points, when appropriate. The result will likely be more concise and cohesive than a point-by-point summary.

Relate it all to a broader context.

Here's one caveat to the above advice: Writing the conclusion based solely on the assumption that your readers probably haven't read the entire paper shortchanges those readers. In a misguided effort to serve their needs, you may end up treating the conclusion as nothing more than one last chance for the readers to "catch up" on the important points they've missed. The opportunity to add something else to the conclusion, something of depth and insight, then gets overlooked entirely.

In other words, you don't serve your readers' needs by viewing them as laggards who need "one last chance." True, many of them are time pressured and impatient. And many don't particularly like reading. But all of them are intelligent. If your conclusion – or any part of the paper – doesn't reflect that, you're not serving your readers. You're patronizing them. Let their intelligence – and your own – guide you as you address, perhaps indirectly, one or some of these questions in your conclusion:

- What one key point do you want your reader to remember after having read your paper?
- Why is this one key point important?
- What are its implications – past, present or future?
- What do you want your reader to think or to do as a result of having read your paper?

Addressing even one of these questions will give your conclusion more depth. But here's a caution: addressing even one of these questions in depth will give your reader the start of another paper. Don't do that to him or her – and don't do it to yourself either. One essay at a time is enough to handle for both reader and writer. Provide just a glimpse of some relevant, but as yet unexplored, territory that your essay points to. That glimpse will add a sense of vitality to your conclusion because now, it doesn't just look backward, recounting important points made earlier in the paper; it also looks forward, providing a glimpse of something important to come.

If a metaphor helps, try envisioning your conclusion as two doors, one closed and one just slightly ajar. The closed door suggests, well, closure. This conclusion recaps the thesis or purpose and main points. The paper is now finished. The slightly ajar door, however, points to unexplored area just beyond the paper's threshold. This conclusion invites you to cross that threshold. (If you're a visual person, check out Figure 7.2, to see if that helps drive home the point).

Exercise 7.5

With that last metaphor in mind, re-read the three example conclusions provided earlier. Do they contain both a closed door and a door that's slightly ajar?

A few other points about the conclusion

- Choose whatever ORDER is most appropriate to present your three Rs. In fact, you don't have to present them separately. If it works, you could integrate them.
- If you include a QUOTATION in the conclusion, make it a particularly good one. Be selective. The conclusion is a high profile section of your paper. It might be one of the few sections that get read carefully, and it will likely be the last section to be read. In other words, the conclusion carries an inordinate weight in terms of the reader remembering – and perhaps assessing – your work. Make it strong, so it will leave a positive impression.
- As with the introduction, the conclusion's LENGTH is generally proportionate to the overall document length. For the typical undergraduate paper, that usually means a paragraph.
- Reconsider starting with "IN CONCLUSION." It's overused, and therefore directly contravenes your mantra of "unpredictable content". And it's probably unnecessary: your readers don't need a signpost telling them they've arrived at the conclusion. They can see for themselves that they're nearing the end of the paper.

WRITING THE SUMMARY OR ABSTRACT

Your paper may not require a **summary** or **abstract** – that brief overview of main points found at the start of document. It's typically used in scientific writing, business reports (where it's referred to as an "executive summary"), and graduate-level papers, less frequently in undergraduate

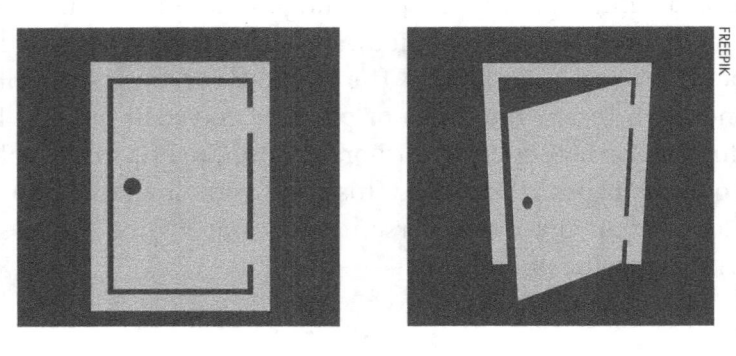

Figure 7.2: Include two "doors" in your conclusion: one closed and one slightly ajar

essays. Sometimes, however, a research assignment will ask you to summarize secondary source material or to compile an **annotated bibliography**,[105] which draws on your summary-writing skills. Cultivating the ability to write a summary or abstract can benefit every writer in every discipline.

Consider the following definitions:

abstract *noun* A smaller quantity, containing the virtue or power of a greater; an epitome.[106]

summary *adjective* early 15c., "Brief, abbreviated; containing the sum or substance only."[107]

And with these two definitions in mind, now consider this question:

What happens when a great "power" is distilled within a small or "abbreviated" space?

Answer: the power is intensified.

That's why the summary or abstract[108] is so important. It requires that you distill the essence of your paper, its key points, into a relatively small space. This process draws upon and strengthens your ability to be discerning, coherent and concise. This process, in other words, gives you an oppor-

---

105. An annotated bibliography is a list of research sources, but with an added element: each entry is followed by a summary of the source, along with your assessment of the source's usefulness or value.
106. Retrieved from http://johnsonsdictionaryonline.com/?page_id=7070&i=64.
107. Retrieved from http://www.etymonline.com/index.php?term=summary&allowed_in_frame=0.
108. From now on, for the sake of simplicity and quite arbitrarily, I'll use the term "summary" alone. You can replace it with "abstract" if you prefer.

tunity to intensify the power of your writing.

Take that opportunity.

And that was an indirect way of saying, pay attention to writing the summary. Don't relegate it to an afterthought, something to be done quickly and with minimal care now that the main work of writing the paper is done. Dismissing the summary as unimportant means missing out on the benefits it can offer.

Those benefits – and a blueprint for writing the summary – are described in the following pages.

Writing the summary strengthens your power of discernment – or "what to include in the summary"

The summary presents the paper's key information, which means you need to discern what falls into the category of "key information." If you're in the sciences, using an IMRAD (Introduction; Methods; Results; and Discussion) structure, your job is straightforward: extract the most important points from each of those categories. Omit background information or examples – unless they're needed to understand the key points. For example, your summary would include the paper's purpose; a short explanation of methods; the main results; and, from the Discussion, an explanation of why those results are important. If you've used them, informative headings (i.e., headings throughout the paper that encapsulate the key points) can help you identify what information to include. Also, pay particular attention to your topic sentences. If you've followed the advice given earlier in this chapter, they can also help you identify key points.

For other fields, the approach is the same, except you'll use other headings or categories to identify key points and structure your summary. Generally, your summary will include the thesis or purpose; the paper's main conclusions – including the overall importance, or broader implications, of those conclusions; and, if applicable, recommendations.

WHAT NOT TO INCLUDE IN THE SUMMARY

- Material that isn't included in the article being summarized.
- Repetition. Even though your summary may be formatted as a paragraph, the rules of paragraphing (e.g., topic sentence, reinforcing details, etc.) don't apply.
- The article title. (Your title page makes referring to the article title redundant.)
- Secondary source **references**. Your summary shouldn't reference any

sources, aside from the one source (i.e., the paper) that it's summarizing.

Three types of readers to address (even when you're writing for only one reader – your instructor)

If you're uncertain about the amount of information to include, remember this tip: the summary is a "stand-alone" document. It should make perfect sense to the reader without him or her having to refer to the paper. Consequently, background information, definitions, or examples may need to be included – or not. To help you decide, approach the summary from the perspective of the readers described below. Keeping their perspectives in mind will help you discern the paper's most important material. And it will also help you discern your readers' interests and needs – a skill that will strengthen your writing generally, even if you're writing for only one reader, the instructor who's grading your paper.

- Readers who want a "head start." Your summary should provide a clear overview of what's to come. All the main points are disclosed right at the start. Therefore, your readers can begin the paper already knowing what to expect, which means they can read more efficiently and closely.
- Readers who want a "short cut." Your summary should include enough information to justify their preference not to have to read the rest of the paper. That might seem counter to your own interests as a writer, but a gratified reader, one who feels the summary provides sufficient information to exempt him or her from having to read the entire paper, is more likely to want to read the rest of the paper. That's the power of clarity – it invites further investigation.
- Readers who want a "screening device" to assess your insights and your academic capabilities. You'll encounter these readers if you're a more advanced or ambitious writer, submitting your ideas for a paper (or a presentation based on your paper) to a conference. Organizers typically decide who to accept or who to reject based on the submitted summaries. If you keep these readers in mind, you're unlikely to include superficial or general statements – a failing so common that it's frequently lampooned.[109] Instead, you're more likely to write a summary like this:

> When a new work group forms, people often make snap judgments about who is qualified to lead. If the players don't already know one another, they tend to afford status to teammates on the

---

109. By *Ph.D. Comics*, for instance; see http://www.phdcomics.com/comics.php?f=1121.

basis of factors such as age, gender, race, attractiveness, and rank. These are characteristics beyond your control, but they don't necessarily predetermine the influence you can have on a group. Anyone, the authors say, can achieve higher status and more influence by getting in the right mind-set before engaging with new teammates.

There are three psychological states that can increase the optimism, confidence, and proactive behavior that people associate with leaders: promotion focus (defined as a focus on goals and positive outcomes), happiness, and a feeling of power. And all it takes to help you enter one of these states is a simple five-minute exercise before starting a group task: Write about your ambitions or a time when you felt happy or powerful. The authors report that study subjects who did exactly that were more likely than others to speak up, steer decision making, and be viewed by their teammates as leaders – both in initial group meetings and in follow-up meetings two days later.[110]

Writing the summary strengthens the coherence of your writing

Coherence is easier to achieve when you can take baby steps, slowly showing how each point is related to the next. A summary, though, offers no time for that. Because it's so short, it requires broad, quick leaps from one disparate category (e.g., purpose) to another (e.g., findings). If you can write coherently under these challenging conditions, then you can write coherently throughout the rest of your paper. That's why the summary is the perfect training ground to help you achieve coherence in your writing.

Exercise 7.6

One way to gauge coherence is to read your work aloud. Try that for the summary presented above. As you read it aloud, note the easy flow from one sentence to the next. Now, drawing on your earlier practice in the second and third exercises in this chapter, identify the transitions that have created that easy flow or coherence.

Writing the summary strengthens your ability to be concise

The length of the summary depends on the length of the original article, but a summary, by definition, is short. The example summary above is

---

110. A. Galinsky and G. Kilduff, "Be Seen as a Leader," *Harvard Business Review*, 91: 12 (December 2013), reprint 1312K.

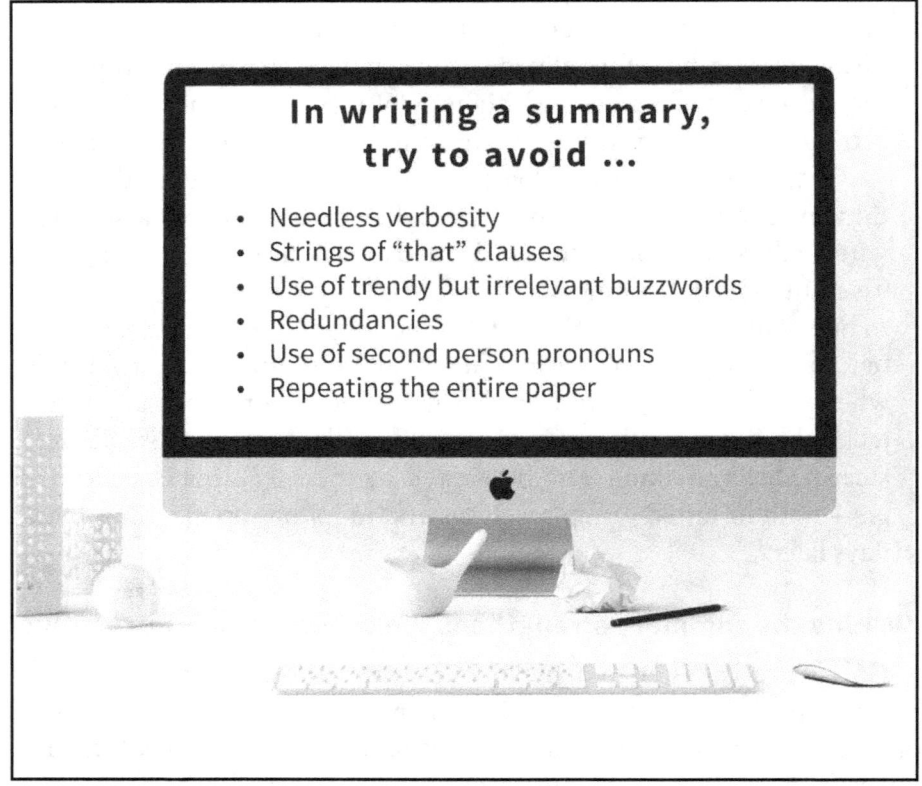

Figure 7.3: Some things to avoid in writing a summary

about 10 percent of the original article's length and would not take up more than one-half to three-quarters of a typed page. Unless you're given other instructions, those are good guidelines.

However, they're also challenging ones to follow – especially since they seem to contradict other advice that's been given throughout this book: provide concrete, precise detail. How do you make it short *and* detailed at the same time? Answer: By using the skills you acquired in Chapter 4 (and a couple more listed below) to write concisely. Those skills will allow you to eliminate extraneous words, creating space for concrete detail.

Here's an example:

> ~~There are~~ (1) three psychological states ~~that~~ (2) can increase the optimism, confidence, and proactive behavior ~~that~~ (2) people associate with leaders: promotion focus (~~defined as~~ (3) a focus on

goals and positive outcomes), happiness, and a feeling of power. ~~And all it takes~~ (3) to help ~~you~~ (4) enter one of these states ~~is~~ a simple five-minute exercise before starting a group task: Write about ~~your~~ (4) ambitions or a time when ~~you~~ (4) felt happy or powerful. ~~The authors report that~~ (5) study subjects who did exactly that were more likely than others to speak up, steer decision making, and be viewed by their teammates as leaders – both in initial group meetings and in follow-up meetings two days later. **(113 words)**

Recall the tips from Chapter 4 on how to write concisely:

1. Re-consider any "There are" prefaces.
2. Avoid a string of "that" clauses.
3. Eliminate redundancies.
4. Avoid using the second person pronoun ("you" or "your") in academic writing. Using it also gives your writing an informal or even casual tone, which may undermine your academic credibility.

And here is one more tip not previously discussed:

5. Save space by cutting references to "the author" or "the study" in the summary. Since this is a summary, it's self-evident that you're referring to the author's views and the study's findings.

Exercise 7.7

With those tips in mind, re-write the above summary excerpt, making it more concise.

Your revision may look something like this:

> Three psychological states can increase the optimism, confidence, and proactive behavior associated with leaders: promotion focus (i.e., a focus on goals and positive outcomes), happiness, and a feeling of power. These states can be fostered before a group meeting by a five-minute writing exercise that focuses on the writers' ambitions or on a time when they felt happy or powerful. Study subjects who did exactly that were more likely than others to speak up, steer decision making, and be viewed by their teammates as leaders – both in initial group meetings and in follow-up meetings two days later. **(98 words)**

BEING CONCISE OFFERS ANOTHER BENEFIT

This particular revision is 15 words shorter than the original. A difference of 15 words may not seem like much – until you consider that you've now opened up space to change one sentence from this:

> … promotion focus (i.e., a focus on goals and positive outcomes), happiness, and a feeling of power. **These states can be fostered before a group meeting by a five-minute writing exercise that** focuses on the writers' ambitions or …

to this:

> … promotion focus (i.e., a focus on goals and positive outcomes), happiness, and a feeling of power. **This study suggests these states can be fostered before a group meeting by a five-minute writing exercise that** focuses on the writers' ambitions or …

Adding three words – "This study suggests" – transforms a misleading generalization ("These states can be fostered") into a statement of fact ("This study suggests these states can be fostered"). After all, one study doesn't conclusively prove anything; it simply points to or "suggests" something. Removing the non-essential words gives you the space – and the encouragement – to insert the essential words.

Of course, you can apply that lesson not just to the summary, but also to the entire paper.

"Always room for improvement" (or a preview of Chapter 8)

And here's another lesson to take away from the last exercise – an exercise in which you were asked to revise a summary that's been presented as an example of how to write a summary: No one's writing is sacrosanct. Good writers acknowledge (and frequently lament) that fact about their own writing. There's always room for improvement, even in published articles. That's why none of the essays or excerpts in this book are presented as models for you to slavishly follow. Instead, they're presented as possibilities for you to consider – and sometimes even to improve upon in your own writing. For more on this, read on to Chapter 8.

SUMMARY

Well-written paragraphs are shaped by one guiding principle: "only connect." They contain the usual elements: focused topic sentences; unity; and sufficient supporting detail. But they also contain elements that go beyond the usual: a predictable structure; transitions; parallelism; and a layout that facilitates reading. Well-written conclusions do more than simply restate the paper's main points. They help you forge a deeper relationship with the reader – and with yourself – by presenting not just what you think but also, on a subtle level, how you feel about the topic at hand. And, finally, the summary offers you a chance to strengthen your writing by focusing on your ability to discern the most important material and to write coherently and concisely.

Chapter 8
Editing

This chapter will help you edit your writing by ...

- Explaining what "editing" actually means
- Providing you with step-by-step editing guidelines
- *Assuring you* that it's all right if you're one of those "edit as you go" writers

There's a difference between what editing means and what most of us would like it to mean. Most of us would like it to mean correcting typos, spelling and grammatical errors. Those sorts of corrections are relatively fast and easy – and a source, therefore, of immediate gratification. But editing involves considerably more. It begins with reviewing, and possibly revising, your paper's ideas, data, information, sources, scope, depth, logic, organization and relevance. And if that list seems exhausting and maybe even disheartening, consider this: editing has the potential to offer long-term gratification – the sort of gratification that comes from knowing you've done more than produce a paper free of typos, spelling and grammatical errors. You've produced a paper of substance. That's a good reason to learn how to edit.

TWO KINDS OF WRITERS. TWO KINDS OF EDITING.

Some writers don't believe in producing "rough drafts." They edit as they write, polishing each sentence, each paragraph, before they move on to the next. They take this approach even though writing instructors and texts – including this one (see Chapter 2) – routinely advise against it.

Others wait until they've covered quite a bit of ground, perhaps even drafted the entire paper, before they start to edit seriously.[111] At the end of their writing session, they have the psychological advantage of an impressive word count and the security of having mapped out, however roughly, if not the entire paper then at least a good portion of it. Moreover, their focused, sustained concentration on getting the entire draft written increases the likelihood they stayed on topic and maintained coherence.

---

111. The "unserious" editing happens almost constantly throughout the writing process – any time you hit the "delete" key, you are, in fact, editing.

If you're one of the first group – a writer who moves slowly because you revise as you write – you likely won't have those advantages. And you likely won't ever change to become the sort of writer who does – the kind who takes quick broad leaps to produce a first rough draft. I'm guessing something within you resists that kind of approach, despite the advice of writing instructors and textbooks. But the "edit-as-you-go" style of writing isn't without its benefits. For example, once the entire paper is completed, any remaining editing is relatively quick to complete.

And there's also another, less obvious benefit. Consider novelist E.L. Doctorow's analogy between writing and driving:

> … it's like driving a car at night: you never see further than your headlights, but you can make the whole trip that way.[112]

With "edit-as-you-go" writers, those headlights are directed at (and often linger on) the sentence or paragraph that's just been written – as opposed to the sentences or paragraphs to come. Consequently, these writers cultivate, by necessity, a faith or a confidence[113] that the writing process itself will lead them where they need to go, that the sentences and paragraphs to come will, indeed, get written. Confidence. That's an advantage that can take you far as a writer – and as a person. It's not to be overlooked.

KEY EDITING PRINCIPLES

No matter which group of writers you belong to, the same editing principles can guide your writing. But be forewarned: they're counterintuitive and challenging – and sometimes environmentally incorrect. Therefore your first inclination may be to resist them. Try, instead, to consider them – they do make good sense – and then to apply them.

Focus on the big picture first

In writing, the "big picture" refers to the document's content – the facts, information, research, data, and ideas being presented. Let these questions guide your editing: Is the content logical and relevant? Is it well structured? Does it provide the expected level of scope and depth? Does it "fit" the assignment instructions? To help answer the first three questions, refer to

---

112. Interviewed by George Plimpton in *The Paris Review*. Retrieved from http://www.theparisreview.org/interviews/2718/the-art-of-fiction-no-94-e-l-doctorow.
113. An etymological detour: "confidence" comes from the Latin, meaning "with faith", i.e., to have faith is to have confidence – a statement not restricted, of course, to a religious context.

Chapters 3 and 5 on structure and logic. To help answer the last two questions, compare what you've written with what you were asked to write. For example, instructions to "summarize," "review the literature," "reflect on," "compare and contrast," "critique," "analyze," and "explain the significance of" all require different approaches and sometimes different writing skills. Make sure your paper delivers what was asked of it. If it doesn't, then revise it. And as you do, you come to understand that editing isn't synonymous with small changes, here or there. It *could* mean small changes, but it could also mean major revisions, even a complete re-write if, for example, you discover that you've summarized other people's ideas when you were asked to develop your own. Or vice versa.

I emphasize "focus on the big picture *first*" because if you're like most people you won't want to. You'll want to start by running the Spell Check or Grammar Check. Or your first inclination will be to delete single words or short phrases, replacing them with phrasing that's more agreeable to you because it's more concise or apt or just sounds better. And all of that has its place in editing. But that place is at the end, not at the start. There's no point in fussing with specific words within a paragraph if the entire point of the paragraph is misplaced and therefore the entire paragraph needs to be deleted. Editing asks you to make those big decisions, and the most logical place to make them is at the start of the editing process.

Once you've focused on the big picture, you can then move to paragraphs (see Chapter 7), grammar (see Chapter 9), spelling, and layout (See Chapter 7).

Guidelines to help you focus on the big picture first

1. Set aside your paper for as long as possible before editing.

We can become emotionally attached to our writing. An insight in the second paragraph makes us feel proud. Some clever phrasing in the conclusion makes us feel witty. Knowing how much time was spent tracking down and incorporating an elusive piece of information makes us feel smart and scholarly. But those feelings are based on a shaky foundation if that insight, clever phrasing and elusive piece of information are only loosely connected to the essay's purpose and need to be significantly revised or even deleted altogether. Our attachment works against good editing when it makes us protect our writing, wanting to keep it exactly as it is.

Attachment also works against good editing when it makes us feel discouraged about our writing. A mundane observation, an awkwardly written paragraph, or a fruitless search for the perfect quotation – these are the experiences of *every* writer. But writers who are emotionally attached to their work risk assigning too much significance to them – as if "mundane," "awkward," and "fruitless" are their own personal failings rather than the expected outcomes of anyone's writing process. Attachment can then make us view editing as a frustrating waste of time. It can prompt us to give up because our writing – or "we" – will never be good enough.

One way to loosen that attachment, and all the misdirected feelings associated with it, is to set your finished work aside for as long as possible before editing. If you can afford it, hours are better than minutes, days better than hours, and – ridiculously optimistic, I know – weeks better than days. Ideally, when you pick up the paper again, you'll be looking at it with a completely fresh perspective, almost having forgotten that you wrote these words. You can now read the paper with a calm objectivity. Achieving that level of detachment means your ego no longer holds your attention, with its relentless insistence that your writing is perfect as is – or, conversely, a terrible mess that can never be corrected. (Ironically, the ego works both ways – building up and tearing down. It's a drama queen that likes extremes only.) Detaching from your writing (and therefore from your ego) will make you a more balanced, objective editor of your own work.

2. Some "nuts and bolts" advice: Hard copy. Double-spaced. Non-justified.

A 13- or 15-inch computer screen doesn't offer ideal conditions for seeing the big picture. For example, scrolling back and forth to check whether a point made at the bottom of page five contradicts something in the middle of page two is more difficult and time consuming than physically setting page five beside page two. Print out your essay draft so that you can edit it as a hard copy instead of an electronic copy. An additional benefit here is the chance to edit your work using a pen or pencil. (If you need a reminder of why that's a benefit, see Chapter 2, p. 16).

Double spacing your draft gives you ample room on the hard copy to make notes to yourself, insert arrows to indicate a changed placement of a paragraph, or cross out and rewrite a single word or an entire passage. Single spacing discourages that kind of effort to improve your paper. Double spacing encourages it.

Some people routinely use **justified text** (i.e., a straight right-hand margin) in their documents. They like the neat, symmetrical way it can frame the text. But that neatness and symmetry require professional software and probably a professional designer. Otherwise, justified text produces uneven spacing between characters. Lines with big spaces become extended and those with small spaces become crammed. All of this makes the text hard to read and therefore difficult to edit. **Non-justified text**, with its uniform spacing, is a better, more readable choice.

3. Start by reading your paper without interruption from beginning to end.

Consider these quotations:

> In 11 studies, we found that participants typically did not enjoy spending 6 to 15 minutes in a room by themselves with nothing to do but think, that they enjoyed doing mundane external activities much more, and that many preferred to administer electric shocks to themselves instead of being left alone with their thoughts....
> —Timothy Wilson et al.[114]

> All of humanity's problems stem from man's inability to sit quietly in a room alone.
> —Blaise Pascal[115]

It's hard to edit your own paper without immediately wanting to do something – to change a word, strike out a phrase, or insert a reference. All these fairly simple tasks clamour for our attention when we try to sit quietly reviewing our written work because, generally, we don't like sitting quietly with only our thoughts – and our essay draft – for company. Most of us have been schooled to believe that sitting quietly is nonproductive. We have a deadline, after all. We need to get to work.

Consider the opposite view: sitting quietly, reading your paper, *is* work. It offers you the opportunity to work hard and be incredibly productive. You cannot focus on the "big picture" of your written work without quietly and consciously reading it through from start to finish. That action – and it *is* an action – is the only way you can assess the paper's overall logic, organization, and sense of coherence. If you stop along the way to fuss with a word, sentence or paragraph, you risk getting stuck in the details and losing sight of the big picture.

The lesson here? Read the entire paper once, consciously, deliberately – and quietly. Then go back and make your changes. If that's an impossible instruction to follow, restrict yourself to quick notations in the margins as your read, indicating what needs to be revisited.

---

114. T. Wilson, et al., "Just Think: The Challenges of the Disengaged Mind," *Science*, 345: 6192 (2014): 75–77.
115. *Les Pensées*, 139 (1669).

4. Show your work to someone else.

Exercise 8.1[116]

Four simple steps:

1. Imagine you're lying outside on a beautiful day, staring up at a blue sky.
2. Hold a drinking straw up to one eye, close the other eye, and now look through the straw, as if it were a telescope.
3. Note what you see: a tiny circle of blue.
4. Remove the straw, open wide both eyes, and note what you see: an expanse of blue, the original tiny circle magnified many times over.

Consider this yet another writing analogy, the explanation of which is below.

We tend to think of writing as a solitary activity, at least for individual (as opposed to group) writing assignments. And certainly writing does required sustained periods of being alone with your thoughts: generating, organizing, researching and composing all by yourself. But there can be more to writing than just your own thoughts. In fact, I'm going to suggest there *should* be more to writing than just your own thoughts. Your own thoughts are influenced and perhaps constrained by all sorts of factors, such as your family background, education, beliefs, what you've read (or haven't read) and even how you're feeling, physically and emotionally, at a particular moment of writing. All these factors might influence what and how you write. All these factors are like the drinking straw that you looked through in the exercise: they direct you to a very specific part of the whole vision that's available to you. They allow you to see only one part of the big picture, only a small circle of that beautiful sky, as opposed to the broad expanse of blue that's out there and available to you, if only you could see it.

How can you see it? One way is to show others what you've written and ask for their feedback. Ask at least one other person to edit your work – and then pay attention to what he or she says. When you do that, you're discarding, just for the time being, that metaphorical drinking straw, and opening both eyes wide, to glimpse someone else's perspective.

If you're lucky, someone else's perspective of your work will directly strengthen it. Your "editor" may suggest modifying your thesis, adding a

---

116. I encountered this exercise in a yoga class, of all places. I don't know who to credit for first developing it.

new example, tightening the structure or deleting a section that's not relevant. He or she may suggest, in other words, needed changes that you couldn't see on your own because you lacked the perspective.

A key word here is "suggest." Asking for someone's perspective means asking for their suggestions or comments on what works, what doesn't work, and what could work better. It doesn't mean asking that person to rewrite your paper or parts of your paper because that, as discussed in Chapter 5, is plagiarism.

Even suggestions that aren't particularly noteworthy – or that are ill advised – can help strengthen your paper. For example, a suggestion you don't agree with and don't intend to implement might nonetheless redirect your focus toward a particular part or aspect of your paper that could be improved, prompting you to revise it. Or you may discover that a passage you thought was completely clear is actually confusing to the reader. John Cleese, the English comedian and writer, explains the unlikely benefit of weak or mundane comments in this description of his own writing approach, one that relies heavily on receiving feedback – or ideas – from other people:

> The really good idea is always traceable back quite a long way, often to a not very good idea which sparked off another idea that was only slightly better, which [led to] ... something which was really rather interesting.... [That's] actually why I have always worked with a writing partner, because I'm convinced that I get to better ideas than I'd ever do on my own.[117]

Cleese's final remark – "I get to better ideas [with a writing partner] than I'd ever do on my own" – points to another reason showing your writing to someone else can strengthen it: over time, this practice helps subdue the pesky, limiting ego that takes offence at editorial suggestions. (If you've ever been irritated, perhaps even made indignant, by an instructor's comments on a paper without taking the time to actually consider the comments, you've experienced the limiting effects of the ego.) Routinely giving your work to others to edit allows you to practice acknowledging, and assessing, their views with objectivity, detachment, and openness. This is wonderful training for any writer.

---

117. John Cleese, as cited in M. Schrage, *Shared Minds: The New Technologies of Collaboration* (New York: Random House, 1990), pp. 39-40.

Now move to the smaller (but still important) matters

After you've finished the "big picture" editing, the above guidelines can also help you edit your paper for the smaller details. To help you get a sense of perspective, those details, and their place in the editing process, are explained in Figure 8.1.

Figure 8.1: An overview of the editing process

1. Begin with the big picture:

Is your thesis or purpose statement clear? Focused? Thoughtful? (i.e., does it reflect an appropriate sense of depth or analysis?)

No or Undecided ➔ See Chapter 2

Yes
⬇

Draft a quick outline of your paper as it's now written: Does this outline follow a logical, even predictable, structure?

No or Undecided ➔ See Chapter 2

Yes
⬇

Assess the depth, complexity, and scope of your paper: Do they meet the assignment instructions and expectations? Consider, for example, whether you've summarized or synthesized; and the number and quality of secondary sources, if any; the extent to which you've incorporated unpredictable content.

Undecided ➔ See Chapters 4 and 5

It's fine
⬇

Ensure you've provided adequate detail and evidence: Is your support logical, convincing, and balanced? If secondary sources are included, are they referenced?

No or Undecided ➔ See Chapters 4 and 5

Yes
⬇

2. Move to the smaller (but still important) matters:
- Paragraphing: Are yours "only connect" paragraphs? (Note: this question also applies to the introduction and the conclusion.)

No or Undecided ➔ See Chapters 6 and 7

Yes

- Sentences: Are they concise and concrete?
        No or Undecided See Chapter 4
            Yes
             ⬇
- Correct grammar and spelling:
             ⬇

Read on for advice on grammar. If you know spelling is a weakness, have someone who's a good speller proofread your work.

SUMMARY

Editing is not the same as proofreading for grammar, typos and spelling errors. Reviewing those elements is part of the editing process, but it's a relatively minor part that comes at the end of the process. The most important – and challenging – part of editing involves reviewing the focus, content and organization of your work. Don't be surprised if your editing results in major changes.

Chapter 9
Grammar

This chapter will help you ...

- Become more confident in your use of the English language
- Ensure that your writing is grammatically correct
- Know how to use a **semicolon**; avoid **dangling modifiers**; decide whether or not a comma's needed in the sentence you just wrote ...

WHY GRAMMAR MATTERS

If you were to tell me you didn't like grammar, I'd understand. I'm not overly enthused about it either. In fact, I get slightly insulted when someone assumes the writing courses I teach revolve around grammar. Something about that assumption, aside from its basic inaccuracy, rankles. Probably it's the fusty image it evokes – the quaint but inconsequential ability to use a semicolon properly, avoid dangling participles, or know the difference between restrictive and nonrestrictive clauses. Surely there are more meaningful talents or knowledge to nurture in this lifetime.

I suspect a lot of people feel that way about grammar, perhaps you, as well. In any case, consider that belief as you do the quick exercise below.

Exercise 9.1

Correct any *grammatical* errors in the following sentences. (Note: you're not being asked to make the sentences more concise or more stylistically agreeable. You're being asked to correct only the grammar – if, indeed the grammar needs correcting. If it doesn't, then leave the sentence alone, and mark it as "correct.")

1. The work is to be divided between you and me.
2. Having never understood the rules, there was little chance of winning the game.
3. She is more intelligent than I, but not as shrewd.
4. The company has always treated their employees with respect.
5. They only had one option: to accept the conditions, however harsh.
6. No other opinions mattered but theirs'.
7. None of them are right, or perhaps none of them is wrong. It's difficult to tell.

See the Answer Guide at the end of this chapter. When you've compared your responses to those in the Answer Guide and figured out your score, ask yourself the most important question of all: how do you feel?

If you got all or most of the answers and your score was high, I'm guessing you feel good – even if just slightly. If, on the other hand, you missed some or most of the answers and your score was low, I'm guessing you feel somewhat deflated, perhaps disappointed – even if just slightly.

And that's a reason to consider the importance of grammar. Knowing its rules and understanding how to apply them can make you feel better about yourself – even if just slightly. Feeling slightly more educated or more confident about your grammar means feeling slightly more certain that your voice, as you write and speak, will be looked upon as credibile. That is not a small matter. We're judged, after all, by how we use the language. If you doubt that, think of all the times you've been engaged in conversation with someone who caught your attention by saying something like "That don't matter" or "I seen the movie." Or maybe it was more subtle: using "I" when it should have been "me" or "good" when it should have been "well". Think about whether your view of that person changed, even slightly, as a result of his or her grammatical slip. Did the grammar negatively influence your perception of that person's background, status, or credibility?

If you said "yes," you wouldn't be alone. The world generally, but more specifically, professors, prospective employers, and potential friends, form a perception of us based on our language. Being proficient in grammar helps us shape that perception so that it works in our favour, not against it. More importantly, being proficient in our use of the language – and that includes knowing our language is grammatically correct – can help shape how we perceive ourselves: educated, confident, and credible.

Those are powerful reasons to learn more about grammar.

A GUIDE TO GRAMMAR

Grammar is a piano I play by ear, since I seem to have been out of school the year the rules were mentioned. All I know about grammar is its infinite power.

—*Joan Didion*[118]

A lot of people write grammatically correct prose without being able to explain why it's grammatically correct. They just know by intuition, by having read a lot, or by having a good "ear" for the language whether or not something is grammatically correct.

118. J. Didion, "Why I Write," *New York Times Book Review*, December 5, 1976.

You may or may not be one of those people. Perhaps you're one of those people only sometimes. Or perhaps you're one of the few who already know the rules and are confident in applying them. Whichever category you fall into, consider, just for a moment, the value of being a complete beginner:

In the beginner's mind, there are many possibilities, but in the expert's there are few. —*Shunyru Suzuki*[119]

When it comes to grammar, having a beginner's mind is helpful:

- It may help you get over any sense of embarrassment or inadequacy you might feel about not knowing the rules.
- It may help you detach from longstanding rules that no longer serve a purpose.
- It may help you occasionally break perfectly good rules for the purpose of strengthening your writing.
- It may help you realize that you need to learn the rules before you can decide to detach from, or break, them.

The parts of speech: A quick overview

Parsing or diagramming a sentence – identifying the different **parts of speech** contained within it – is a bit of a dying skill. Knowing the parts of speech, though, will help you more easily understand the rest of the chapter. On the following page, Figures 9.1 and 9.2 set out the parts of speech, using Joan Didion's words on page 148 as the organizing framework.

The top grammar mistakes – and how to avoid them

The following isn't intended as a comprehensive guide to grammar. Other books serve that purpose. The function of this section is to identify the most common grammatical errors and explain how to avoid them, as simply as possible.

As for those errors that aren't included in this section, here's a tip: English grammar is mostly based on logic.[120] When you're uncertain about a grammatical point that you've never been taught or read about, apply your analytical skills and figure out the answer logically. That's another benefit of grammar: it strengthens our ability to be logical.

---

119. S. Suzuki, *Zen Mind, Beginner's Mind* (Boston: Shambhala Publications, 2006), p. 2
120. There are a few exceptions, such as the rules about split infinitives and never ending a sentence with a preposition. However, those rules, as we'll see later on, are changing.

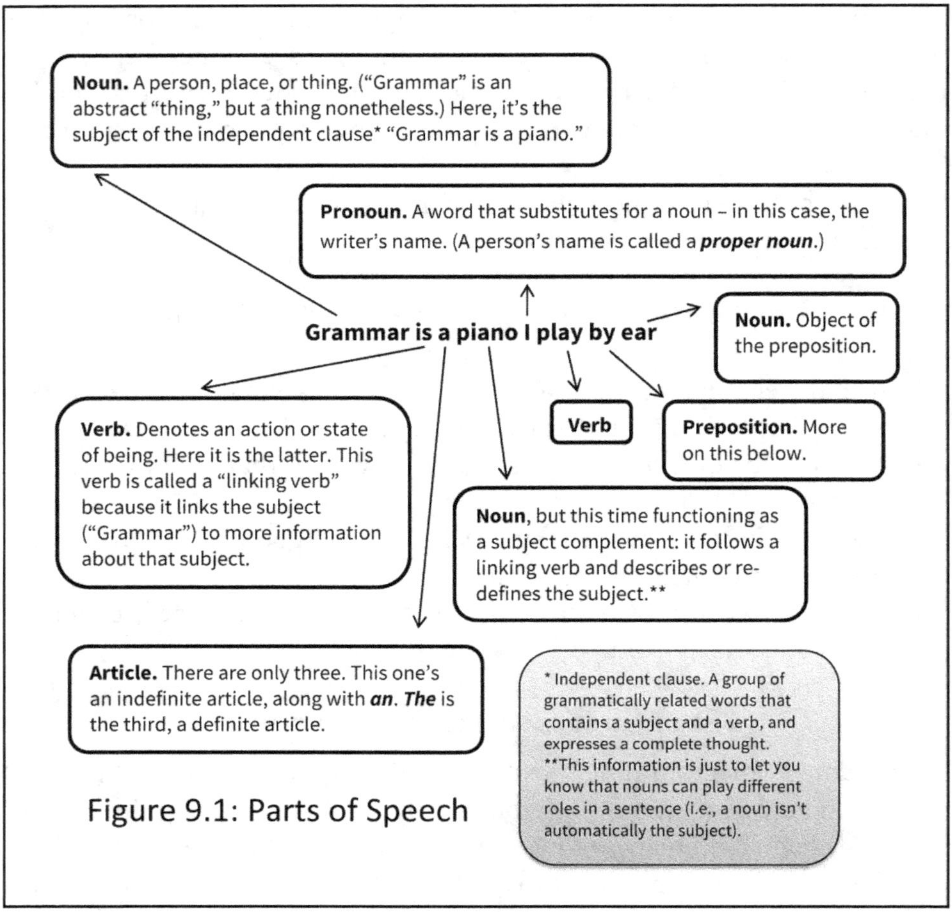

Figure 9.1: Parts of Speech

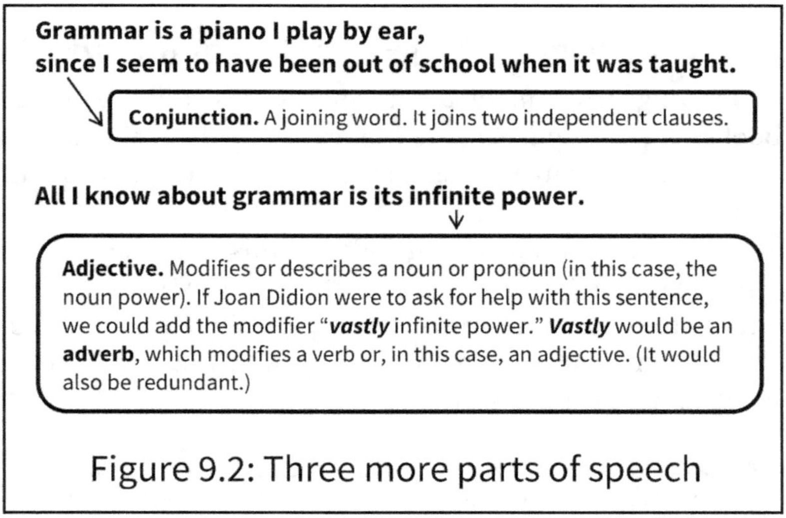

Grammar is a piano I play by ear

- **Noun.** A person, place, or thing. ("Grammar" is an abstract "thing," but a thing nonetheless.) Here, it's the subject of the independent clause* "Grammar is a piano."
- **Pronoun.** A word that substitutes for a noun – in this case, the writer's name. (A person's name is called a **proper noun**.)
- **Noun.** Object of the preposition.
- **Verb.**
- **Preposition.** More on this below.
- **Verb.** Denotes an action or state of being. Here it is the latter. This verb is called a "linking verb" because it links the subject ("Grammar") to more information about that subject.
- **Noun**, but this time functioning as a subject complement: it follows a linking verb and describes or re-defines the subject.**
- **Article.** There are only three. This one's an indefinite article, along with **an**. **The** is the third, a definite article.

* Independent clause. A group of grammatically related words that contains a subject and a verb, and expresses a complete thought.
**This information is just to let you know that nouns can play different roles in a sentence (i.e., a noun isn't automatically the subject).

Figure 9.2: Three more parts of speech

**Grammar is a piano I play by ear,
since I seem to have been out of school when it was taught.**

- **Conjunction.** A joining word. It joins two independent clauses.

All I know about grammar is its infinite power.

- **Adjective.** Modifies or describes a noun or pronoun (in this case, the noun power). If Joan Didion were to ask for help with this sentence, we could add the modifier "**vastly** infinite power." **Vastly** would be an **adverb**, which modifies a verb or, in this case, an adjective. (It would also be redundant.)

SUBJECT-VERB AGREEMENT ERRORS

In a nutshell: "Agreement" means consistency. Read the examples below to see what that means.

Subject-verb agreement

This is the singular subject
⬇
EXAMPLE: A singular SUBJECT REQUIRES a singular verb.
⬆
This is the singular verb

This is the plural subject
⬇
EXAMPLE: Plural SUBJECTS REQUIRE plural verbs.
⬆
This is the plural verb

"And" usually indicates a plural subject, which is known as a "compound subject"[121]
⬇
EXAMPLE: Example #1 AND Example #2 ILLUSTRATE subject-verb agreement.
⬆
This is the plural verb

In each of the examples above, the subject "agrees with" its verb.

Subject-verb agreement troubleshooting

If you have trouble identifying the subject, first identify the verb. For most people the verb is fairly straightforward to locate. It's the word(s) that denotes an action or a state of being. Once you've identified the verb, ask yourself, "Who or what does this verb refer to?" By answering that ques-

---

[121]. Sometimes, "and" joins two words that are considered one unit. In that case, you would use a singular verb, even though the subject appears to be plural. That's one reason (out of several) that questioning the grammar of a police officer who asks, "What IS your NAME and ADDRESS?" would be unwise. Another common example is any compound subject preceded by "Each" or "every" – as in "**Each** RULE and its inevitable EXCEPTION IS important" or "**Every** RULE and its inevitable EXCEPTION NEEDS to be memorized." (If you're not a native English speaker, you have good reason to be irritated right now.)

tion, you've identified your subject. For instance, in the first example above, you would ask, "Who or what 'requires' a singular verb?" The answer is "A singular subject." Now strip away the modifiers "A" and "singular" and you're left with "subject." That's the sentence's subject.

But not all sentences are so simple.

EXAMPLE: The **consequences** of the agreement that **we** *have negotiated* during the past year *seem* straightforward.

Some sentences, such as the one above, have more than one subject and more than one verb. The same approach applies, though:

1. Find the verb: *have negotiated*
2. Ask: "Who have negotiated?"
3. Answer: **we**. That's your subject.

1. Find the verb: *seem*
2. Ask: "Who or what 'seem' straightforward?"
3. Answer: the **consequences**. That's your subject.

TIP: You can double check that "consequences" is the subject of "seem" by applying this rule of thumb: a subject is seldom found within a prepositional phase.

Quick (and entirely serious) definition: **Prepositions** are those small words that describe anywhere a monkey can be or go: *in* the tree; *at* the seashore; *above* my head; *against* the lamp post; *up* the river; *with* the donkeys; *to* the market; *through* the crowd; *toward* the sunset; *at* my side; *for* a ride; etc.

Their function? To introduce a noun (person, place or thing) or a pronoun (a noun substitute). The result is a prepositional phrase that acts as a modifier within the sentence. In the example above, the small words are the prepositions; the entire phrase is the prepositional phrase.

Back to the tip ("a subject is seldom found within a prepositional phrase"): Sometimes you can identify the subject through the process of elimination. Cross out all the prepositional phrases in your sentence. The subject will likely be contained within whatever is left.

EXAMPLE: The consequences ~~of the agreement~~ that we have negotiated ~~during the past year~~ seem straightforward.

With "agreement" and "year" now eliminated as possible subjects, your job of identifying the correct subject just got easier.

Remember that tip as you read the following examples:

This is the singular subject *This is the singular verb*
⬇ ⬇

EXAMPLE: The INSTRUCTOR, together ~~with the students~~, IS PARTICIPATING ~~in the literacy fundraiser~~. *["Literacy fundraiser" and "students" are eliminated as potential subjects because they are contained within prepositional phrases.]*

This is the plural subject *This is the plural verb*
⬇ ⬇

EXAMPLE: The STUDENTS, accompanied ~~by the instructor~~, ARE PARTICIPATING ~~in the literacy fundraiser~~. *["Literacy fundraiser" and "instructor" are eliminated as potential subjects because they are contained within prepositional phrases.]*

If you can identify the subject, but aren't sure whether it's singular or plural, you're probably dealing with one of these cases:

1. Two subjects joined by "nor" or "or": Choose whichever subject is closest to the verb.

This is the subject closest to the verb. It's plural
⬇

EXAMPLE: Neither the instructor nor his STUDENTS ARE PARTICIPATING in the literacy fundraiser.
⬆
This is the plural verb

This is the subject closest to the verb. It's singular
⬇

EXAMPLE: Either the students or the INSTRUCTOR IS PARTICIPATING in the literacy fundraiser.
⬆
This is the singular verb

*2. A subject that is a **singular indefinite pronoun**: anyone, somebody, anybody, everybody, everything, each, either, neither, one, no one, something, everyone, nobody, nothing, anything, someone.*

Give a singular indefinite pronoun a singular verb. (Hint: pronouns that end in "one" or "body" are singular.)

The subject is a singular indefinite pronoun
⬇
EXAMPLE: EVERYBODY *IS PARTICIPATING* in the literacy fundraiser.
⬆
This is the singular verb

The subject is a singular indefinite pronoun
⬇
EXAMPLE: NEITHER *WANTS* to be left out.
⬆
This is the singular verb

3. A subject that is a **plural indefinite pronoun**: *both, few, several, others, many*. Give a plural indefinite pronoun a plural verb.

All three subjects are plural indefinite pronouns.
⬇
Examples: MANY *ARE* participating.
　　　　　FEW *HAVE* declined.
　　　　　SEVERAL *SHOW* enthusiasm.
⬆
All three verbs are plural

4. A subject with an indefinite pronoun that can be either singular or plural, depending on the context: *all, any, more, most, none, some*. Decide whether the indefinite pronoun is singular or plural based on the context. That's infuriatingly vague, I know, so here's another tip: if the pronoun refers to something that can be counted, use a plural verb. If the pronoun refers to something that cannot be counted, use a singular verb.

"food" is not countable, so the indefinite pronoun "none" takes a singular verb
⬇
EXAMPLE: NONE of the food *IS* ready yet.
⬆
This is the singular verb

"tacos" are countable, so the indefinite pronoun "none" takes a plural verb
⬇
EXAMPLE: NONE of the tacos ARE ready yet
⬆
This is the plural verb

5. A subject that is a **collective noun,** such as team, class, family, committee, faculty, or group. Again, decide whether the collective noun is singular or plural based on the context. For example, if your collective noun emphasizes the individuals within the group, use a plural verb. If your collective noun emphasizes the group as one unit, use a singular verb. Sometimes this is a judgment call, and sometimes it's easier to rewrite the sentence (i.e., write "team members" rather than "team" to clarify your focus is on the individuals rather than on the group.)

The collective noun "team" acts as one unit here – as a group, it meets on Monday mornings, so it takes a singular verb
⬇
EXAMPLE: The TEAM MEETS on Monday mornings.
⬆
This is the singular verb

The collective noun "team" refers to individual team members having settled their differences among themselves (i.e., from the context, it seems as if individual team members disagreed with each other. Therefore, the subject takes a plural verb).
⬇
EXAMPLE: The TEAM HAVE SETTLED their differences.
⬆
This is the plural verb

If you have trouble distinguishing between singular and plural verbs, you're not alone. Even native English speakers sometimes hesitate, wondering, for example, if "seem" or "seems," "suggest" or suggests" is the singular form. The "s" at the end of the verb can be confusing, because with nouns it suggests a plural form – but that's not the case with verbs.

Try this trick: place "It" in front of the verb, and then say aloud whatever verb form immediately comes to mind. It will likely be the correct singular form. Conversely, place "They" in front of the verb, and then say aloud whatever verb form immediately comes to mind. It will likely be the correct plural form.

For example, which would you write (or say): "It seem straightforward" or "It seems straightforward"? "They suggests this strategy" or "They suggest this strategy"? If you're fluent in English, you will automatically choose the second sentence in each pair as the correct one. If you're not yet fluent in English, this challenge is just one more reminder that English grammar is sometimes counterintuitive.

Exercise 9.2
Subject-verb agreement exercise
(or "you can't always rely on how it sounds")

Choose the correct answer[122] – and use logic as your guide when it's an unfamiliar example, not covered in the above explanations:

1. I know that either Stephen or Edward (has have) prepared the presentation slides.
2. Neither of us (knows know) the answer.
3. (Is Are) there any questions?
4. She is one of the many competitors who (is are) succeeding.
5. Anna is the only one of the many competitors who (is are) succeeding.

PRONOUN PROBLEMS

Pronouns – those words that substitute for nouns, such as *I, me, she, him, it, them*, etc. – can be complicated to explain. There are so many different types, and so many rules governing them. This doesn't have to mean, though, that they're complicated to understand – and to use properly.

Exercise 9.3

Read the excerpt[123] below and identify the faulty pronoun use:

> "Cheers," she said as I left, "and don't forget you're seeing Matt and I on Monday."

---

122. See the correct answers at end of this chapter.
123. S. Faulks, *Engleby* (London: Vintage Books, 2008), p. 152.

I thought for a moment she'd said "matineye," an East End pronunciation of "matinee." Was I meant to review it?

Then I remembered Matt was the production editor.

"Me won't forget," me muttered as me went downstairs.

You would never actually make the mistake in the last sentence, of using "me" when it should be "I." In a sentence like that, you know the right pronoun to choose – "I" vs. "me" – without even thinking. Not all sentences, though, are so straightforward, and that's where understanding the rules can help: they guide us toward the grammatically correct choice, so we can confidently rewrite the excerpt's first sentence to read "you're seeing Matt and **me**" (as opposed to the grammatically incorrect "you're seeing Matt and **I**").

In the spirit of building up your grammatical confidence, learn the following pronoun rule:

Your pronoun choice depends on the pronoun's function in the sentence.

If the pronoun is functioning as a subject,[124] choose from this list only: *I, you, she, he, it, we, they, who*. These pronouns belong to the **subjective case**.

If the pronoun is functioning as an object, choose from this list only: *me, you, her, him, it, us, them, whom*. These pronouns belong to the **objective case**.

How to figure out if the pronoun is functioning as an object?

A **direct object** is the noun or pronoun that is being acted upon. To determine whether a sentence contains a direct object, find the verb and then ask "what" or "whom."

Choose "me" because the pronoun functions as an object here.
↓
EXAMPLE: You ARE SEEING (*I   me*) on Monday.
↑
Here's the verb. Ask "who" or what" is being seen. The answer leads you to the direct object.

Now it's easier to see the grammatical sense behind "You are seeing

---

124. A subject is the part of the sentence that is being or doing something. If you need an update on how to identify it, re-read the section on subject-verb agreement troubleshooting.

Matt and me [*not "I"*] on Monday."

An **indirect object** is the noun or pronoun that receives the action of the verb. It may be preceded by "for" or "to" – or those prepositions may be implicitly understood. An indirect object always requires a direct object, and it always comes after the verb.

                                        Choose "me" because the pronoun
                       Direct object   *functions as an object here.*
                            ↓   ↓

EXAMPLE: Please GIVE the BOOKS to (*I* *me*).
                      ↑

Verb. Ask "who" or "what" is being given. The answer leads you to the direct object: books. Now ask "who" is being given the books. The answer leads you to the indirect object.

Now it's easier to see the grammatical sense behind

Please give the books to Gwen and me [*not "I"*]

OR

Please give Gwen and me [not "I"] the books ["to" is implied in this sentence].

PRONOUN CASE TROUBLESHOOTING

Pronoun case problems tend to occur in the following situations:

1. *The pronoun is paired with another pronoun or noun.* In those cases, repeat the sentence to yourself, but, as you do so, eliminate the other pronoun or noun. (Remember, a person's name is also a noun, a proper noun.) The correct answer will then probably be obvious:

"Please give the books to ~~Gwen and~~ I" sounds odd.
"Please give the books to ~~Gwen and~~ me" sounds normal.

Exercise 9.4

Try the same strategy with these sentences:

1. The director gave the job to (her   she) and Terry.

2. (He Him) and Hugo will complete the first assignment.

3. That arrangement will allow Albert and (I me) to start the second assignment.

4. Sean and (I me) are the project consultants. (Note: we could flip the introduction of this sentence around to read "(I me) and Sean are the project consultants," but grammatically-correct people like to be polite, so they place the other person's name first.)

5. (We Us) consultants require more stringent guidelines.

6. More input into the curriculum should come from (we us) students.

Now double-check your answers by identifying whether each pronoun functions as a subject or an object.

• • • • •

2. "I" gets mistaken as being more grammatical – or more refined – than "me." Maybe the word "me" stirs up childhood memories of being corrected anytime you asked an ungrammatical question like, "Can my friends and me go to the movies?" or "Can me and Tom work together on this project?" For whatever reason, the word "I" gets elevated in some people's minds as the more grammatical, educated choice. They end up writing sentences like, "Between you and I, the hiring decision has already been made," when they really should write, "Between you and **me**, the hiring decision has already been made."

Tip: Remember the earlier advice given in the section on subject-verb agreement errors – a subject is very seldom found within a prepositional phrase. "Between" is a preposition, signaling the start of a prepositional phrase. Therefore, "I" is an incorrect choice in that sentence because it's a *subject* pronoun, and subjects aren't usually found in prepositional phrases. That leaves "me," an object pronoun, as the only correct choice.

Exercise 9.5

Try applying this tip to these sentences:

1. A decision will be made by Mike and (I me) shortly.

2. The bonus was divided equally between Ryan and (I me).

3. Because the work was assigned to Christine and (I   me), it will be completed soon.

4. He went with Brian and (I   me) to the concert.

The mistake of viewing some pronouns as more grammatical or refined than others may also account for the misuse of "myself":

INCORRECT: *Please report any problems to either Karen or myself.*
INCORRECT: *Jerry and myself will be responsible for the program.*

CORRECT: Please report any problems to either Karen or me.
CORRECT: Jerry and I will be responsible for the program.

TIP: If you can substitute "myself" with either "I" or "me" in a sentence, then do so.[125] That's the grammatically correct choice. Reserve "myself" for those situations where "I" or "me" do not work.

EXAMPLE: I, myself, am responsible for the program.
EXAMPLE: I did the work by myself.

In the examples above, "I" or "me" can't substitute for "myself" – not if you want the sentence to make sense.

3. *The choice is between "who" and "whom."* Some people view "whom" as pretentious and outdated. The language evolves, they argue, and so should the rules. Others, perhaps with a bit of nostalgia, argue for it:

"Whom" may indeed be on the way out, but so is Venice, and we still like to go there.[126]

Before you choose a side, learn how to use "who" and "whom." Then, at least, your choice to either embrace or discard "whom" will be an informed one.

TIP: "Who" acts as a subject. You can associate it with *he*. "Whom" acts

---

125. I never knew about this rule until I stumbled across it in an online document from Bow Valley College, Learning Resource Services.
126. M. Norris, *Between You and Me: Confessions of a Comma Queen* (New York: Norton, 2015), p. 89.

as an object. You can associate it with *him*.

Now reconfigure the sentence to insert *he* or *him* into it. If *he* sounds natural, the correct choice is "who." If *him* sounds natural, the correct choice is "whom."

The original sentence	The reconfigured sentence	The answer
(Who Whom) should we contact?	Should we contact him? ("Should we contact he" does not sound natural)	**Whom** should we contact?
(Who Whom) do you think knows the answer?	Do you think he knows the answer?	**Who** do you think knows the answer?
The instructor is someone (who whom) I used to know.*	I used to know him.	The instructor is someone **whom** I used to know.
Can you recommend (who whom) I can ask for advice? **	Can I ask him for advice?	Can you recommend **whom** I can ask for advice?
Do the next example yourself.		
The answer depends on (who whom) is an expert in the field.		

*This example contains two clauses: "the instructor is someone" and "(who whom) I used to know)." Reconfigure only the relevant clause – the one that contains "who/whom".

** The same point applies to this sentence, also – and to the last one that you'll do yourself.

Once you know the rules, you can then decide whether or not to reject "whom." Or you might decide to reject "whom" selectively – perhaps only when you're speaking. That would be understandable. In the midst of a heated discussion, after all, the grammatically incorrect "Who do you think you are?" probably carries more impact than the delicately grammatical "Whom do you think you are?"

But perhaps that's a special case, involving tone. For a more general overview, re-read aloud the above exercise sentences that contain "whom," and then ask yourself how you feel. Your proficiency with the language should never make you feel uncomfortable or awkward or pretentious. It should make you feel confident. If it doesn't, then take to heart Emerson's famous quotation:

A foolish consistency is the hobgoblin of little minds.[127]

In other words, if you have a good reason to apply the "who" vs. "whom" rule inconsistently, go ahead and do so. (If you want to be on the safe side, though, consistently apply the rule when you're writing a class assignment.)

Pronoun-antecedent agreement

If you understood the earlier section on subject-verb agreement, you'll understand **pronoun-antecedent agreement**. It's based on the same principle: one part of the sentence must "agree with" another part.

In this case, the two parts that have to agree are the pronoun and its antecedent. A pronoun always substitutes for a noun or a pronoun. That noun or pronoun is called the antecedent.

Example: Claire likes to read. She has many books.
↑ ↑
antecedent   *pronoun*

The pronoun ("She"), singular and feminine, agrees with the **proper noun** it's replacing ("Claire"), singular and feminine.

Example: Kevin likes to read. He has many books.
↑ ↑
antecedent   *pronoun*

The pronoun ("He"), singular and masculine, agrees with the proper noun it's replacing ("Kevin"), singular and masculine.

Example: Wilma and Dennis like to read. They have many books.
↑ ↑
plural antecedent   *plural pronoun*

The plural pronoun ("They") agrees with the plural proper nouns it's replacing ("Wilma" and "Dennis").

Pronoun-antecedent agreement is simple – except when it's not. Try the exercise below.

---

127. R.W. Emerson, *Essays, First Series*: "Self Reliance."

Exercise 9.6

Using the above three sentences as your guide, fill in the blanks:

Each family member likes to read. _____ many books.

The _____ pronoun ("_____") agrees with the singular noun ("member") it's replacing.

If you followed the simple agreement rule, you filled in the blanks by writing:

Each family member likes to read. *He or she has* many books.

The *singular* pronoun (*"he" or "she"*) agrees with the singular noun (*"member"*) it's replacing.

Your answer would be technically correct, but it probably didn't seem correct as you were writing it, and as you re-read your answer, it probably sounded awkward. Moreover, once you're on the path of "he or she" or something like it, such as "he/she" or "(s)he," the awkwardness escalates, opening the door to "him/her" and "himself/herself".

We've already established awkwardness and good writing don't go together; therefore, in a case like this consider three options:

OPTION #1. Change the antecedent, so that it's plural rather than singular (don't forget to change the verb form, as well):

EXAMPLE: ~~Each member~~ *The family members* like to read. ~~He or she has~~ *They have* many books.

Option #1 can be a simple, quick solution: in the example above, it doesn't change the sentence's meaning or undermine its clarity. It works.

It doesn't always work *well*, though.

    singular antecedent   *singular pronoun*
        ⬇   ⬇

EXAMPLE: EVERYONE remembers his/her first love. In fact, he/she may treasure that memory.   ⬆

                      singular possessive pronoun

"Everyone," you'll recall from the section on subject-verb agreement, is singular. (Even if you don't recall that, you can still figure out it's singular by the singular verb it takes – "remembers.") Here, the sentence is grammatically correct, but the "his/her" and "he/she" construction is awkward.

Making the antecedent plural results in something like,

"All people remember their first love [*or should that be "loves"?*]. In fact, they may treasure that memory [or should it be *"those memories"?*].

Sometimes Option #1 just doesn't work stylistically or needlessly complicates matters, even though it's grammatically correct. That's when you consider other options.

OPTION #2. If necessary, use "they" and "their" as singular pronouns:

EXAMPLE: Everyone remembers their first love. In fact, they may treasure that memory.

Use "they" and "their" as singular pronouns when making everything plural is too complicated and awkward. (This advice, by the way, is considered erroneous in some circles – but they're becoming smaller and smaller these days, so the chances of your encountering them are slim.[128])

Another advantage of the singular "they" or "their" is its gender neutrality. Not everyone identifies as "he" or "she" or is comfortable being labeled "him" or "her." Since the English language lacks a singular gender-neutral pronoun, "they" and "their" are a satisfactory, if not completely perfect, solution.[129]

OPTION #3. Avoid the problem entirely by revising the sentence, so that the pronoun is eliminated:

REVISION: A person's first love is a long lasting, often cherished, memory.

Exercise 9.7

Correct the pronoun antecedent agreement errors below. If you decide to use the **"singular they/their"** solution, explain why – if only to yourself.

[128]. Some style guides, such as the APA's, still view the singular "they" as an error.
[129]. I've deliberately omitted "one" as a possible solution to our pronoun problems here: "One remembers one's first love. In fact, one treasures that memory." It would be grammatically correct, but some people find it pretentious.

(That's not a bad practice, generally.)

1. University of Guelph is known as Canada's Food University. They are noted for their food-related academic programs and research.

2. Neither of the women wants their contribution to be made public.

3. Both Ken and Tom had his name added to the list of donors.

4. I wanted to join the club, but their fees were prohibitively expensive.

5. Everyone is required to bring their textbook to class tomorrow.

Vague Pronoun Reference

A pronoun takes the place of a noun or another pronoun. Make sure it's clear which noun or pronoun is being replaced. The big culprit here is often "This" when it's used as a "stand-alone" word.

EXAMPLE: Many students pay a lot of money for textbooks they hardly read. This is wrong.

"This" is a vague pronoun reference here because we're not sure what it refers to. Is it wrong that students pay a lot of money for texts they don't read? Or is it wrong that they don't read the texts? A revision corrects the problem:

REVISION: Many students pay a lot of money for textbooks they hardly read. This waste of money is wrong.

OR

REVISION: Many students pay a lot of money for textbooks they hardly read. This lack of effort is wrong.

Other words that often become vague pronoun references are "which," "they," and "it."

EXAMPLE #1: I brought my umbrella, even though they're forecasting sunny skies.

↑

Who are they?

REVISION: I brought my umbrella, even though the forecast calls for sunny skies.

EXAMPLE #2: The protagonist is a sensitive individual with a history of violence, which adds to his complexity.

Does "which" refer to the fact that he's both sensitive and violent, or just the fact that he's violent?

REVISION: The protagonist is both sensitive and violent, a combination that adds to his complexity.

EXAMPLE #3: The report included a lengthy appendix. It was comprehensive and well documented.

Does "it" refer to the report or to the appendix?

REVISION: The comprehensive, well-documented report included a lengthy appendix

OR

REVISION: The report included a lengthy appendix that was comprehensive and well documented.

"That" vs. "Which"

Some people think the distinction between "that" and "which" probably doesn't make a difference – except to make the person who knows the distinction feel a bit more educated and knowledgeable. The real difference, therefore, is mostly in your mind. That's a pretty big difference.

Read these two sentences to see the distinction between "that" and "which":

The course **that seemed interesting** is completely full.

This is essential to the meaning of the sentence (i.e., "The only course in the entire calendar that interests me is full!").

The course, **which seemed interesting**, is completely full.

This is not essential to the meaning of the sentence (i.e., "This course is full.

Too bad. It might have been interesting.")

"That" introduces a **restrictive clause**. You don't have to remember that term unless you particularly want to. You just have to remember the meaning behind it: "that" introduces something essential, something that "restricts" or defines the sentence's meaning. Another way of putting it: "that" introduces something that plays a starring role in the sentence.

"Which" introduces a **non-restrictive clause**:[130] something that is not essential to the sentence's meaning. If it were cut, you would still understand the main point of the sentence. Another way of putting it: "which" introduces something that plays a secondary role in the sentence.

TIP: In keeping with their essential status, clauses introduced by "that" are never separated from the rest of the sentence by commas.

"That" ≠ ,

In keeping with their non-essential status, clauses introduced by "which" are typically separated from the rest of the sentence by commas.

"Which" = ,

EXAMPLE: Commas **THAT ARE INDISCRIMINATELY SPRINKLED THROUGHOUT THE ESSAY** distract the reader. ↑

Not a comma in sight. This clause is essential to the sentence's main point.

EXAMPLE: Commas, **WHICH ARE INDISCRIMINATELY SPRINKLED THROUGHOUT THE ESSAY**, are clearly the writer's favourite piece of punctuation.

Separated from the rest of the sentence by a comma at the start and at the end, this clause is not essential. It adds detail, nuance and maybe even tone, but it's not needed to understand the sentence's main point.

SPEAKING OF COMMAS …

A lot of people claim they've been taught that commas are like breathing: insert a comma whenever you have to stop to take a breath. But as the eminently practical *New York Times* editor Mary Norris points out, "Basing

---

130. A clause is a grammatically related group of words that contains a subject and a verb.

the rules on lung capacity is just too subjective."

Here are some (mostly objective) rules about commas:

1. Never separate a subject from its verb with a single comma.

EXAMPLE: The main reason Joe didn't major in English literature, was post-modernism.
↑
delete the comma

2. Never use commas to separate an essential element of the sentence from the rest of the sentence. This rule extends the earlier "that" vs. "which" discussion by introducing a new term: **appositive**. Appositives define or further identify something, usually a nearby noun. (And, again, you don't have to remember that term if you don't want to. You just need to recognize one when you see it.)

In a nutshell: If the appositive is not essential to the sentence, use commas to separate it from the rest. If the appositive is essential to the sentence, don't use any commas.

In fact, the essential vs non essential rule can be broadly applied here:

Essential ≠ ,
Non Essential = ,

An appositive: it defines "post-modernism". This definition is a bit of extra detail here. It's not needed to understand the main point. Therefore, it gets separated from the rest with commas.
↓
Example: Post-modernism, A COMPLEX LITERARY THEORY, was the main reason my nephew Joe did not major in English.
↑
An appositive: it identifies "nephew". This identifier is essential if you want to clarify which of your many nephews is being referred to. Therefore, "Joe" does not get separated from the rest with commas.

An appositive: it identifies the dog. It's not enclosed in commas because "Lucy" is essential to the sentence (i.e., there's more than one dog in this household).
↓
EXAMPLE: My dog LUCY, A TERRIER-CROSS, is the dominant dog in the household.
↑
An appositive: it further defines "Lucy." It's enclosed in commas

because it's not essential to the sentence's meaning.

3. **Use a comma before a co-ordinate conjunction** *that joins two complete sentences.* An old elementary-school tip: to remember the seven co-ordinate conjunctions, think of the acronym FANBOYS: **f**or, **a**nd, **n**or, **b**ut, **o**r, **y**et, **s**o.

EXAMPLE: **I like apples, and I like pears.**
⬆   ⬆
two complete sentences

EXAMPLE: **It was a hard lesson, but it was one that I needed to learn.**
⬆   ⬆
two complete sentences

EXAMPLE: **The holiday was beautiful, so we were sorry to see it end.**
⬆   ⬆
two complete sentences

4. *Use a comma to separate an introductory element from the main part of the sentence. It can be one word, often a transition:*

Therefore, the Civil War was inevitable.
However, more research is needed to confirm this conclusion.
Consequently, the project deadline has been extended.

The inevitable exceptions to the rule: If the word is a co-ordinate conjunction, do not place a comma after it, unless it's the first of a pair of commas. (It's easier to show this exception than to explain it. See the two examples below.)

No comma here
⬇

EXAMPLE #1: But not everyone agrees that co-ordinate conjunctions can be used to start a sentence.[131]

---

131. Starting a sentence with a co-ordinate conjunction is not acceptable to some people. In the two example sentences, they might substitute "But" with the more formal "However" and "And" with "Furthermore." Others (and I'm one of them) make a judgment call, using the word that just "sounds" better in that particular sentence and that fits the level of formality expected in that particular paper.

A pair of commas after a co-ordinate conjunction
⬇   ⬇

EXAMPLE #2: But, as you all know, some people view a sentence that starts with a co-ordinate conjunction as both grammatically incorrect and inappropriately informal.

It can be a phrase:

As a result, the contracts have been renewed.
In the meantime, we will continue our research.
Depending on the success of our grant application, we may investigate an overseas collaboration.

Something you probably already knew (or figured out by now): If that "introductory" sentence or phrase were placed in the middle of the sentence, it would be separated with a pair of commas:

The Civil War, therefore, was inevitable.
We will continue, in the meantime, our research.

It can be a clause:

Because it's raining, I brought you an umbrella.[132]
Since they're reluctant to collaborate on this project, we'll work on it independently.
Although I had my share of doubts about this venture, I am pleased by the outcome.

5. *Use commas to separate items in a series (sometimes).*
If you don't remember what a "serial comma" is and how to use it, revisit Chapter 7, p. 118, for a quick and easy explanation.

Exercise 9.8

1. Explain why both sentences in this pair could be punctuated correctly:

My nephew, Ken, lives in Waterloo.

---

[132]. Contrary to what you might have thought you were taught back in elementary or high school, a sentence can start with "Because." Just make sure it's a complete sentence. If you need further convincing, look to the American poet Emily Dickinson: "Because I could not stop for Death, Death kindly stopped for me."

My nephew Ken lives in Waterloo.

2. Add or delete commas where necessary. If you come to an example that hasn't been explained in the text, figure it out based on the rules we've covered so far.
(a) *According to some people texting has made punctuation obsolete.*
(b) *However Jerry's favourite piece of punctuation is, the semicolon.*
(c) *Zachary on the other hand is particularly fond of dashes and parentheses but he also likes the tilde a little known piece of punctuation.*
(d) *The narrator of the story, Maureen is portrayed in a mysterious light which adds an element of suspense to the novel.*
(e) *The booklist contained these three titles:* The Catcher in the Rye, A Perfect Day for Bananafish *and* Franny and Zooey.
(f) *More mistakes are made using too many commas, than too few.*

Semicolons and Colons

This section could be called "punctuation for advanced students or for those who are particularly interested in the finer points of English grammar." It would be more accurate, though, to call it "easier than you probably thought." People tend to make mistakes with these two pieces of punctuation, but there's no need to. They're not difficult.

Semicolons have two uses, both of them judgment calls:

1. *A "heavy-duty" serial comma:* Use the semicolon (instead of a comma) to separate items in a series or in a list when those items consist of more than one word or contain internal punctuation.

EXAMPLE: Before I brought home my dog Molly from the Humane Society, I was told to purchase the following items: a pet carrier, portable, with a removable floor; a six-foot leash, preferably leather; non allergenic biscuits; and plenty of compostable "poop" bags.

NOTE: You could substitute commas instead of semicolons in the above sentence, but semicolons make the sentence a bit easier to read by clearly delineating where one item ends and the next one begins.

2. *A "subtle" period:* Use the semicolon (instead of a period) to separate two sentences that are closely related.

EXAMPLE: First, Patricia rototilled her front yard; then, she added a special compost mixture to the soil.

EXAMPLE: The case was complex; however, the jury arrived at a quick verdict.

EXAMPLE: He is an acclaimed author with a recent best-seller; therefore, he drew a large crowd to his public reading.

Some notes about semicolons:

- You could substitute periods instead of semicolons in the above sentences, but semicolons send a subtle message to the reader: these two sentences have a close connection.
- Never use the semicolon to separate three or more sentences in a row. Limit yourself to just two.
- Another grammatical term that you don't need to remember: **conjunctive adverb**. In the example sentences above, "then," "therefore" and "however" are conjunctive adverbs. They are connecting words that signal the start of a new sentence and, therefore, they need to be preceded by a period or a semicolon.

For example, the following sentences are incorrect:

Replace this comma with a period or semicolon
⬇

EXAMPLE: First, Patricia rototilled her front yard, then she added a special compost mixture to the soil.

Replace this comma with a period or semicolon
⬇

EXAMPLE: The case was complex, however, the jury arrived at a quick verdict.

Now you know how to correct this sentence:

EXAMPLE: She was challenged by the workload, however, she was determined to finish the assignment.

The error in the above three examples is called a **comma splice** (i.e., two sentences that are separated by a comma, instead of a period or semicolon).

TIP: To ensure the semicolon is being used correctly as a "subtle period," check to make sure that what comes before it is a complete sentence and what comes after it is a complete sentence.

Colons introduce something: a list, phrase, clause, complete sentence or quotation. They send this message to the reader: "Now, I'm going to explain further what I just wrote."

EXAMPLE: Macbeth's tragedy stems from one cause: "vaulting ambition, which o'erleaps itself."

EXAMPLE: The following stakeholders were consulted: students, faculty, and industry professionals.

EXAMPLE: Despite scientific evidence to the contrary, some politicians still dismiss climate change: it is, they argue, a hoax, fuelled more by emotions than by facts.

What comes after the colon can be anything, grammatically speaking. What comes before it, though, should be a complete sentence. (There's no real logic to this particular rule. It's just something to remember.)

SENTENCE FRAGMENTS

A sentence fragment is an incomplete sentence punctuated as if it were a complete sentence.

Like this.

Journalists, bloggers and writers of personal essays may deliberately use the occasional sentence fragment to emphasize a point or to adopt a conversational, casual tone that will engage the reader. However, students writing an academic paper don't have this option. For them, sentence fragments send only one message to the instructor: grammatical error.

EXAMPLE: Having been betrayed by his own family, the main character now immerses himself in grief and thoughts of revenge. **Unable to reach out to anyone for help.**

↑

fragment

EXAMPLE: Having been betrayed by his own family, the main character now immerses himself in grief and thoughts of **revenge, unable** to reach out to anyone for help.

fragment corrected

EXAMPLE: Having been betrayed by his own family, the main character now immerses himself in grief and thoughts of **revenge. He is** unable to reach out to anyone for help.

fragment corrected

As illustrated above, there are usually two ways of correcting a fragment:

1. Attach it to the main sentence, which typically involves replacing the period with a comma.
2. Rewrite it as a sentence. (Remember, a sentence contains a subject and its verb; and it makes complete sense all by itself. "Unable to reach out to anyone for help" doesn't fill either of those criteria.)

RUN ONS

A lot of people think that a run-on sentence means a really long sentence. It doesn't – and a really long sentence, all by itself, doesn't constitute a grammatical error, anyway. A **run on** refers to two or more sentences that have no punctuation at all separating them:

EXAMPLE: She liked dogs he liked cats the relationship was doomed from the start.

Complete sentences with no punctuation to separate them = Run-on

Correcting a run-on can be as simple as adding periods at the end of each sentence:[133]

EXAMPLE: She liked dogs. He liked cats. The relationship was doomed from the start.

---

133. Invoking the "once you know the rules, you can break the rules" principle, some experienced writers will use a comma to separate two sentences if the two sentences are very short (e.g., "She liked dogs, he liked cats."). Until you've established that you're an experienced writer, however, you're better off demonstrating that you know the rules.

Exercise 9.9

Explore different ways of correcting the "She liked dogs" example above by using at least one of the following in each of your revisions: a semicolon; a colon; a co-ordinate conjunction; and a conjunctive adverb. (Remember: revising doesn't have to mean slavishly following the order and the wording of the original.)

APOSTROPHES

Some people think the **apostrophe** is doomed, a victim of texting. But in the writing world there's no strong groundswell of support for getting rid of it anytime soon. Learn how to use it.

1. Use an apostrophe to indicate possession by

(a) placing **'s** *at the end of a singular noun:*

Khalil's dissertation topic
The manager's decision
The class's new teacher
James's report[134]

(b) placing **'** *at the end of a plural noun that ends in "s":*

The thirty students' presentations
The families' group picnic

(c) placing **'s** *at the end of a plural noun that does not end in "s":*

The children's toys
The women's fitness club
The men's yoga class

In cases of joint possession, add the apostrophe to the last noun only:

Maureen and Jerry's car

---

134. The last two examples – singular nouns that already end in "s" – have another option: add an apostrophe at the end of the word (e.g., the class' new teacher; James' report).

2. Use an apostrophe to indicate a **contraction** (i.e., to indicate that at least one character has been deliberately omitted from a word or number):

> will not → won't
> who is → who's
> 2016 → '16
> it is → it's

Contractions can lend an informal or conversational tone to a piece of writing. That's why they're used seldom, if at all, in academic writing.

3. Use an apostrophe to indicate the plural of upper and lower case letters. Here, we're getting finicky, but since we're on the subject of apostrophes, you might as well learn it:

The word "commitment" is often misspelled with three t's .
The number of c's vs. l's in "broccoli" makes it a difficult word to spell.
His report card contained mostly A's.

Envision those letters without the apostrophes – "three ts"; "number of cs vs. ls"; "mostly As" – and you can see why apostrophes are needed for clarification.

4. *Do not use an apostrophe*

(a) *with possessive personal pronouns (e.g., yours, her, his, its, ours, theirs)*:

The fault is yours, not theirs.
The dog wagged its tail.   } **No apostrophes!**

(b) *to pluralize a number, an abbreviation, or a noun*:

The 1900s
Students in their 20s
PhDs   } **No apostrophes!**
Tuesdays are my favourite day.
The Smiths are an interesting family.

TIP: "it's" and "its" often get confused. To ensure your use is correct, silently replace the two with "it is" or "it has" (e.g., "It's been a long day." Silent check: "It has been a long day." The use is correct. Or: "The novel's complexity is both it's strength and it's weakness". Silent check: "It is strength"? "It is weakness"? The sentence needs to be corrected: "The novel's complexity is both its strength and its weakness.")

Exercise 9.10

Correct any punctuation errors in the following sentences.

(a) I know who's essays have received Bs and Cs but I don't know whose responsible for selecting the winning entry. (5 errors)

(b) According to the menu "kid's eat free on Wednesday's": furthermore this restaurant is famous for "it's local cuisine." (6 errors)

(c) The term, "digital immigrants", refers to people who have not been immersed in the digital world since childhood; meaning, they didnt grow up with computers'. (5 errors)

(d) My three favourite fruits are: lemons; apples; and pears. (3 errors)

(e) Their report is better than ours'; which seems unfair, because we put in a weeks' worth of preparation. (4 errors)

(f) According to his account the 1960's were highly overrated, and often mythologized. (3 errors)

(g) A great deal has been written about the subject therefore I won't have trouble finding secondary source material. (2 errors)

(h) Carpel tunnel syndrome once a relatively uncommon medical ailment has become almost commonplace. A consequence of hours spent on the keyboard or on video games. (3 errors)

MISPLACED MODIFIERS

A modifier describes something or someone – and therefore it should be placed as close as possible to that "something" or "someone." When it's not, it's misplaced, and that can cause misunderstanding.

Here's an example so famous that it no longer needs referencing:

EXAMPLE: The report presents statistics about the survey respondents **broken down by age and sex**.
↑
Modifies "statistics." Misplaced because it's not close to "statistics."

CORRECTED: The report presents statistics broken down by age and sex about the survey respondents.

Here are some more subtle examples of misplaced modifiers:

EXAMPLE: I **only** needed one good reference.
↑
Modifies "one good reference," so it should be placed beside "one good reference."

CORRECTED: I needed only one good reference.
OR
CORRECTED: I needed one good reference only.

EXAMPLE: Some people view grammar as confusing and outdated, **with all its arcane terminology**.
↑
Modifies "grammar", so it should be placed beside "grammar."

CORRECTED: Some people view grammar, with all its arcane terminology, as confusing and outdated.

DANGLING MODIFIERS

Dangling modifiers are common, subtle, and difficult to grasp at first. That means you'll feel particularly gratified, and maybe even a bit smug, when you figure them out. Here's a way of understanding them:

Every modifier describes something or someone.

Make sure the "something" or "someone" being described is clearly present in the sentence – as opposed to being implied.

If the "something" or "someone" being described is not clearly present, the modifier is said to be "dangling" (i.e., it's not attached to what it's supposed to modify).

EXAMPLE: **While jogging down the road at dusk,** the sunset looked beautiful. ↑
    Modifier ... but what does it modify? Who was jogging down the road?

CORRECTED: While jogging down the road at dusk, **I** was captivated by the beautiful sunset.
                  OR
CORRECTED: As **she** jogged down the road at dusk, the sunset was beautiful.
                  OR
CORRECTED: The sunset was beautiful as **he** jogged down the road at dusk.

Here are some more subtle examples of dangling modifiers:

EXAMPLE: **After reviewing the literature**, our hypotheses were developed ↑
    Modifier ... but what does it modify? Who reviewed the literature?

CORRECTED (SEVERAL OPTIONS):
    After reviewing the literature, we developed our hypotheses.
    After we reviewed literature, we developed our hypotheses.
    We developed our hypotheses after reviewing the literature.

EXAMPLE: **By developing stronger volunteer networks,** *it* creates a more cohesive community. ↑   ↑
    Modifier ... but what does it modify? Who is developing these networks?

Technically, this example has more than just a dangling modifier problem. There's also the matter of that strange, disconnected "it," a reminder of the earlier rule on vague pronoun references.

CORRECTED (SEVERAL OPTIONS):
    By developing stronger volunteer networks, our community becomes more cohesive.
    By developing stronger volunteer networks, we build a more cohesive community.
    We build a more cohesive community by developing stronger volunteer networks.

PARALLELISM

Parallelism is partly a matter of craft – knowing the grammatical rule –

and partly a matter of style – knowing what sounds pleasing to the reader's ear. Read the three examples below to see what I mean.

> Some are born great, some achieve greatness, and some have greatness thrust upon them. —Malvolio in *Twelfth Night*

> No matter that you have a Ph.D. and have read all of Henry James twice. If you still persist in writing, "Good food at it's best," you deserve to be struck by lightning, hacked up on the spot and buried in an unmarked grave.[135]

> Parallelism adds style and coherence to your writing.

If you read those examples aloud, your voice might have naturally and intuitively *found* the parallel structure of the sentences: the grammatical symmetry that results when different parts of a passage share the same structure.

You can achieve this symmetry by repeating close together

- the same word or derivatives of the same word (e.g., in the example above: "some" "great"; "greatness")
- the same sequence of words (e.g., a pronoun immediately followed by a verb: "some are"; some achieve"; "some have"; or a verb immediately followed by a preposition: "struck by"; "hacked up"; "buried in")
- the same type of word (e.g., in the third example above, both items in the series are nouns: "style" and "coherence." Contrast this with "Parallelism adds style to your writing, and there's more coherence." The error here is known as faulty parallelism.

TIP: Pay particular attention to parallelism when you're listing items in a series or developing headings for your paper (see Chapter 7, p. 120 for more on this).

ACTIVE VS. PASSIVE VOICE

In active voice, the subject is doing the acting. In passive voice, the subject is being acted upon. Active voice is generally preferred in writing because it tends to be more straightforward and concise, but there are times

---

135. L.Truss, cited in Matthew J.X. Malady, "Are Apostrophes Necessary?" *Slate*, May 23, 2013. Retrieved from http://www.slate.com/articles/life/the_good_word/2013/05/apostrophes_and_when_to_use_them_punctuation_necessary_at_all_not_really.html.

when **passive voice** is more appropriate.

EXAMPLE: **Harry** drives Zachary to school every morning.
↑
Harry, the subject, is doing the action (i.e., driving). That's active voice.

EXAMPLE: **Zachary** is driven to school every morning by Harry.
↑
Zachary, the subject, isn't doing the action. He's being "acted upon" (i.e., driven). That's passive voice.

Use active voice unless you have a reason not to. For example:

PASSIVE VOICE: The survey respondents were not told the purpose of the study.
ACTIVE VOICE: The researchers did not tell the survey respondents the purpose of the study.

Passive voice is probably preferable in the above example because the focus is on explaining how the study was carried out. Using active voice here would subtly shift the focus to who carried out the study, which is likely not important in this context. In other words, use passive voice when you want to focus on the action and downplay who carried out the action.

TIP: Active and passive voice has nothing to do with verb tense, and everything to do with focus.

Exercise 9.11

1. Correct any misplaced or dangling modifiers:

(a) He was born in northern Ontario where he lived all his life in the dead of winter.
(b) In order to write the paper, it was necessary to do some secondary research.
(c) Even after studying all night long, the test was still challenging.
(d) Few political analysts can predict the outcome of the election accurately.

2. Circle and connect all the examples of parallelism in the excerpt below:

We watch a 30-second ad in exchange for a video; we solicit a friend's endorsement; we freely pour sentence after sentence, hour after hour, into status updates and stock responses. None of this depletes our bank balances. Yet its cumulative cost, while hard to quantify, affects many of those things we hope to put at the heart of a happy life: rich relationships, rewarding leisure, meaningful work, peace of mind.[136]

3. Place a check mark beside the sentences that are in passive voice. Rewrite them, so that they are in active voice. (And note whether your rewrite results in a more direct, concise sentence. That's the goal.)

(a) The narrative plods dully along.

(b) An interesting reaction is observed when the two chemicals are mixed.

(c) Adverse climate changes throughout the world are aggravated by lack of action on the part of government policy makers.

(d) Employee motivation and morale are being undermined by the ongoing layoffs and reduced benefits.

(e) Expenses increase when energy costs rise.

---

136. T. Chatfield, "The Attention Economy," *Aeon*, October 7, 2013. Retrieved from http://aeon.co/magazine/technology/does-each-click-of-attention-cost-a-bit-of-ourselves/.

ANSWER GUIDE TO CHAPTER 9 EXERCISES
Exercise 9.1
1. Correct. (Tip: see Pronoun Problems, objective vs. subjective case.)
2. Having never understood the rules, **she** (or **he** … or **anyone**) had little chance of winning the game. (Tip: see Dangling Modifiers.)
3. Correct. (Tip: see Pronoun Problems, objective vs. subjective case.)
4. The company has always treated **its** employees with respect. (Tip: see Pronoun-Antecedent Agreement.)
5. They had **only** one option: to accept the conditions, however harsh. (Tip: see Misplaced Modifiers.)
6. No other opinion mattered but **theirs**. (Tip: see Apostrophes, possessive personal pronouns.)
7. None of them are right, or perhaps none of them **are** wrong. It's difficult to tell. (Tip: see Subject-Verb agreement, indefinite pronouns.)

Exercise 9.2
1. I know that either Stephen or Edward (**has** have) prepared the presentation slides.
2. Neither of us (**knows** know) the answer.
3. (Is **Are**) there any questions?
4. She is one of the many competitors who (is **are**) succeeding.
5. Anna is the only one of the many competitors who (**is** are) succeeding.

Exercise 9.4
1. The director gave the job to (**her** she) and Terry.
2. (**He** him) and Hugo will complete the first assignment.
3. That arrangement will allow Albert and (I **me**) to start the second assignment.
4. Sean and (**I** me) are the project consultants. (Note: we could flip the introduction of this sentence around to read "(I me) and Sean are the project consultants, but grammatically-correct people like to be polite, so they place the other person's name first.)
5. (**We** Us) consultants require more stringent guidelines.
6. More input into the curriculum should come from (we **us**) students.

Exercise 9.5
1. A decision will be made by Mike and (I **me**) shortly.
2. The bonus was divided equally between Ryan and (I **me**)
3. Because the work was assigned to Christine and (I **me**), it will be com-

pleted soon.
4. He went with Brian and (I **me**) to the concert.

Exercise 9.7

1. University of Guelph is known as Canada's Food University. ~~They are~~ **It is** noted for ~~their~~ **its** food-related academic programs and research.
2. Neither of the women wants ~~their~~ **her** contribution to be made public.
3. Both Ken and Tom had ~~his name~~ **their names** added to the list of donors.
4. I wanted to join the club, but ~~their~~ **its** fees were prohibitively expensive.
5. Everyone is required to bring **their** textbook to class tomorrow. (You could change this to "Everyone is required to bring ~~their~~ **his or her** textbook to class tomorrow" or "Everyone is required to bring ~~their~~ **the** textbook to class tomorrow." You could also leave it as is. It may be a case where the "singular they/their" works.)

Exercise 9.8

Explain why both sentences in this pair could be punctuated correctly:

My nephew, Ken, lives in Waterloo.
This is correct if the writer has only one nephew. "Ken," in that case, is a non-essential appositive.

My nephew Ken lives in Waterloo.
This is correct if the writer has more than one nephew. "Ken," in that case, is an essential appositive.

Add or delete commas where necessary. If you come to an example that hasn't been explained in the text, figure it out based on the rules we've covered so far.

↓

(a) According to some people, texting has made punctuation obsolete.

↓

(b) However, Jerry's favourite piece of punctuation is the semicolon.
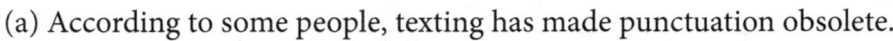
no comma

(c) Zachary, on the other hand, is particularly fond of dashes and parentheses, but he also likes the tilde, a little known piece of punctuation.

(d) The narrator of the story, Maureen, is portrayed in a mysterious light, which adds an element of suspense to the novel.

(e) The booklist contained these three titles: *The Catcher in the Rye*; *A Perfect Day for Bananafish*; and *Franny and Zooey*.

(f) More mistakes are made using too many commas than too few.

no comma

Exercise 9.9

Explore different ways of correcting the "She liked dogs" example above by using at least one of the following in each of your revisions: a semicolon; a colon; a co-ordinate conjunction; and a conjunctive adverb. (Remember: revising doesn't have to mean slavishly following the order and the wording of the original.)

No answers needed for this one because there are so many possibilities. Don't be reluctant to explore them. That's one of the joys of writing.

Exercise 9.10

Correct any punctuation errors in the following sentences.

(a) I know ~~who's~~ **whose** essays have received ~~Bs~~ and ~~Cs~~ **B's and C's**, but I don't know ~~whose~~ **who's** responsible for selecting the winning entry. (5 corrections)

(b) According to the menu, "~~kid's~~ **kids** eat free on ~~Wednesday's~~ **Wednesdays**"; furthermore, this restaurant is famous for "~~it's~~ **its** local cuisine." (6 corrections)

↓   *no commas*   ↓
(c) The term "digital immigrants" refers to people who have not been immersed in the digital world since childhood,
↑
meaning, they ~~didnt~~ **didn't** grow up with ~~computers'~~ **computers.** (5 corrections)

(d) My three favourite fruits are lemons, apples and pears. (3 corrections)
↑
No colon here; and no semicolons needed in the rest of the sentence. The list is simple enough; a comma will suffice.

↓
(e) Their report is better than ~~ours'~~ **ours,** which seems unfair because we put in a ~~weeks'~~ **week's** worth of preparation. (4 corrections) ↑
no comma
(f) He said the ~~1960's~~ **1960s** were highly overrated and often mythologized. ↑   ↑
no comma   *no comma*
(3 corrections)

↓   ↓
(g) A great deal has been written about the subject. Therefore, I won't have trouble finding secondary source material. (2 corrections) (Note: you could also use a semicolon to separate the two sentences. If so, you wouldn't capitalize "therefore.")

↓   ↓
(h) Carpel tunnel syndrome, once a relatively uncommon medical ailment, has become almost commonplace, a consequence of hours spent on the
↑
keyboard or on video games. (3 corrections)

Exercise 9.11

1. Correct any misplaced or dangling modifiers:

(a) He was born in northern Ontario, where he lived all his life in the dead of winter.
ANSWER: He was born *in the dead of winter* in northern Ontario, where he lived all his life.

(b) To write the paper, it was necessary to do some secondary research.
ANSWER (and this is just one possibility): In order to write the paper, *I* had to do some secondary research.

(c) Even after studying all night long, the test was still challenging.
ANSWER (and this is just one possibility): Even after studying all night long, *she* still found the test challenging.

(d) Few political analysts can predict the outcome of the election accurately.
ANSWER: Few political analysts *can predict accurately* (or "*can accurately predict*") the outcome of the election.

2. Find all the examples of parallelism in the excerpt below:

> We watch a 30-second ad in exchange for a video; we solicit a friend's endorsement; we freely pour sentence after sentence, hour after hour, into status updates and stock responses. None of this depletes our bank balances. Yet its cumulative cost, while hard to quantify, affects many of those things we hope to put at the heart of a happy life: rich relationships, rewarding leisure, meaningful work, peace of mind.

3. Place a check mark beside the sentences that are written in passive voice. Revise them, so that they are in active voice. (And note whether your rewrite results in a more direct, concise sentence. That's the goal.)

(a) The narrative plods dully along. *[Active voice]*

(b) An interesting reaction is observed when the two chemicals are mixed. *[Passive voice. Answer (and this is just one possibility): Mixing the two chemicals results in an interesting reaction.]*

(c) Adverse climate changes throughout the world are aggravated by lack of action on the part of government policy makers. *[Passive voice. Answer (and this is just one possibility): The government policy makers' lack of action aggravates adverse climate changes throughout the world.]*

(d) Employee motivation and morale are being undermined by the ongoing layoffs and reduced benefits. *[Passive voice. Answer (and this is just one possibility): The ongoing layoffs and reduced benefits are undermining employee motivation and morale.]*

(e) Expenses increase when energy costs rise. *[Active voice]*

SUMMARY

Understanding grammar isn't just about knowing the rules. It's also about strengthening the credibility of your sentences – and therefore your ideas. Those are two good reasons to learn grammar.

Chapter 10
How to "Get" a Good Grade

This chapter will help you ...

- Revise your definition of a good grade
- Understand ... *really* understand ... why a good grade is worth pursuing
- Figure out a strategy to increase your chances of achieving a good grade

I'm guessing you skipped ahead to read this chapter. If you did, I have just one suggestion: if you haven't already done so, go back and first read Chapter 1. It lays some groundwork that will make this chapter easier to understand. And then, if you like, come back and read this as your second chapter. That wouldn't be such a bad thing – reading this chapter out of order. Your writing probably doesn't unfold in a neat, linear order, so why expect your curiosity or your interests to line up and march in step like soldiers in a row? Breaking rank now and then is good for the soul – even necessary, if you're a counterintuitive writer.

THE CONVENTIONAL DEFINITION OF "A GOOD GRADE"

Most of us define a good grade in a narrow way. We see it as a letter, probably ranging from B+ to A+, or as a number that indicates the instructor's high assessment of our work. And there's another aspect of the good grade: we typically feel good about ourselves, perhaps proud, when the instructor "gives" us, say, an A+ on a reflection paper or an 85% on a research essay. That's the power of a good grade.

But that's also one of the problems of a good grade – at least as defined above.

Why the conventional definition may not be enough (Exercise 9.1)

Choose the question you've asked – and been asked – multiple times over the years:

(a) "What grade did you earn?"

(b) "What grade did you get?"

Your answer just illustrated the problem with the conventional definition of a good grade. It's widely – and mistakenly – perceived as something we "get" rather than something we "earn." Someone else gives us the good grade. Consequently, any good feelings we have about getting a good grade are vulnerable – if a good grade can be "given" this time, it can be withheld the next time. Therefore the feeling of pride in having received an A+ or an 85% is short-lived, lasting until the next assignment gets submitted. How we feel then is bound to depend on the next grade given.

If that pattern seems familiar, you're probably a student who cares about good grades. You're also probably stressed quite a bit whenever you submit an assignment, because you've given someone else – your instructor – a power that he or she shouldn't have: the power to control how you feel about yourself.

And by the way, your instructor doesn't want that power. To a certain extent, writing elicits a subjective response from the reader. The same phrase could prompt one person to smile and another to smirk, simply based on individual preference. Controlling for that bias makes objectively grading a paper enough of a challenge already, even with a detailed rubric. No instructor wants the added burden of knowing a student's state of mind depends on his or her paper "getting" an A as opposed to an A–, or an A– as opposed to a B+.

That's why instructors have two preferences when it comes to grades:

1. They prefer you pay less attention to the grade on the paper and more to the instructor's comments;
2. They prefer you respond to the grade and the comments in an impartial, objective manner.

Those two preferences might be a good basis for revising the conventional definition of "a good grade."

Broadening the definition of "a good grade":
(i) "… pay less attention to the grade on the paper"

I'm not suggesting you dismiss the conventional definition of a good grade. You need the letter or the number grade because it's a universal indicator of the paper's quality. The rest of the world understands and respects it – and you have to live with the rest of the world. It's also a good measure for you, personally, letting you know with certainty how your instructor views your paper.

Consider, though, adding another component to your definition of a good grade, one that goes beyond the first two letters of the alphabet or a narrow range of numbers between 75 and 100 that someone else assigns to your paper. Those are external measures of a good grade. Try completing your definition by adding an internal measure:

I've earned a good grade when the paper I've submitted makes me feel confident.

In other words, try measuring the quality of your submitted assignment by the feeling it evokes within you. A feeling of confidence is a measure of a good grade. Aim for that feeling.

Now confidence is not to be confused with boastfulness or arrogance. A person can be quietly, humbly, even self-deprecatingly, confident. Confidence is a state of mind that comes from having faith in yourself – in this case, faith that you've given your best effort in writing this paper. And of course, the benefits of self-confidence are many, extending into, and potentially enriching, all areas of your life. Self-confidence is a gift you can give yourself by knowing you've done your best. Let it be the measure of a good grade for your next writing assignment.

The connection between confidence and writing well

Many people think that writing well revolves around proper grammar and spelling and the use of stylistic flourishes, so that the writing "sounds" good. And, yes, those are aspects of good writing. But they're not the most important aspects. They're like the icing on the cake. The actual "cake" itself is what you have to say and the connection you forge with others (and with yourself) because of what you have to say. How exactly to forge those connections is a core theme throughout this text, but it essentially comes down to this: for every writing assignment, make a commitment to dig deeper, understand more fully, and broaden your perspective. Commit to being at a higher level of awareness and insight than you were before you started the writing assignment. Commit, in other words, to trying hard. That's what writing well requires you to do. And that's why writing well – or even making a sincere attempt to write well – can help bolster your confidence.

Broadening the definition of "a good grade": (ii) "... respond to the grade and the (instructor's) comments in an impartial, objective manner"

Embracing and applying this new definition of a good grade will likely result in higher grades (in the conventional sense) on your writing assignments. I've used the qualifier "likely" because, of course, no one can guarantee it. However, perhaps that guarantee doesn't matter so much anymore. Ideally, the process of writing your paper has made you confident enough that if your instructor assesses it as less than good, you don't react with extreme negativity. You're disappointed but your innate sense of confidence prevents you from being angry, offended, demoralized or devastated. Your confidence allows you to consider the comments, ask for help if necessary, or even for a second reading, if appropriate. Conversely, if your instructor assesses your paper as good or excellent, you respond with the same balanced equanimity. You're pleased, but your feelings are not unduly influenced by the opinion of others. Your confidence isn't dependent on an "A" paper. It comes from within.

A GOOD GRADE REQUIRES THAT YOU ...
Avoid the path of least resistance

Anyone who has ridden a bicycle knows what the path of least resistance is like. It's the paved straightaway: no bumps, no twists, and definitely no hills. It's the fastest way to get from Point A to Point B with the least amount of effort. That's why a fair number of people take it.

In writing, the path of least resistance involves doing the work with one goal in mind: to get it over with as quickly and as easily as possible. But that single-minded goal will likely result in a paper that lacks the depth, research and care associated with good grades – because depth, research and care aren't generally associated with "quick" and "easy."

The alternative path is considerably different: twisting, bumpy, and one hill after another. In writing, the alternative path can be a hard slog, its moments of coasting and sailing along equal to – or maybe outnumbered by – periods of slow, straining progress where you feel as if you're fighting against gravity to make it up the hill – and not always winning. That's why a lot of students who have to write essays avoid it.

Figure 10.1 shows what this alternative path looks like, compared to the path of least resistance.

After viewing the two paths, ask yourself this question: which one leads to the better, more all-encompassing, view?

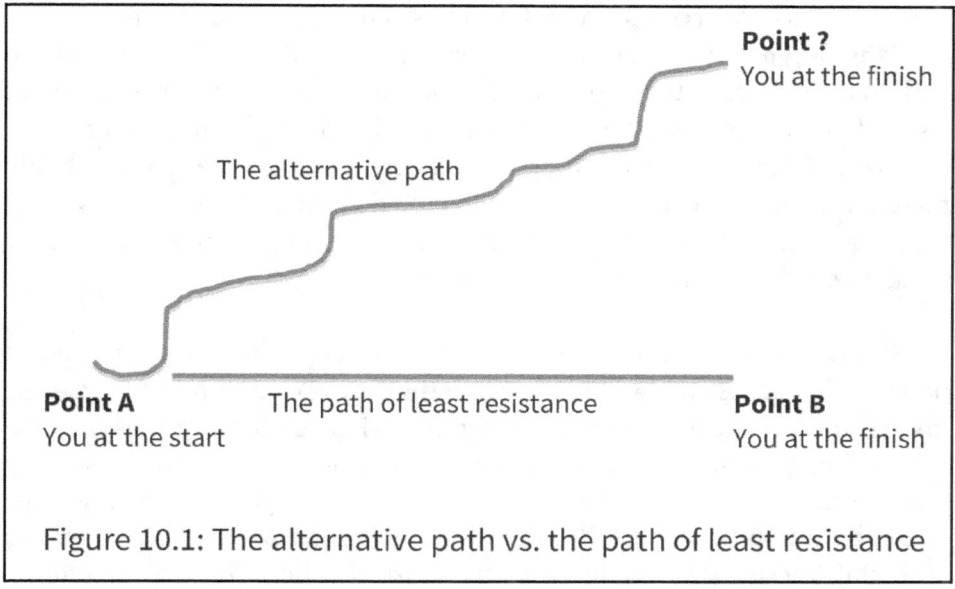

Figure 10.1: The alternative path vs. the path of least resistance

Take that path.

In terms of writing your paper, it means you'll have to work longer and harder. But it also means you're more likely to earn a good grade.

Cultivate self-discipline

Working longer and harder requires self-discipline – which isn't an enticing prospect for a lot of people. In their minds, "self-discipline" conjures an image of sacrifice, tedium and denial of pleasure. A self-disciplined person is often seen as no fun at all. But does that common image tell the entire story? That's the sort of question a counterintuitive writer asks, and this is the sort of answer a counterintuitive writer may uncover:[137]

Discipline comes from the Latin word *disciplina*, meaning learning and knowledge. A self-disciplined person, in other words, is on the path to greater understanding and knowledge.

That's a path worth following.

In other words, if aspiring to be disciplined doesn't motivate you, try aspiring to be knowledgeable or to be a constant learner. It's the same thing. It's also within the capability of everyone, and it may give you the push you need to choose the path to a good grade, as opposed to the path of least resistance.

---

137. I came across this idea while reading a book on yoga: Donna Farhi, *Bringing Yoga to Life* (New York: HarperCollins, 2005).

A GUIDE TO BECOMING A SELF-DISCIPLINED WRITER

Manage your time. Start your paper well before its due date because the path to a good grade takes longer than the path of least resistance. Map out a schedule of when you'll work on the paper, allowing yourself more time than you think you'll need, in case something unexpected arises – a family matter, last-minute concert tickets, a bad cold – that cuts into your writing time, or in case the writing is more time consuming than you originally anticipated. And then stick to that schedule.

Pay attention to the details. Sometimes a well-written paper receives a poor grade because the writer answered the wrong question or ignored the instructions. Read and follow the assignment instructions, not just regarding the big details, such as topic, purpose and depth, but also the smaller ones: format requirements (font size; spacing; title page); referencing style; and submission procedure (hard copy or electronic). Understanding and following these details right from the start will help focus your efforts, shape your thoughts, and guide your research (if research is required).

Ask the right person for help when you need it. It's quick and easy to ask a classmate, a friend or the person who took the course last semester what exactly the instructor wants from a particular writing assignment. However, there's no guarantee the answers will be correct. You're guaranteed a correct answer only if you go directly to the instructor or the teaching assistant. If you still have questions after reading all the instructions, ask him or her. (And because you started the assignment well in advance, you won't ask your questions via an email the night before the paper is due).

Refer to the grading rubric. Your assignment likely has a grading rubric, detailing the instructor's general expectations along with the specific requirements for a good grade. Aim for that good grade by explicitly tailoring your paper to meet those expectations and requirements.

Persevere. At times, it's hard, frustrating, boring, and time consuming. At times, the question "When am I ever going to use this?" overshadows everything. When that happens, remind yourself of the answer: "Right now." With each stage of the writing process, from pre-writing to revision, you're doing more than writing a paper. You're getting an opportunity to broaden your knowledge, sharpen your analytical skills, expand your vocabulary and, most importantly of all, forge a connection with your reader – and with yourself. In other words, you're building skills and cultivating qualities that will strengthen you, both intellectually and emotionally.

And if all of that sounds hopelessly idealistic and so far removed from that 2,500-word paper that's due in two weeks, think about this question from the American poet, Mary Oliver: "Tell me, what is it you plan to do with your one wild and precious life?"[138]

By now you know that the act of writing can generate your deepest insights, so write down an answer to her question.

Now, the chances that you wrote, "I plan to be a writer" are slim. You probably wrote something else, something that sets you apart, as completely different, from everybody else. But I'm guessing one common element connects all our answers: whatever we intend to do with our lives, we all want to be successful at it.

Writing is one way of cultivating the qualities that will make you successful – no matter what you plan to do with your "one wild and precious life." And getting a good grade, especially a good grade as defined above, gives you a glimpse of what success feels like. It feels good. With every paper you write, keep chasing after that feeling.

It's worth quite a bit more than a good grade.

---

138. Mary Oliver, "The Summer Day," in *New and Selected Poems* (Boston: Beacon Press, 1992).

Glossary

Abstract Briefly states the source's key points only. No new ideas or information is added. The length may vary, but typically it is about 10% of the original source. In non-academic writing, it is usually referred to as a "summary" and in business writing as an "executive summary."

Active voice A sentence in which the subject is doing the acting is said to be written in active voice. Contrasts with passive voice in which the subject is being acted upon. Generally, active voice is more direct and concise than passive voice.

ADD Q An acronym for **A**uthor, **D**ate, **D**epth, and **Q**uality of writing. Critically examining these four factors can help someone assess the credibility of information found on the Internet.

Adjective A part of speech: modifies or describes a noun or pronoun.

Adverb A part of speech: modifies or describes an adjective or a verb.

Annotated bibliography A list of research sources, formatted according to a specific style guide (e.g., APA; MLA), but with an added element: each entry is followed by a summary and assessment of the source.

Antecedent The noun that a pronoun refers to.

APA (American Psychological Association) A referencing format widely used with the social and physical sciences. Sometimes referred to as "APA style."

Apostrophe A punctuation mark used to indicate either possession or a contraction (i.e., a missing character from a word or number).

Appositive A part of speech, referring to a word, words, or a phrase that defines or identifies something, usually a nearby noun or phrase.

Article A part of speech. There are only three articles: "the," "a," or "an." "The" is a definite article. "A" and "an" are indefinite articles.

Block-by-block structure A way of organizing your paper or a section of it. It's particularly useful for papers that compare or assess something. For example, all the similarities (or advantages or strengths …) are presented in one large block, followed by a second block that presents all the differences (or disadvantages or weaknesses), or vice versa.

Circular reasoning A type of faulty logic, characterized by lack of progression of thought. A point is made. The evidence to support it is simply a reworking or rewording of the original statement (e.g., "Writing is important because it plays a significant role in our lives").

Clause A group of grammatically related words that contains a subject and a verb.

Clock plan A chronological essay structure, where the material is organized according to time frames, typically (but not always) past, present and future.

Coherence A logical flow from sentence to sentence, paragraph to paragraph, and section to section. The ideas, data, or examples are arranged in such a way that they connect easily to each other.

Collective noun A noun that refers to a group (e.g., team, class, family, committee, faculty, group). A collective noun may "take" a singular or plural verb, depending on the context.

Colon A punctuation mark that serves to introduce or to provide further information about someone or something.

Comma splice A grammatical error that refers to two sentences being separated by a comma, instead of by a period or a semicolon.

Common knowledge Content that is already familiar to the general public or to readers within your discipline. In a research essay, "common knowledge" does not need to be referenced; however, determining whether something falls within this category is a judgment call. When in doubt, the information should be referenced to avoid the risk of perceived plagiarism.

Conjunction A part of speech: a "joining" word. It joins two independent clauses. (Independent clause: a group of grammatically related words that contains both a subject and a verb.)

Conjunctive adverb A connecting word that signals the start of a new sentence (or independent clause) and that also acts as a transition, indicating the relationship between those two sentences or independent clauses (e.g., "therefore"; "however"; "then"; "otherwise").

Constructive pessimist In this context, a writer who focuses on identifying weaknesses and gaps in the rough draft in order to anticipate – and then constructively address – the readers' objections.

Contraction A word or number that uses an apostrophe to indicate a missing character. Typically used in informal or conversational writing, but gaining some, albeit limited, acceptance in academic writing.

Co-ordinate conjunction A part of speech, referring to a word that joins two or more nouns, phrases, or clauses that are grammatically similar. A co-ordinate conjunction that joins two complete sentences (or two independent clauses) is preceded by a comma. An old elementary-school tip: to remember the co-ordinate conjunctions, think of the acronym FANBOYS: **f**or, **a**nd, **n**or, **b**ut, **o**r, **y**et, **s**o.

Dangling modifier A grammatical error that occurs when a word or phrase modifies something or someone implicitly rather than directly (i.e., the person or thing being modified isn't actually stated).

Databases Huge repositories of subject-based information. Libraries subscribe to them, allowing their users free access to all the information they contain. Many of them allow the user to organize bibliographic information, formatting it into different reference styles, such as MLA or APA.

Deductive approach A method of reasoning: the essay begins with its conclusion (or thesis); the rest of the paper then provides support for that conclusion. Often seen as the counterpart to the inductive approach.

Direct object The noun or pronoun that is being acted upon. To determine whether a sentence contains a direct object, find the verb and then ask the question "What?" or "Whom?" For example, in the sentence "I wrote the book," the direct object is "book."

Editing Reviewing and revising the document's focus, organization, scope, depth, logic, relevance, accuracy and correctness.

Ethos A Greek term, referring to an argument that depends heavily on the writer being perceived as credible, as someone whose opinion and judgment can be trusted.

Free writing A technique to generate ideas (and enthusiasm) that involves writing "freely," without regard for grammar, spelling, punctuation, paragraphing or even focus. Sometimes cited as a way of addressing writer's block (for those who believe in writer's block), but presented here as a way of overcoming procrastination.

Globe plan A "spatial" essay structure. The essay material is organized according to physical spaces (e.g., east to west, north to south, top to bottom, left to right, etc.).

Google (verb) To research information on the Internet, probably using the search engine Google. An effective way of identifying general – but potentially biased and/or inaccurate – information sources (e.g., newspapers, magazines, personal and corporate websites and blogs). An ineffective way of identifying credible academic sources, including those that are peer-reviewed, when compared to searches conducted through Google Scholar and library databases.

Google Scholar (scholar.google.ca) A specialized version of Google that searches out only scholarly or academically credible information.

Handwrite, the value of Research studies involving elementary students indicate a link between handwriting and increased neural activity in certain parts of the brain, suggesting that a person might generate ideas and words more quickly by handwriting than by typing on a keyboard. This finding has been supported, anecdotally, by published writers.

Headings A word, phrase or even a statement that introduces a section of a document. Headings can be generic (e.g., "Background," "Discussion," "Conclusion") or informative (i.e., a heading that reflects more specifically the content being introduced). Both types can reinforce the principle of "predictable structure" by alerting the reader as to what's coming up.

IMRAD An acronym for **I**ntroduction; **M**ethods; **R**esults; and **D**iscussion, a method of organization widely used for research papers in the sciences.

Indirect object The noun or pronoun that receives the action of the verb. It may be preceded by "for" or "to" – or those prepositions may be implicitly understood. An indirect object always requires a direct object, and it always comes after the verb (e.g., "I submitted the essay to the instructor": the indirect object here is "instructor"; the direct object is "essay.")

Inductive approach A method of reasoning: the paper begins with a purpose statement, a question or an hypothesis (an educated guess), presents evidence, and then analyzes it to determine what patterns, inferences, or conclusions can be drawn. Often seen as the counterpart to the deductive approach.

Informative headings In contrast to generic headings (e.g., "Introduction," "Background," etc.), informative headings are unique to a particular paper (i.e., they encapsulate key points of the paper).

In-text citation An abbreviated reference within the text of a research article. The full reference can usually be found in the list of sources provided at the end of the paper.

John Swales' model A template (step-by-step guide) on how to structure the introduction of a research paper: explain importance of topic; selectively summarize existing research; identify gaps or questions in the research; show how this paper addresses those gaps or questions. Often used in the natural and social sciences.

Justified text Characterized by a document having a straight right-hand margin, so that the text is symmetrically framed on the page. For nonprofessional publications, however, justified text often results in uneven spacing between characters. Consequently, it may be more difficult to read and to edit than non-justified text.

Layout How the text is physically arranged on the paper or the screen. Elements of layout such as the deliberate use of white space, bulleted lists, and headings can facilitate reading and comprehension.

Logos A Greek term, referring to an argument based on reason, intellect or logic (as opposed to emotion, pathos, or the writer's credibility, ethos).

Madman, The A person who is mind mapping or free writing. The term was coined by author Betty S. Flowers to emphasize that the writer should not censor his or her thoughts, ideas or impressions at the start of the writing process.

Mind mapping Diagrammatic brainstorming with arrows and perhaps colour (i.e., the writer is not limited to words; drawing pictures is also allowed). A technique to generate ideas, particularly at the start of a writing project. Completely non-linear.

MLA (Modern Language Association) A referencing format widely used within the humanities. Sometimes referred to as "MLA style."

Non-justified text Characterized by a document having a ragged or uneven right-hand margin and uniform spacing. The latter makes it easier to read and to edit than justified text with uneven spacing.

Non-restrictive clause A clause that is not essential to the meaning of the sentence (i.e., if it were deleted, you would still understand the sentence's meaning). A non-restrictive clause is separated from the rest of the sentence with commas.

Noun A part of speech: a person, place or thing.

Objective case (pronoun) The form of a pronoun depends on its function in the sentence. If the pronoun is functioning as an object (as opposed to a subject), choose from this list only: *me, you, her, him, it, us, them, whom*. These pronouns belong to the objective case.

Parallelism A grammatical and stylistic device that refers to the similar or perhaps identical construction of sentences or phrases. This similarity adds coherence, a sense of style, and clarity.

Paraphrasing Restating your source's material, retaining the same amount of detail but using your own words and sentence structure. No new ideas or information is added. Note: paraphrasing that follows too closely the original source's wording or sentence structure is considered plagiarizing, even though the information has been referenced.

Parenthetical citation An abbreviated reference that's enclosed within parentheses in the text of a research article. The full reference can usually be found in the list of sources provided at the end of the paper.

Parsing To identify the different parts of speech in a sentence, figuring out their relationship to each other. A bit of a dying skill these days.

Parts of speech Words can be categorized according to the eight basic parts of speech: noun, verb, adjective, adverb, preposition, conjunction, article, and pronoun.

Passive voice A sentence in which the subject is being acted upon is said to be written in passive voice. Contrasts with active voice in which the subject is doing the acting. Passive voice is often criticized as being indirect and wordy, but it's an appropriate choice when you want to emphasize the action itself, rather than the actor.

Pathos A Greek term, referring to an argument based on emotion (e.g., the writer appeals to the reader's heart, perhaps by addressing important values or beliefs, or by sharing personal stories that highlight a sense of common humanity). Contrasts with logos, an argument based on logic, and with ethos, an argument based on the writer's credibility.

Peer-reviewed The gold standard for research essay citations. "Peer-reviewed" means specialists in the field have critiqued the article for its scholarly value and reliability.

Personal essay A reflective, opinion-based essay. First person pronouns (i.e., "I," "you," "we"), personal examples and narratives all figure prominently in this kind of writing. The tone tends to be conversational and relaxed. A style appropriate for journal writing assignments, newsletters, blogs and other forms of social media writing.

Phrase A group of grammatically related words that does not contain a subject and a verb.

"Ping-pong" structure A particularly useful way of structuring essay content when the objective is to compare and contrast; present strengths and weaknesses; or discuss advantages and disadvantages. For example, a strength would be immediately followed by its corresponding weakness, an advantage by its corresponding disadvantage, and so on, until all the strengths and weaknesses or advantages and disadvantages have been explained.

Plagiarism Using someone else's ideas or language without adequately crediting them. Considered a highly serious instance of academic misconduct, unacceptable in any situation, whether accidental or intentional.

Plural indefinite pronoun A plural pronoun that doesn't refer to specific people, places or things (e.g., both, few, several, others, many). Plural indefinite pronouns "take" a plural verb.

Post hoc, ergo propter hoc A type of faulty logic. This well-known Latin phrase literally translates as "after this, therefore because of this," referring to the mistaken notion that if one event follows another, the first event inevitably caused the second one. In other words, if B follows A; then A must have caused B. Essentially, a faulty cause and effect relationship.

Preposition A part of speech: introduces a phrase that acts as a modifier. TIP: for some examples of prepositions, imagine anywhere a monkey could go or be (e.g., **on** the table, **in** the car, **by** the seashore, **with** the elephants …).

Prepositional phrase A grammatically related group of words that starts with a preposition and that acts as modifier. TIP: for examples of prepositional phrases, imagine anywhere a monkey could go or be (e.g., on the table, in the car, by the seashore, with the elephants…).

Problem-solution A common and useful way of structuring essays that can work in tandem with the ping-pong and block-by-block structures.

Pronoun A part of speech: a word that substitutes for a noun.

Pronoun-antecedent agreement The grammatically correct practice of ensuring that a pronoun and its antecedent are both either singular or plural. The exception to this rule occurs when a gender neutral pronoun is required. In those situations, the plural pronoun "they" or "their" increasingly gets pressed into action even though the antecedent is singular. (See SINGULAR "THEY" OR "THEIR.")

Proper noun A type of pronoun: the name of a person, an operation/organization, a place, etc. The first letter is capitalized (e.g., "Guelph" is a proper noun; "Lucy," my dog's name, is a proper noun.)

Purpose statement A purpose statement may or may not directly disclose the paper's specific conclusions. Instead, it may simply describe the route the paper will take to arrive at its conclusions. Depending on the discipline and the type of document, a purpose statement may be the opening sentence or two of the document, or it may come at the end of the introduction.

Reading your own work aloud A good practice generally. Listening to how the words sound can allow the writer to assess coherence, word choice, conciseness and tone.

References The research sources cited within a body of writing.

Referencing The practice of acknowledging your research sources, typically using an established format.

Research essay An essay that contains primary and/or secondary source research material. This research is referred to, or "referenced," throughout the paper and in a list at the end of the paper in accordance with a recognized style guide (e.g., APA, MLA).

Restrictive clause A clause that is essential to the meaning of the sentence (i.e., it "restricts" the meaning of the sentence). A restrictive clause is never separated from the rest of the sentence with commas.

"Rubber stamps" Commonly used words, phrases and even complete sentences (e.g., "Please find enclosed"; "In today's world"; "If you have any further questions, please do not hesitate to contact me"). Writing characterized by rubber stamps is weak because it lacks originality of expression and perhaps even thought.

Run on A grammatical error, referring to two or more sentences that are not separated by the proper punctuation – typically a period or a semicolon.

Semicolon A punctuation mark that has two distinct uses: to separate items in a series or in a list when those items consist of more than one word or contain internal punctuation; and to separate two sentences that are closely related.

Sentence fragment A grammatical error that refers to an incomplete sentence being punctuated as if it were a complete sentence.

Signal phrase An alternative to an in-text parenthetical reference or citation. A signal phrase incorporates the citation within the sentence (e.g., "According to Pawlowski (2003)…").

Singular "they" or "their" Refers to the practice of using "they" or "their" to refer to a singular noun. This practice can help the writer avoid an awkward construction (e.g., "he/she"; "him/her") or gender bias, but it is considered by some to be grammatically incorrect because the plural pronoun ("they" or "their") does not agree with its singular antecedent.

Singular indefinite pronoun A singular pronoun that doesn't refer to a specific person, place or thing. TIP: pronouns that end in "one" or "body" are singular (e.g., anyone, somebody, anybody, everybody, everything, each, either, neither, one, no one, something, everyone, nobody, nothing, anything, someone). Singular indefinite pronouns "take" a singular verb.

Subjective case (pronoun) The form of a pronoun depends on its function in the sentence. If the pronoun is functioning as a subject (as opposed to an object), choose from this list only: *I, you, she, he, it, we, they, who*. These pronouns belong to the subjective case.

Subject-verb agreement The subject of a sentence should agree with its verb (i.e., a singular subject "takes" a singular verb; a plural subject "takes" a plural verb).

Summary Briefly states the source's key points only. No new ideas or information is added. The length may vary, but typically it is about 10% of the original source. In academic writing, it is usually referred to as an "abstract." In business writing, it is often referred to as an "executive summary."

Synthesizing Integrating information or ideas from different research sources to point out a connection among the sources, illustrate a relationship or introduce a new perspective. It showcases not just the writer's understanding of these different sources, but also his or her ability to expand upon them.

Thesis statement The point of view or the specific argument that is presented and supported in an essay. It summarizes the paper's conclusions right at the start, usually in a sentence or two at the end of the introduction.

Three, importance of in essay structure. Essays often follow a three-part structure to build momentum and to help ensure reader interest and comprehension.

Topic sentence States the main point of the paragraph, often, but not always, in the first sentence of the paragraph. May be omitted if the paragraph continues a point made in the previous paragraph or if a narrative or story is being related.

Transitions Connecting words or phrases that show how sentences within a paragraph are related or how individual paragraphs are related to one another. Transitions can be direct (e.g., "However", "For example", "Furthermore"), or they can be subtle (the use of synonyms, pronouns, or repetition).

Triangle plan A commonly used essay structure: the paper is organized around three main aspects of (e.g., personal, financial, academic) or perspectives on (e.g., student, parent, professor) the topic.

Unity Each paragraph focuses on one main point only, which is related to the essay's overall thesis or purpose.

Unsupported generalization A type of faulty logic: a general statement is made without sufficient evidence to support it.

Vague pronoun reference A grammatical error that results when the pronoun's antecedent is not clear (i.e., it's not clear who or what the pronoun is referring to).

Verb A part of speech: denotes a state of action or being.

Voice A glimpse of the writer behind the words – witty, uncertain, fearful, optimistic, angry, hesitant, courteous, etc. Ideally, this glimpse of the writer's personality doesn't overpower the words, but adds nuance and depth to them.

Wikipedia One of the most consulted websites in the world, but generally perceived as lacking academic credibility and therefore not recommended as a reference in a research paper. It can, though, be a helpful starting place that provides a general orientation to the subject matter, highlights relevant trends, and identifies useful sources for further research.

Writer's block Commonly viewed as an affliction of uncertain duration that prevents someone from starting, continuing or finishing a piece of writing. This text, however, borrows A. Patchett's view: writer's block is a myth, a synonym for procrastinating when confronted with a challenging writing assignment.

Writing template A step-by-step guide on how to structure a document. Offers the advantage of strengthening the paper's coherence, but may contain the risk of promoting a "paint-by-numbers" approach, where one essay or research paper reads like another.

Index

Abstract, 75, 129–136
Active voice, 33, 50, 180–181, 197
ADD/ADDQ (acronym), 72–73, 197
Adjective, definition, 150, 197
Adverb, conjunctive, 199; definition, 150, 197
Amis, Kingsley, 4n
Annotated bibliography, 130, 197
Antecedent, 162–164, 197
APA, 75, 197
Apostrophes, 175–177, 197
Appositive, 168, 197
Article, definition, 150, 197
Bacon, Francis, 8
Bad Writing Contest, 94–95
Bad writing, 94–95
Berninger, Virginia, 16
Block-by-block (writing structure), 35, 36, 198
Circular reasoning, 69–70, 198
Clarifying, 59–60
Clause, 51, 198
Cleese, John, 144
Clock plan, 31, 101, 198
Cohen, Leonard, 3, 4, 29
Coherence, 113, 115, 116, 133, 180, 198
Colon, 122, 173, 198
Comma splice, 173, 198
Comma, 167–171
Common knowledge, 58, 119, 198
Conciseness in writing, 49–56, 67, 135, 136
Conclusion, 123–129
Confidence, and writing, 191
Conjunction, co-ordinate, 169, 170, 175, 185, 199; definition, 150, 198
Conjunctive adverb, 199
Constructive pessimist, 64, 197
Contraction, 176, 199
Co-ordinate conjunction, 169, 170, 175, 185, 199
Counterintuitive principle, 1–7, 10, 71, 193
Crick, Francis, 49, 50, 116–117, 125
Dangling modifier, 178–179, 181–182, 199
Databases, 74, 75, 76, 92, 199

Davidson, Cathy, 38
Deductive approach, 104–106, 110, 111, 199
Didion, Joan, 148
Direct object, 157, 199
Doctorow, E.L., 139
Easterbrook, Gregg, 126
Editing, 138–146, 200; kinds of, 138–139; principles, 139–144
Ego, in writing, 23
Einstein, Albert, 1, 2
Elbow, Peter, 14n, 15, 115, 127
Emerson, R.L., 162
Engagement, 103–104
Ethos, 58, 64–67, 200
"Everyone," use of, 164
Feedback from others, 143–144
Feel good about self, as writing goal, 5–6
Find your focus, 20–23
Finding Forrester, 11
Fischer, Norman, 23
Focus on the big picture, 139–142, 145
Forster, E.M. 34
Free writing, 13, 200
Frost, Robert, 1, 2
Girard, Eric C., 63
Gladwell, Malcolm, 29, 65
Globe plan, 31, 200
Google Scholar, 75–76, 200
Google (verb), 74–75, 200
Grade, definition of "good," 189–195
Grammar, 147–188; importance of, 147–148; logic and, 149
Handwriting, 16, 200
Headings, 37, 38, 200; informative, 120, 131, 201
Hemingway, Ernest, 14
"I" vs. "me," 159–160
IMRAD (acronym), 120, 131, 201
Indirect object, 158, 201
Inductive approach, 104–106, 110, 111, 201
Informative headings, 120, 131, 201
Internet research, 68, 72–76
In-text citations, *see* PARENTHETICAL

CITATIONS
Introduction, 93–111, 127
Inverted triangle model, 95–96; modified, 96–97, 110, 111
Invisible thread, 112–113
"Its" vs. "it's," 177
Jobs, Steve, 1, 2, 48, 49
John Swales' model, 108, 201
Journalistic style, 63–64
Justified text, 141–142, 201
Kant, Immanuel, 43
Keillor, Garrison, 18
King, Stephen, 15, 94
Kingwell, Mark, 45–47
Kubrick, Stanley, 126
Layout, 119–120, 123, 202
Lewis, Sinclair, 4
Logic, errors in, 68–72
Logos, 58, 66, 67, 202
Maclean's magazine, 44
"Madman, The," 16, 202
Metaphor, 45
Mind mapping, 16, 20, 25, 28, 34, 202
Misplaced modifiers, 177–178, 181–182
MLA, 75, 202
Modifiers, *see* DANGLING MODIFIERS, MISPLACED MODIFIERS
Monkey mind, 13
Munro, Alice, 1, 2
Non-justified text, 142, 202
Non-restrictive clause, 169, 202
Noun, collective, 155, 198; definition of, 150, 202; proper, 162, 205
Object, indirect, 158; direct, 157, 199
Objective case (pronoun), 157–159, 202
Oliver, Mary, 195
One key point, 128
"Only connect" paragraphs, 113–115, 118, 123, 145
Openings, attention-grabbing, 97–99
Organizational patterns, 31
Paragraph layout, 119–120, 123
Paragraph length, 119, 123
Paragraphing, 112–137
Parallelism, 114–117, 120, 123, 179–180, 202
Paraphrasing, 76–82, 84–85, 203
Parenthetical citations, 66, 102–103, 201, 203
Parsing, 149, 203
Parts of speech, 149–150, 203
Passive voice, 53, 180–181, 203
Patchett, Ann, 9, 10, 47–48
Path of least resistance, 192–193
Pathos, 58, 61, 64, 66, 67, 203
Peer review, 74, 203
Perfect paper pressure, 93–94
Personal essay, 20, 103, 203
Personal experiences, 48–49
Phrase, definition of, 204; *see also* PREPOSITIONAL PHRASES
Ping pong (writing structure), 35, 36, 204
Pinker, Stephen, 57, 98
Plagiarism, 68, 76–81, 204
Plath, Sylvia, 18, 19
Plural indefinite pronoun, 154, 204
Pollan, Michael, 120
Post hoc, ergo propter hoc, 70–71, 204
Predictable structure, 33–34, 114, 123
Preposition, 152; definition of, 150, 204
Prepositional phrases, 53, 114, 123, 152, 204
Problem-solution (writing structure), 35, 36, 204
Procrastination, 4
Pronoun, 156–159; definition of, 150, 205; first person, 100–101, 103; plural indefinite, 154, 204; objective case, 157–159, 202; personal possessive, 176; second person, 135; singular, 163; singular indefinite, 153–154, 206; subjective case, 157–159, 206
Pronoun-antecedent agreement, 162–164, 205
Proper noun, 162, 205
Purpose statement, 24–30, 35, 38, 99, 145, 205
Purpose, 127
Quotations, 120–122
Reading your work aloud, 126, 133, 205
References, 81, 205; APA, 75, 197; MLA, 75, 202; *see also* PARENTHETICAL CITATION
Restrictive clause, 167, 205
Risk-taking in writing, 83–84
Rowling, J.K., 16
"Rubber stamps," 54, 205–206
Run ons, 174–175, 206

Seinfeld, Jerry, 1, 2
Self-discipline, 193–194
Semicolon, 171–173, 206
Sentence fragment, 109, 173–174, 206
Serial comma, 118, 170
Signal phrases, 102–103, 206
Simic, Charles, 18
Simplicity in writing, 37, 49–56, 67
Singular indefinite pronoun, 153–154, 206
Sokal, Alan, 51
Spicer, Keith, 31
Stone, Robert, 16
Stout, Karen A., 61
Structure of essays and papers, 31–41
Subject, 153–158; joined by "or" or "nor," 153
Subjective case (pronoun), 157–159, 206
Subject-verb agreement, 151–156, 206–207
Summary, 129–136, 207
Supporting arguments, 64
Supporting evidence, 56–58, 64, 66, 69, 118–119, 123; balanced approach to 59–60
Suzuki, Shunyru, 149
Sword, Helen, 52
Synthesis guide, four-step, 68
Synthesis, 84–92, 128, 207
"That" vs. "which," 166–169

Theme, 8, 22–23
Thesis statement, 24–30, 35, 38, 99, 145, 207
Thesis, 41, 127
"They/their" as singular pronouns, 164–165, 206
Three "Rs," 127–128
Three key points/structure, 32–33, 41, 207
Titles, 44–45, 67
Toor, Rachel, 18, 20
Topic sentence, 112, 114, 123, 207
Transitions, 115–117, 123, 207
Triangle plan, 32, 34–35, 36, 101, 207
Unity, 115, 123, 207
Unpredictable content, 42–49, 67
Unsupported generalizations, 68–69, 208
Vague pronoun reference, 165–166, 208
Verb, definition of, 150, 208; singular or plural, 155–156
Voice, 13–15, 18, 109, 208
Watson, James, 49, 50, 116–117, 125
"Who" vs. "whom," 160–162
Wikipedia, 21, 73–74, 208
Williams, W.C., 57, 61
Word count, fixating on, 83
Write to discover what you know, 12–13
Writer's block, 9–10, 208
Writing plan, two-part, 8, 10–11, 13, 15–16
Writing templates, 108, 208
Yeats, W.B., 11, 12, 33–34

www.ingramcontent.com/pod-product-compliance
Lightning Source LLC
Chambersburg PA
CBHW071821080526
44589CB00012B/882